AI and Business

AI and Business: Mapping the Present for Harnessing the Future

BY

RAHUL PRATAP SINGH KAURAV
FORE School of Management, New Delhi, India

AND

SURABHI KOUL
FORE School of Management, New Delhi, India

emerald
PUBLISHING

United Kingdom – North America – Japan – India – Malaysia – China

Emerald Publishing Limited
Emerald Publishing, Floor 5, Northspring, 21-23 Wellington Street, Leeds LS1 4DL.

First edition 2026

Printed and bound by CPI Group (UK) Ltd, Croydon, CR0 4YY

British Library Cataloguing in Publication Data
A catalogue record for this book is available from the British Library

ISBN: 978-1-83708-889-8 (Print)
ISBN: 978-1-83708-888-1 (Online)
ISBN: 978-1-83708-890-4 (Epub)

INVESTOR IN PEOPLE

To my late father, whose wisdom still guides me.
And to my mother, whose prayers carried me here.
—Rahul Pratap Singh Kaurav

To my parents, especially my late father, whose dream of writing a book lives on through these pages. This is as much his story as it is mine.
—Surabhi Koul

Contents

About the Authors

Dr. Rahul Pratap Singh Kaurav is an accomplished academician, a researcher and an author with a demonstrated expertise in marketing analytics, artificial intelligence (AI)-driven research methodologies and digital transformation in education and business. Currently serving as an Associate Professor at the FORE School of Management, New Delhi, Dr. Kaurav brings more than 17 years of academic experience. His research portfolio spans journal articles, book chapters and authored or edited books, many of which examine the intersection of marketing, technology and data analytics. He has published extensively on AI applications in tourism, marketing and human resource management, offering cutting-edge insights into how intelligent technologies can transform consumer experiences, organisational efficiency and decision-making processes.

Dr. Kaurav is proficient in both quantitative and qualitative analytics platforms and has contributed to major research projects funded by AICTE and ICSSR. He actively supervises doctoral students and consults on projects leveraging AI and machine learning for data-driven solutions. His collaborative works with leading international scholars and institutions, including BITS-Pilani and Taylor's University, Malaysia, University of Liverpool, UK, reflect his global perspective on the transformative role of AI in business and education. With a passion for integrating AI tools into research and pedagogy, Dr. Kaurav continues to champion innovation, offering readers an evidence-based understanding of AI's evolving potential in marketing, analytics and beyond.

Dr. Surabhi Koul is an accomplished academician, a researcher, and an educator with demonstrated expertise in the area of Marketing. Currently serving as an Associate Professor of Marketing at FORE School of Management, New Delhi, she brings nearly a decade of academic experience, including prior faculty roles at NMIMS Navi Mumbai and BITS Pilani. Dr. Koul has established a robust research portfolio, comprising approximately 20 international publications. Her research focuses on emerging Gen Z consumption patterns, as well as understanding the new-age consumer tools like SoLoMo-commerce, AI-enabled shopping assistants, and influencer-mediated platforms. In the classroom, she champions co-value creation, fostering interactive, experiential learning where students and faculty collaborate as partners in knowledge construction. Her teaching interests lie in Branding, AI & Marketing, and Product Management. With a passion for integrating innovative consumer research methods and pedagogy, Dr. Koul continues to pioneer evidence-based insights at the intersection of marketing, technology, and education.

Preface: Why This Book, Why Now

We are standing at a unique inflection point in human history – where lines of code influence billion-dollar decisions, where machines learn and adapt faster than entire industries and where AI is no longer a futuristic concept but a present reality. Whether you're leading a multinational enterprise, managing a start-up, teaching in a classroom or just entering the workforce, you are already part of this transformation.

This book was born from one simple, pressing question we kept hearing in **corporate meetings, student interactions and coffee chats**: '*How do we actually use AI in business?*' Not the hype, not the jargon, but real strategies, practical tools and honest reflections. Across sectors – from healthcare to retail, logistics to education – organisations are experimenting with AI. But many still face hesitation, confusion or fear of falling behind.

We wrote this book for the curious students, the reflective policymakers, the hands-on managers and, of course, the risk-taking entrepreneur. It speaks to all who are eager to understand not just *what* AI is but *how* to apply it responsibly and intelligently. The world of business is not becoming digital; it already is. The next step is to make it *intelligently digital.*

This book is designed to serve as a core or supplementary text for a wide range of management and executive programs. It is particularly relevant for courses such as Artificial Intelligence for Business, AI and Marketing, Digital Transformation, Technology and Innovation Management, Strategic Management, and Executive Education modules on AI-driven decision-making. The integrated blend of conceptual foundations, industry cases, and managerial frameworks makes it suitable for MBA, PGDM, executive education, and advanced postgraduate programs, while also supporting practitioner-oriented learning and applied research.

Inside, you'll find a mix of foundational concepts, future-forward trends, ethical reflections and real-world 40+ case studies. But more than that, you'll find a guiding philosophy***: AI is not about replacing people – it's about augmenting human potential***.

To quote no one in particular but many in spirit: '*You don't need to be a coder to shape the future, but you do need to understand how code is shaping it.*' This book is your invitation to step in – not tomorrow but today.

Welcome to the new era of business intelligence. Let's build it together.

Acknowledgements

The creation of this book has been an intellectually stimulating and deeply collaborative journey. Along the way, I have had the privilege of engaging with colleagues, students and mentors whose insights and encouragement made this work possible.

I am especially thankful to ***Dr. Subir Verma***, Director of FORE School of Management, New Delhi, for fostering an academic environment where innovation is encouraged and scholarship is supported. His belief in interdisciplinary work, focused on the technology, and commitment to intellectual curiosity were vital in bringing this project to life.

I owe particular gratitude to my ***co-author, Dr. Surabhi Koul***, for her insightful ideas and steady support, especially during the slower, more uncertain phases of this project. Her thoughtful curation of content, willingness to explore perspectives beyond the conventional and instinct for identifying what truly matters have added depth and originality to this book. Working with her has been both a professional and creative privilege.

To all the scholars and writers whose academic contributions have shaped the way I think, write and question – thank you. Your work has laid the foundation for much of what I've come to believe and has subtly guided the writing of this book. In particular, I would like to acknowledge the enduring influence of Peter Gentsch, Christopher Penn, Ethan Mollick and Paul Roetzer – whose writings and insights have profoundly impacted my academic journey and this work.

I am profoundly grateful to my family – whose unwavering love forms the quiet strength behind all my pursuits. To my **beautiful wife, Neeraj, and kids, Himanshi and Tanishk**, thank you for your tireless patience, your understanding and the countless hours you sacrificed so I could focus on this work. Our late-night coffee and snack sessions were more than moments of comfort – they were a constant source of encouragement and joy that carried me through.

Finally, to all those who contributed in ways both visible and invisible – your support is sincerely appreciated. If any names have been inadvertently omitted, please accept my apologies and my heartfelt thanks.

Rahul Pratap Singh Kaurav, *PhD*

Writing a book is never a solitary pursuit; it is shaped by the guidance, encouragement and silent support of many people who walk beside you. This journey has been deeply personal and profoundly collaborative. As I look back, I am filled with gratitude for those who believed in this vision, stood by me through the long nights and endless edits and made this milestone possible.

I extend my deepest gratitude to **Prof. Subir Verma**, Director FORE School of Management, for his encouragement and belief in this endeavour. You have always reminded us to '*take a step ahead of technology*', and that thought has guided me throughout the development of this work. Your visionary leadership continues to inspire and push us towards meaningful innovation.

To my co-author and dear friend, **Dr. Rahul Pratap Singh Kaurav**, thank you for being a true collaborator in every sense. It was you who initiated this and reminded me every time that I can do it. Your insights, partnership and camaraderie made this process not only enriching but also enjoyable. A special mention to my colleague, **Prof. Faisal Ahmed**, for his timely guidance and valuable inputs at critical junctures of this writing process. Your mentorship and perspective added depth and clarity when it was needed most.

I owe heartfelt thanks to my **mother and mother-in-law**, whose values and love have shaped me. A special mention to my **late father**, whose dream of writing a book has found life through these pages. In many ways, I feel I have lived his dream through this work.

And of course, to my **loving husband, Nitish,** thank you for being my unwavering support system. From stepping in during the busiest days to patiently typing long paragraphs as I dictated, you've been my quiet strength behind every word. Your presence made the impossible seem possible.

Finally, to everyone who contributed, whether in ways seen or unseen, your support has meant more than words can express.

Surabhi Koul, *PhD*

Chapter 1

Introduction to Artificial Intelligence

Artificial intelligence is more than a mere tool created for the ease of mankind. It is a mirror that reflects the challenges we face and the solutions we desire. It can be understood as the evolving narrative of human ingenuity in the business world.

Case Study: The Evolving Landscape of Generative AI (Gen AI) Applications in 2025

In 2025, Gen AI has matured from a convenience to an essential tool for personal life activities, jobs and integrated business processes. In Zao-Sanders' (2025) article in the Harvard Business Review, the author discusses this transformation and offers a detailed account of what he considers the top 100 Gen AI use cases from a user viewpoint in 2025. This modern study suggests a fairly balanced partitioning of Gen AI application usage across personal and work-related spheres, with many use cases serving both domains concurrently.

Key Insights

1. Balanced Utilization Across Domains: The applications of Gen AI technology tend to be rather evenly split across personal and business considerations, suggesting it is generic in nature and widely accepted.
2. Multi-Purpose Use: The roles of Gen AI span across content generation, data analytics, personal virtual assistants, aiding in business intelligence and several other functions.
3. Integration into Daily Workflows: Gen AI has been incorporated seamlessly into the functioning of the industries in spheres such as marketing, customer support and product engineering, which has

(*Continued*)

AI and Business, 1–29

Published under exclusive licence by Emerald Publishing Limited
doi:10.1108/978-1-83708-888-120261001

(*Continued*)

automated routine functions, resulting in increased productivity and innovation and great value to business processes and work culture.

4. Addressing Emotional Support Needs: Gen AI is not just limited to technical aspects, but an increasing application of Gen AI for human emotional needs is growing in areas such as therapy and self-improvement training, indicating a growing attention to human concerns.

Implications for Business

The effects of Gen AI on business processes are apparent, including the anticipated widespread integration of Gen AI by the year 2025. Organizations that fully harness these technologies stand to gain in productivity, customer engagement and competitive advantage. Moreover, applications of Gen AI that emphasize human interactions suggest the need for ethics beyond responsibility in placing AI calls for ethical boundaries on its use.

If employed effectively, artificial intelligence (AI) can optimize workflows with optimum results. It is proven to be a significant practical force which is accessible today. From elementary marketing to customer service and even business at retail, finance, healthcare and education, AI serves as a core component in every process as companies seek to enhance efficiency, expand operations and remain competitive. Its impact can be measured in areas like powering decision engines, automating monotonous work and analyzing unprecedented volumes of previously inaccessible data.

AI's evolution into a powerful business tool starts with understanding what it really is, along with its components like machine learning (ML) and deep learning (DL). Therefore, the chapter provides a clear snapshot by deconstructing the characteristics of AI. Readers will delve into the categories of AI systems, starting from narrow and task-focused systems to the more advanced speculative superintelligent agents. Covering AI's historical journey and unpacking its fundamental concepts equips you to engage critically with contemporary issues concerning its place in business and its potential for redefining the future.

Defining AI

In the course of doing any kind of business, an advanced technology is being used today called AI, and it is applied in a very generic and loose manner, confused with robotics and automation or business processes driven by algorithms. The domain of AI as a science is, in fact, much deeper and multidimensional. As defined, AI is the capabilities of modern technologies to enable machines to replicate tasks performed by humans, including reasoning, learning, perception and problem-solving, more quickly.

The primary definitions, dating back to the inception of AI, continue to greatly shape the understanding of the field today. One of the AI founding fathers, John McCarthy,[1] defined it as 'the science and engineering of making intelligent machines.' A more pragmatic definition stems from Stanford's AI Index, which refers to AI as a set of technologies designed to perform tasks requiring human-like skills. These definitions have one aspect in common: the use of computation to replicate or augment human intelligence.

Distinguishing AI From Related Terms

AI is frequently confused with some of its practical applications, such as ML, DL or even data science. Such distinctions are important to avoid confusion about the concepts in question.

(1) AI is the overarching term that refers to the intelligent behaviour exhibited by machines.
(2) ML is a branch within AI that is concerned with algorithm development for predicting or decision-making based on the learnt data.
(3) DL is a subfield of ML that deals with sophisticated image and speech recognition using multi-layered neural networks.
(4) While data science is not a form of AI, it enables data manipulation, cleaning and analysis, which is essential for training AI models.

The understanding of these differences is critical for recognizing the role of AI in the broader digital transformation strategy and how different tools interact within the AI system.

Fig. 1.1 aids in clarifying the confusion that most people have regarding the terms in AI. DL, which is at the centre of Fig. 1.1, is a branch of ML. It concentrates on sophisticated neural networks that perform high-level computations for tasks such as image and voice recognition. ML, in turn, is a branch of AI, which is the broad definition that encapsulates every single system that simulates human cognitive functions. All of this is encircled with data science, another supporting field which facilitates AI and ML by providing means for data collection, cleaning, preparation and data analysis. Such a discipline can neither be classified as a branch of AI nor as any form of AI. Nonetheless, data science serves as a pivotal foundation for the operation and efficiency of AI systems.

Even though the classification of AI and its related domains aids understanding of the context of the field, one must also remember that 'algorithms' and 'models' are two other terms which need a clearer comprehension. While these terms are often used interchangeably, they have distinct features.

---

[1]https://www.pro5.ai/blog/what-is-artificial-intelligence

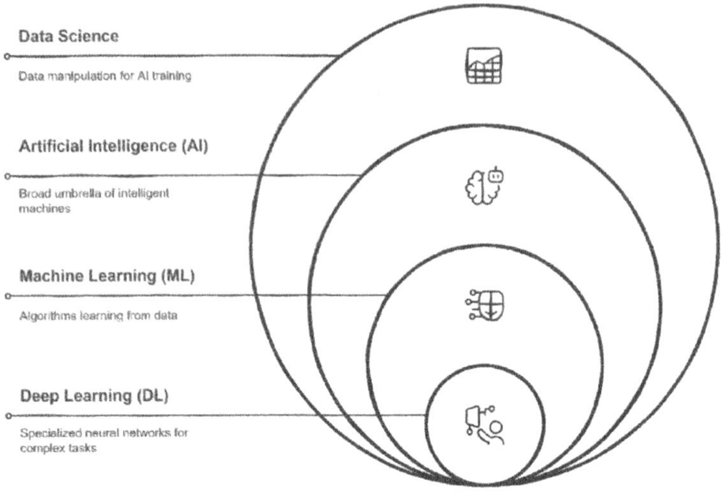

Fig. 1.1. Hierarchy of AI and Related Concepts.

An algorithm refers to a predefined rule set that dictates how a model training system learns from its data. It defines the process of learning – the 'how' aspect of the procedure. In contrast, a model defines what the system receives from an algorithm after data analysis is performed. The model is what gets used in actual operations to predict or make automated decisions in the real world.

Using a kitchen analogy, the algorithm is demonstrated by the recipe, while the model is the completed dish, which is made by following the instructions using specific ingredients (data).

The comprehension of the distinction is critical for the business leaders and managers who are at the forefront in interacting with the AI vendors or analytics teams. The investments do not happen just in the algorithm but in the models that are built with the help of the algorithms. These models can be built for any purpose, such as forecasting sales, credit scoring or the detection of fraud (refer Table 1.1).

The 4A Framework: Core Characteristics of AI in Business

To illustrate AI's practical importance in business, an emphasis on four notable characteristics is essential. These traits constitute what we refer to as the 4A Framework: Autonomy, Adaptability, Agility and At Scale. Collectively, these explain the reason why AI is not solely an appendage technology but rather a core foundational enabler of a company's competitive edge.

(1) Autonomy: As the companies implement the AI system, it requires nearly zero human input. The technology is such that it automates all the functions and requires no external support. For example, AI chatbots, when

Table 1.1. Key Differences Between Algorithms and Models.

Aspect	**Algorithm**	**Model**
Definition	A set of rules for learning from data.	The trained result derived from using data and algorithms.
Role	Guides the learning process.	Executes predictions, classifications or decisions.
Nature	Static and reusable across tasks.	Dynamic and updated with retraining.
Example	Decision Tree, Linear regression	Customer churn prediction model

employed by companies, respond to several queries on a regular basis. This facilitates round-the-clock services and significantly reduces operational costs.

(2) Adaptability: The AI system is designed such that it can learn from past interactions and data and curate responses over the period. With the help of old data and new inputs, different information is stored and analyzed in the system. Based on this information, modifications are needed in the results produced. This is fruitful, especially in an environment which is rapidly changing. A good example of this is a retail business which is based on predictive data modeling and suggest changes for enhanced user engagement.

(3) Agility: AI technologies have the ability to process vast amounts of data and provide instant insights and decisions to be made, simultaneously. The effectiveness of analyzing large data sets is particularly useful in stock exchange trading or real-time bidding for digital advertisement spaces. Also, in the logistics area, AI can revise delivery schedules based on real-time traffic and weather conditions.

(4) At Scale: Once the training is complete, AI can be published across borders, businesses and customer groups with minimal system configuration changes needed. The whole organization can be run on the same AI technology with little to no changes needed across several branches. This is beneficial as it does not require constant revisions in the system.

Fig. 1.2 presents the four characteristics that add business value to AI: autonomy, adaptability, agility and scale. Each capability brings with it unique advantages when integrated within organizational operations. The 4A

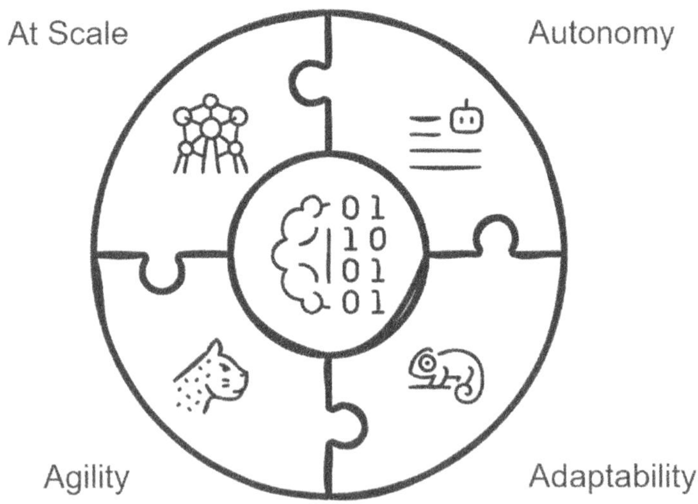

Fig. 1.2. The 4A Framework of AI Characteristics.

Framework outlines an easy way to understand AI's strategic importance in today's businesses. Autonomy refers to AI's ability to function without the supervision of a human, which is automating monotonous tasks fully disengaged from people. Adaptability focuses on learning; being able to function optimally within shifting contexts and environments over time exhibits a form of broad intelligence that many associate with living beings. With operational integration of AI technology into workflows, businesses gain all of these characteristics as individual strategic advantages. The 4A framework provides a straightforward method to understand the strategic implications of AI in business today. Agility encompasses rapid pace in data processing and delivery of outcomes deemed useful by stakeholders. And finally, at scale refers to successful performance regardless of scope: small or large organization, within departments and across branches around the world. Collectively, these attributes highlight why AI is not just regarded solely as a piece of technology but rather as a transforming asset for any organization.

Why This Matters for Business

These are the main reasons AI has become a strategic focal point for numerous enterprises. Unlike older forms of automation that execute monotonous tasks, AI's ability to respond to complex stimuli and recognize intricate patterns makes it much more capable than any rule-based automation. It achieves seamless centralization in decision-making, offers insight at the needed moments with empirical data analysis grounded in the underlying facts, and interaction with customers is scalable and personalized at unprecedented levels.

In addition, AI functions do not stop at backend operations. AI functions don't merely end with backend activities. These involve front-end positions like digital imitative human assistants and proactive systems that service user needs. Now that we view the AI development timeline, it is clear that the capabilities we enjoy today are a culmination of years of growth, research, mistakes and successes. In order to maximize AI, companies need to grasp its origins in the technology timeline and appreciate where the technology is heading.

A Brief History of AI

Tracing the Roots of Intelligence in Machines

Just like human imagination and scientific rigour go through various stages, AI includes a broad range of engineering, social science and technologies. The development of AI was founded on traditional logic, philosophy and reasoning, which further shifted to the computing breakthroughs of the 21st century.

Early Philosophical and Mathematical Origins

The idea of intelligent machines started a long time ago in myths such as the automata in Egypt and China or the mechanical slaves of Hephaestus in Greek mythology. However, it was not until the 20th century that these ideas evolved into formal thinking about intellect and computation.

In 1950, Alan Turing posed the famous question, "Can machines think?" In his paper Computing Machinery and Intelligence, he proposed the Turing Test – a machine's ability to demonstrate conversational human-level intelligence – as a benchmark for evaluation. This question, albeit theoretical, provided the core pillar of research for AI development.

The Birth of AI as a Discipline (1956–1970s)

The field officially commenced in 1956, when John McCarthy, Marvin Minsky and Claude Shannon, alongside others, organized the Dartmouth Conference. It is widely acknowledged as the birth of AI. McCarthy called it 'artificial intelligence,' envisioning a field developed for machines capable of learning and demonstrating intelligence in every possible way.

The period of the 1960s and 1970s was characterized by heightened optimism. Scholars constructed symbolic AI systems, referred to as 'good old-fashioned AI' (GOFAI), which relied on formal logic and rules to solve problems. Human-computer interaction was demonstrated, superficially, with programs like ELIZA, which was a precursor to chatbots and functioned as a psychotherapist. Early enthusiasm was affected by the limited capabilities of these systems. Deficient in learning mechanisms, they faltered in the face of real-world complexity and ambiguity.

The First AI Winter (Mid-1970s to Mid-1980s)

Interest and investment plateaued with expectations outpacing technological developments, marking the beginning of the first AI winter. Many AI projects did not produce significant value, prompting governments and private entities to reduce investment. Problems arose due to insufficiency in computing resources, inflexibility of scalability, and fixed, overly regimented systems that depended on pre-established guidelines.

The Rise of ML and Expert Systems (1980s–1990s)

As expert systems emerged in the 1980s, AI became popular once again. These new computer programs mimicked decision-making procedures on the basis of rule-based reasoning offered by human specialists. As a result, they began to be used in fields like medicine, as can be seen through the diagnostic system MYCIN, and finance.

At the same time, another method was gaining momentum: ML. Unlike rule-based AI, ML-enabled machines detect patterns in data without being programmed for it. The 1990s were a successful decade for ML algorithms owing to their steady improvement through greater access to data and better statistical techniques.

Deep Blue, the Internet and Growing Public Awareness (1990s)

The year 1997 was a milestone in the history of AI, as IBM's Deep Blue beat chess world champion Garry Kasparov. It not only highlighted the technical capability of AI then but also represented a public milestone that proved the level to which AI had come and can compete with human skills in strategic thinking.

In parallel, the onset of the internet was generating increasingly high quantities of data, which presented new opportunities for AI. As a result, there was a growing shift in focus from symbolic AI to more practical approaches, transforming the very core of research.

The Rise of Big Data and DL (2000s–2010s)

The 2000s witnessed a massive growth in the availability of data, the power of computation and increasing algorithmic sophistication. With the advancement of neural networks and DL, we have conquered powerful AI that utilizes ML, sprinting ahead with algorithms like CNN (Convolutional Neural Networks), changing the landscape of image, audio and speech recognition.

With the successful road to advancements in technologies, a turning point was achieved in 2012 when AlexNet, which is a DL model, outran other competitors in the ImageNet challenge. It showcased unprecedented accolades in the domain of AI DL by achieving milestones in cross-AI visioning, redefining the scope of computer vision. As a result, DL was adopted on a larger scale not only for cross-domain language processing but also for self-driving cars and smart assistants for voice recognition at warp speeds.

Around the same time, AI entered the market of consumer applications like Siri, Google Assistant, Alexa, Spotify, etc., and thus AI gradually became a part of a person's everyday life.

From AlphaGo to GPT: The Modern AI Boom (2016–2023)

The AI division proved its superiority in unstructured and innovatively logical challenging solutions. In 2016, DeepMind's AlphaGo defeated Go champion Lee Sedol. The win was a reflection of the effective learning and creativity of AI, a feat that people thought was a decade away.

OpenAI's GPT-3, launched in 2020, changed the landscape of text composition, as it was able to produce text effortlessly and with human-like grace. This sparked the onset of generative AI, which reshaped content writing, programming and marketing. Following it, we had ChatGPT, DALL·E and then GPT-4, which showed the expansion of AI capabilities from single to broader task focus. This also initiated intense ethical dilemmas concerning AI governance, ranging from accountability for the fake content and job cuts to discriminatory algorithms. These debates are still at the forefront of the discourse on AI governance legislation.

Looking Ahead

As we move further into the 2020s, AI is no longer restricted to technology laboratories and corporate offices. It is now being used to develop business and marketing strategies, manage client relations, and conduct business analysis and risk assessment. Not only does AI serve as a catalyst when integrated with cloud storage, generative systems and large-scale data analytics, but it also transforms into a strategic asset.

Even so, a lot of work still remains to be done. The next chapters in the evolutionary saga of AI will demand bold leaps of technology while at the same time creating sustainable protocols in managing the governance surrounding the risks of implementation of the devices and tools by corporations.

Fig. 1.3 presents major turning points in the development of AI – from early theoretical work and the coining of the term 'AI' to landmark achievements such as Deep Blue, AlphaGo, and the rise of generative AI models like GPT-3 and ChatGPT. It highlights how AI evolved through innovation, setbacks and resurgence to become a strategic technology in the modern era.

Core Concepts of AI

> Foundations that Power Intelligence [How AI learns → How it's structured → How it scales → How it's applied]

To the unfamiliar, AI might seem like pure magic, but it derives its capabilities from several approaches that are clearly defined and highly organized. This encompasses how AI systems are taught, their internal configuration, and how they amplify their power to accomplish intricate functions. This section explains

Fig. 1.3. Timeline Key Milestones in AI History.

three core concepts that constitute the fundamentals of AI in business use cases: learning paradigms, neural networks and DL.

Learning Paradigms in AI

Data has become the nucleus of attention in today's world. It is the new oil, foundations and bank. AI systems bank on various learning paradigms to get information, understand patterns and provide outputs. The exponential amount of data extraction also helps it to improve over time. It is crucial to understand these paradigms for evaluating how AI systems can be applied across different business functions. The three most common types are supervised learning, unsupervised learning and reinforcement learning.

Supervised Learning

In supervised learning, an algorithm is trained on a labelled dataset, that is, a dataset with both the inputs and the correct outputs. The intention is for the model to develop inputs to outputs and predict outcomes for new, unseen data. For example, in predictive analytics, a telecom company can use past data of customers showing features like contract length, service issues and call usage to analyze whether a customer is likely to churn or not. Some of the popular algorithms in supervised learning are listed below:

- Linear Regression.
- Decision Trees.
- Support Vector Machines (SVM).

Unsupervised Learning

In contrast with supervised learning, unsupervised learning is concerned with data that has no labels. The algorithm attempts to discover the underlying patterns or inherent structures present in the data. This becomes especially helpful when there are no pre-defined categories. There are instances when retailers make use of unsupervised learning to classify customers into distinct segments for targeted marketing based on their purchasing patterns. A list of popular algorithms in unsupervised learning is provided below:

- K-Means Clustering.
- Principal Component Analysis (PCA).
- Hierarchical Clustering.

Reinforcement Learning

The roots of reinforcement learning can be traced back to behavioural psychology. Learning occurs when an algorithm receives feedback in the form of either rewards or penalties as it interacts with the environment. The algorithm, over time, discovers the optimal way to achieve its goal. For example, some e-commerce platforms use reinforcement learning for dynamic pricing which allows the system to optimize revenue by adjusting product prices relative to the demand, competitor pricing and customer interaction in real-time. Below are some popular reinforcement learning algorithms.

- Q-Learning.
- Deep Q-Networks (DQN).
- Policy Gradient Methods.

The table (Table 1.2) provides a comprehensive overview of the learning framework. This view fosters the development of an understanding of how AI technologies function and evolve. With respect to supply chain logistics or advertisement viewership analysis, the learning method applied defines the strategic level of AI technology employed.

Neural Networks: The Computational Brain of AI

At the core of contemporary AI systems lie neural networks. Neural networks emulate the architecture and operation of the human brain as they incorporate numerous interconnected nodes called 'neurons' that process and relay information in layers. This enables machines to perform increasingly sophisticated tasks such as pattern recognition, language interpretation and outcome forecasting.

Basic Structure of a Neural Network

A neural network typically consists of the following three classifications of layers:

(1) Input Layer: This layer receives raw data, such as the customer's age, income and browsing history.
(2) Hidden Layers: Receives inputs that have been pre-processed and transforms them using weighted connections and activation functions. A hidden layer may be singular or multiple, based on the degree of the problem's sophistication.
(3) Output Layer: Final prediction or classification is generated, e.g. 'likely to purchase' or 'not likely.'

The output from a neuron is transformed through activation functions. Transformations result in modifying each neuron's output by applying a given function (these functions can be linear/non-linear) and hence each linkage of a neuron is linked with the given weight and bias. As information flows through the network, the weights, which are numeric thresholds defining each neuron's

Table 1.2. Comparison of Learning Paradigms in AI.

Learning Type	Input Data	Goal	Example Use Case
Supervised learning	Labelled (X, Y)	Predict outcomes	Customer churn prediction
Unsupervised learning	Unlabelled (X only)	Find structure/patterns	Customer segmentation
Reinforcement learning	Feedback via rewards	Optimize decision-making over time	Dynamic pricing, robotics

signal capacity and output power, are iteratively refined during the training phase of the network to enhance accuracy in predictions.

How Neural Networks Learn: Backpropagation

Neural networks learn by employing a method known as backpropagation. Once the network has made a prediction, it checks how accurate it is against the actual outcome and computes an error. Techniques like optimization and gradient descent are used for further fine-tuning. The cycle repeated several times, in epochs, the error is progressively reduced, thereby making the model more capable. Consider a scenario where a bank trains a neural network to detect fraudulent transactions by inputting historical transaction data. With each training session, the network gets better at identifying subtle changes that signal fraudulent activity.

Cognitive Mimicry and Pattern Recognition

Neural networks have emerged as one of the fastest learning technologies due to their ability to imitate human pattern recognition. A person can recognize a familiar face even from different angles or in different lighting, and in the same manner, neural networks can be trained to recognize the same product in different marketing images, or even categorize sentiment on social media in multiple languages.

This capacity for pattern recognition is invaluable in fields such as:

- Marketing: Sentiment analysis, recommendation engines.
- Healthcare: Medical image diagnosis, patient risk prediction.
- Finance: Credit scoring, fraud detection.

Neural networks (Fig. 1.4) have transformed AI from rule-based systems into learning machines capable of adapting to new and complex environments. As we move towards increasingly sophisticated applications, understanding their architecture and functioning is crucial for any professional involved in AI-driven business strategies.

DL: Scaling Intelligence

If neural networks are the brain of AI, DL is its supercharged engine. DL refers to a class of neural networks with multiple hidden layers, allowing machines to analyze vast datasets and extract complex patterns far beyond the capabilities of traditional models. What makes DL transformative is its ability to automatically learn representations from raw data – be it images, text or speech – without human-designed features.

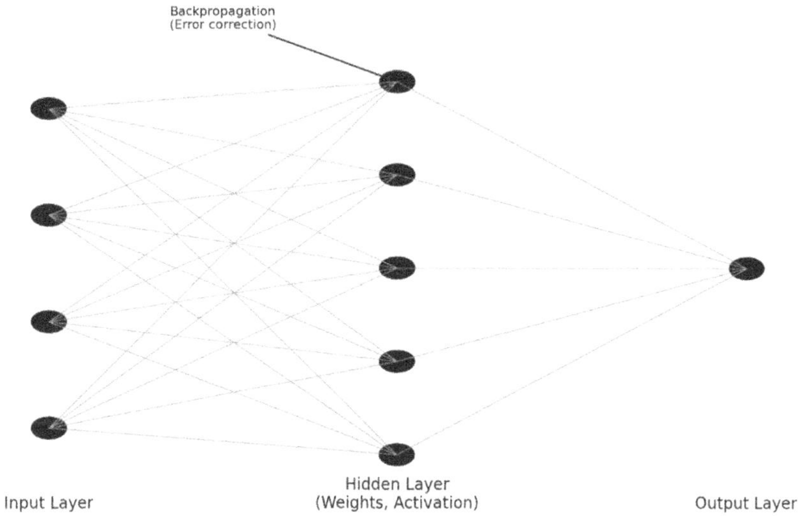

Fig. 1.4. Structure of a Basic Neural Network.

What Makes DL 'Deep'?

The 'deep' in DL comes from the depth of layers in the network. While traditional neural networks may have one or two hidden layers, DL models use dozens or even hundreds of layers, each refining the input progressively to capture more abstract features. This depth gives the network the ability to understand intricate relationships in data. A frequent use case is in image recognition, earlier layers may detect edges, the next may form shapes, and deeper layers recognize complete objects like cars or faces.

This layered learning approach is especially suited for unstructured data, such as voice recordings, handwritten notes, product photos and customer reviews (see Table 1.3).

The Role of Computational Power

DL became practical only with advancements in computational infrastructure, particularly the use of Graphics Processing Units (GPUs) and Tensor Processing Units (TPUs). These processors allow for the parallel computation required to train massive models on large datasets.

Cloud-based platforms (like AWS, Google Cloud and Azure) and open-source libraries (such as TensorFlow and PyTorch) have further democratized DL by reducing the barrier to entry for businesses and researchers.

Table 1.3. Common Deep Learning Architectures and Applications.

Architecture	Purpose	Example Applications
Convolutional Neural Networks (CNNs)	Image processing and spatial recognition	Facial recognition, retail shelf monitoring
Recurrent Neural Networks (RNNs)	Sequence and time-series data	Stock forecasting, chatbot dialogue
Transformers	Language understanding	Translation, summarization, large language models

Business Use Cases

DL is already embedded in many tools and services used in business today:

(1) Natural Language Processing (NLP): Businesses use NLP-based DL models for chatbots, automated summarization, voice assistants and sentiment analysis in customer feedback.
(2) Image and Video Analysis: Retailers deploy computer vision models to monitor shelves, recognize inventory patterns or support visual search in e-commerce.
(3) Fraud Detection and Security: In banking and insurance, DL models detect fraudulent transactions by spotting subtle, high-dimensional patterns in user behaviour.
(4) Generative AI: Tools like DALL·E, ChatGPT and Synthesia are powered by DL architectures (notably transformers). They help businesses generate content, automate design and develop interactive media.

Challenges of DL

Despite its power, DL is not without limitations:

- Requires large labelled datasets to train effectively.
- High computational cost and energy consumption.
- Models are often black boxes – difficult to interpret or audit.
- Susceptible to bias if the training data is unbalanced.

As a result, businesses must weigh the benefits of DL against its operational complexity and governance requirements.

DL represents the next frontier in AI, enabling machines to perform tasks that once seemed exclusively human. Whether it's writing text, classifying images or understanding natural language, DL models are reshaping how businesses operate, communicate and innovate at scale.

Types of AI: Understanding Scope and Capability

Not all AI is created equal. While much of what we interact with today falls under one broad category, AI exists on a spectrum of intelligence and autonomy. Understanding the different types of AI – Narrow AI, General AI and Super-intelligent AI – is essential for appreciating both its current impact and its future potential.

Narrow AI: The Specialist

Also known as Weak AI, Narrow AI refers to systems designed to perform a specific task or solve a well-defined problem. These systems may surpass human performance in that specific domain, but they lack broader reasoning or adaptability outside their area of expertise. Narrow AI is everywhere in business today, here are some examples:

- Google Search uses AI to provide personalized, context-aware search results.
- Netflix and Spotify leverage recommendation engines to tailor content based on user behaviour.
- Amazon Alexa and Apple Siri interpret voice commands and respond with relevant information – but only within their programmed scope.
- Fast fashion brand Zara uses narrow AI to predict trends and manage inventory in real time. AI models analyze sales data, weather patterns and social media mentions to guide production. The result is less overstock, faster turnover and a better match between supply and customer demand.

While Narrow AI is largely context-specific, it is still highly efficient and is widely deployed. Asking Siri to give an analysis of an abstract philosophical essay or translate it into Mandarin will expose the narrow intelligence and context-specific approach of the system. Narrow AI lacks the profound deductive reasoning capabilities, as **it was never meant to reason in such abstract terms.**

General AI: The Theoretical All-Rounder

Artificial General Intelligence (AGI), or Strong AI, is still a theoretical construct. It refers to machines that can perform any intellectual task a human can, with equal or greater proficiency. This means possessing:

- reasoning ability;
- learning across domains;
- adaptability to new situations;
- self-awareness and emotional understanding (in theory).

AGI is what we often see in fiction:

- HAL 9000 in 2001: A Space Odyssey.
- Data from Star Trek.
- J.A.R.V.I.S. from Iron Man.

While no real-world AGI exists yet, leading organizations such as OpenAI, DeepMind, Meta and Anthropic are exploring research frontiers in this direction. These efforts raise profound ethical, social and economic questions.

Reflection Prompt

If a machine can learn any task a human can – and even do it better – who should be responsible for its decisions? The developer? The business using it? The machine itself?

AGI has certain challenges to it in not just engineering but also in areas like governance, accountability and trust. AGI is not like narrow AI, which is more constrained and predictable. It can develop emergent capabilities, making it difficult to predict its behaviour or even control it.

Superintelligent AI: The Hypothetical Apex

Super-intelligent AI refers to machines that outclass human ingenuity, reasoning, emotional capabilities and even scientific inventions on all fronts. This is an intensely controversial topic between specialists, ethicists and even futurists of the world.

Several prominent voices have raised concerns about the existential risks posed by machines whose goals could be counter to human values such as Nick Bostrom (author of Superintelligence) and Elon Musk. Some argue that those fears are overblown along with perpetuating distraction from present day troubles like algorithmic bias or data privacy.

The development of Superintelligent AI is often regarded as the 'end game' in the field of AI. While it is not possible to achieve this at the moment, the existence of such systems has created debate concerning AI alignment, implementing measures that allow superior AI systems to operate within human interests.

Case Story: AlphaFold – Approaching General Intelligence?

In 2020, DeepMind's AlphaFold produced a solution to the protein folding problem – a puzzle that molecular biologists have spent half a century trying to unravel. This achievement did not only surpass the ability of human experts; it drastically shifted the playing field of what machines are capable of contributing towards science.

Although AlphaFold is considered a form of Narrow AI, the lack of human algorithmic assistance in generalizing to different structures of proteins makes it seem like we are getting closer to developing machines that are capable of human learning and reasoning.

Note: This story is constructed by the author with the help of publicly available industry and academic sources. The information is intended for education purposes and does rationalize some elements in order to make complex themes more clearer.

Source

https://www.nature.com/articles/s41586-021-03819-2;
https://pmc.ncbi.nlm.nih.gov/articles/PMC9442638/;
https://www.youtube.com/watch?v=B9PL__gVxLI&ab_channel=Yannic Kilcher

While the only part of business operations today harnessed is Narrow AI, the development towards AGI and beyond is as real as it gets. The augmentation of technology makes clear the direction that industry, government and society are shifting towards. Companies need to adopt a policy of vigilance and, rather, take a stance where they lead the charge in adopting AI responsibly.

AI Agentics: From Tools to Semi-Autonomous Actors

AI systems are evolving from passive tools that only function upon receiving an action to proactive agents capable of social interaction and autonomous decision-making, marking the onset of AI Agentics.

What Is AI Agentics?

To put this in a definition, it is the capacity of an AI system to perform actions autonomously and proactively, as an agent. This differentiates it from command-response systems, which are still reliant on human input. **AI agents can:**

- Monitor their environment.
- Initiate actions on their own.
- Adapt based on feedback.
- Collaborate with humans or other agents.
- In essence, agentic AI systems don't just follow commands – they participate in decisions.

The following are some key characteristics of agentic AI systems:

(1) Autonomy: Agentic AI can function without the direct supervision of a human. One example is an AI customer service agent who can automate ticket triaging, responding to queries, escalating unresolved issues and do follow-ups.
(2) Proactivity: Agentic systems set out to achieve objectives or respond to triggers in their environment. Unlike human-operated marionettes, AI-driven marketing tools can autonomously enact campaigns triggered by real-time data and customer activity.
(3) Learning and Adaptation: Various methods of perceiving new data – from supervised to unsupervised to reinforcing cognitive functions – entail the evolution of agentic AI in response to feedback.
(4) Social Interaction: With the ability to perceive emotion, context or intent, advanced AI agents can reason human interactions with customers, colleagues or other AI systems and adapt accordingly.

AI Agent — A software entity that perceives its environment, makes decisions, and acts autonomously to achieve specific objectives, often with the ability to learn and interact socially.

Case Story: Amelia by IPsoft – The Cognitive Digital Worker

At several global banks and telecom companies, a cognitive agent named Amelia handles customer service and back-office operations. Unlike basic chatbots, Amelia understands natural language, learns from previous interactions, and even recognizes customer frustration to reroute or escalate issues. She isn't just a tool – she's treated as a digital co-worker, working side-by-side with human employees.

Note: This story was developed by the author based on publicly available academic and industry sources. It is intended for educational purposes and may simplify or generalize certain aspects for clarity.

Source

https://amelia.ai/wp-content/uploads/2016/10/Amelia-in-Action.pdf;
https://www.horsesforsources.com/storage/app/uploads/public/593/7f0/a88/5937f0a88d666390091336.pdf;
https://www.wire19.com/2019-be-year-aiops-meets-chatops-uday-chinta-ipsoft/

Having defined AI Agentics and outlined its core characteristics, we now turn to its emerging applications and the strategic implications businesses must consider when AI moves from execution to participation.

Reflection Prompt: From Agent to Ally?

- If AI agents become part of decision-making loops in marketing, HR or operations – should they be given names, roles or even status within teams?
- Some firms now introduce their agents with identities: 'This report was prepared with the help of Ava, our AI marketing analyst.'
- Is this smart branding or premature anthropomorphism?

AI Agentics signals a paradigm shift – from intelligent tools to proactive digital actors. This evolution will not just change workflows but will reshape organizational structures, human roles and the ethics of decision-making. For forward-thinking leaders and learners, understanding and preparing for this transformation is no longer optional – it is essential.

The Table 1.4 offers a structured comparison of the four major types of AI – Narrow AI, General AI, Superintelligent AI and Agentic AI. It describes their range, fundamental competencies, achievement level and customary uses. This overview comparison sheds light on the differences in the complexity and independence of AI systems, their varying types, and their relevance to business needs and the level of technology.

Global AI Hubs: From Research Labs to Business Frontlines

The reach of intelligent systems has expanded well beyond academic research centres and the imagination of science fiction writers. They have now taken over executive offices and cloud ecosystems where billions of users interact daily. At the pinnacle of the diverse ecosystem shift are AI lifecycle hubs of innovation in AI, technology companies and research labs, which are applying available research breakthroughs with practical implementation. These institutions go beyond developing algorithms and crafting plans on how enterprises should operate, compete and strategize in the upcoming years.

OpenAI remains one of the most recognizable names in the industry. With the release of each new model, public expectations of AI capabilities are constantly evolving. OpenAI's models have progressively advanced from fluency and premise comprehension in text to multimodal functions with voice, vision and reasoning in GPT-4o. Regardless of these advancements, organizations now employ these models for generating marketing content, automating report writing, summarizing meetings, and even providing emulated customer service. OpenAI's efforts in AI alignment – guiding an AI's functionality within defined limits – have sparked nationwide debate concerning the ethics and governance of AI technologies.

The most extensive deployment of OpenAI features for commercial use was executed by Microsoft through integrating Azure OpenAI Services with the company's flagship enterprise product: Microsoft Copilot. Word, Outlook, Excel, PowerPoint and Teams have all been enhanced with Copilot, which actively engages users to transform traditional productivity software into dynamic and intelligent partners. A sales professional can now ask Excel to generate predictive forecasts or ask Word to draft a proposal based on meeting notes. This integration exemplifies how AI shifts from a tool to a business partner.

Anhropic, another start-up in the United States, follows a contrasting approach. As part of its Claude models, it practices AI safety and reasoning transparency through 'constitutional AI,' where AI behaviour is bound by a pre-defined set of rules. Claude is being integrated into applications such as Slack and Notion, providing companies with customizable and safer generative AI tools. This is particularly appealing to institutions with high governance, compliance and trust requirements.

In Canada, Cohere is uniquely positioned after launching privacy-first, enterprise-grade LLMs. Usability is not in attention-grabbing chat interfaces but rather deeply embedding LLMs in secure organizational frameworks, making them pliable to internal data and logic. Domain-specific customization means data control makes Cohere a growing preference for the finance and legal industries.

Table 1.4. Comparison of AI Types and Their Characteristics.

Type of AI	Scope	Capabilities	Real-World Status	Example Applications
Narrow AI (ANI)	Task-specific, single domain	Executes well-defined tasks, often better than humans in that domain	Widely implemented	Chatbots, recommendation engines, spam filters
General AI (AGI)	Multi-domain, general-purpose reasoning	Mimics full human cognitive capabilities across tasks and contexts	Theoretical	None (conceptual: like HAL, J.A.R.V.I.S.)
Superintelligent AI (ASI)	Beyond human-level intelligence	Surpasses human intelligence in all domains; potentially self-improving	Hypothetical/ Futuristic	Speculative (no current examples)
Agentic AI (AI agentics)	Semi-autonomous and interactive systems	Autonomous, proactive, adaptive, socially interactive; acts with intent	Emerging, real use cases	Digital co-workers, autonomous marketing agents, smart CRM bots

While North America has led in foundational breakthroughs, Europe is the champion for open, ethical and universally available AI technology. Hugging Face, a platform born in France, has made models, datasets and training resources accessible to everyone. Now, anyone from developers and researchers to start-ups can transparently build, modify and deploy models using the platform. With unrestricted access, AI innovation is accelerated, while verification – which is especially noteworthy for regulation-heavy organizations – becomes easier.

Asia has marked its AI development with precision and state-directed ambitions in the further east. China is now experiencing competition in the LLM sector as DeepSeek has emerged to develop bilingual models excelling in English and Mandarin. This allows Chinese companies to access indigenous alternatives to GPT within the frameworks of AI sovereignty and security. DeepSeek models are currently being used to power local search engines, productivity applications and customer engagement solutions in Chinese enterprises.

China is no longer trying to play catch up with their super apps that are fully integrated into societies. This is due to China's tech giants such as Baidu and Tencent having developed LANGUAGE MODELS with ERNIE and Hunyuan respectively. These are powered with regionally tailored data, enabling them to understand culture and administrative dialects. A major distinction of these models is their functionality beyond traditional chatbot systems – they provide moderation, trading and assistive services in real-time.

At the same time, DeepMind, continuing its scientific accomplishments with AlphaGo and AlphaFold, has now entered the business AI competition with Gemini. Gemini is designed to outperform Bard's capabilities and is set to function in multiple modalities: text, speech, image and code. It is also integrated with Google Workspace, Search and YouTube, aiming to provide contextual support throughout user journeys, such as summarizing videos, planning projects or debugging code. For enterprises, it serves as a unified interface that adapts to the applications they utilize, streamlining tasks within familiar environments.

NVIDIA may not be a model developer in the traditional sense, but it is certainly the backbone of this ecosystem. Almost all large-scale OpenAI or DeepSeek LLMs rely on this firm's GPUs and software stacks for training development and scaling. In addition, enterprises can leverage NVIDIA NIM and DGX Cloud to deploy AI models with low-latency performance and streamlined accessibility, even on-premises. NVIDIA does not offer the brain of AI to sectors like autonomous vehicles, finance or genomics, but rather the nerve centre.

Lastly, we can say that innovation is no longer in silos. Newer players such as Mistral (France), MosaicML (USA) and TII (UAE) are creating open-weight models which compete with proprietary systems. They are pioneering a more modular, open and configurable AI, particularly for businesses with differentiated data, workflows and value systems.

Table 1.5 presents a comparable summary of leading AI platforms to better understand how AI innovation is unfolding across the globe. It sheds light on the flagship model of each platform, their focal strategy, relevance to business and differentiating features, thereby showing the contributions of various organizations towards the development of AI across industries and applications.

Table 1.5. AI Innovation Platforms Comparison.

Platform	Flagship Model	Focus	Impact	Business Relevance	Differentiator
OpenAI	GPT-4, GPT-4o	Multimodal LLMs, reasoning, alignment	Widespread adoption via ChatGPT, APIs	Marketing, customer support, automation	Leading language capabilities, ChatGPT reach
Microsoft	Copilot	Enterprise productivity, AI in office tools	Embedded across MS Office, Azure	Document drafting, Excel analysis, presentations	Seamless integration with enterprise software
Anthropic	Claude 2, Claude 3	Constitutional AI, safe and steerable outputs	Adopted in Slack, Notion and Zoom	Privacy-sensitive applications, content summarization	Focus on transparent and ethical responses
Google DeepMind	Gemini	Multimodal search, productivity, creativity	Integrated with Google Workspace, Search	Team collaboration, writing, summarization	Context-aware AI with real-time data access
Meta	LLaMA 2, LLaMA 3	Open-source LLMs, multilingual NLP	Used in research and lightweight apps	Language localization, academic research	Open access and global language coverage
NVIDIA	NIM, DGX Cloud (infra)	AI infra, deployment, acceleration	Used across AI labs and enterprises	Model training, inference, analytics at scale	Hardware-software synergy, real-time performance
Hugging Face	Transformers Hub	Open-source model hosting and training	Backbone for custom AI development	Model fine-tuning, deployment pipelines	Community-driven, model-agnostic tools

(Continued)

Table 1.5. *(Continued)*

Platform	Flagship Model	Focus	Impact	Business Relevance	Differentiator
Cohere	Command R+	Enterprise-focused LLMs, RAG-based	Integrated into vertical-specific tools	Legal, finance, healthcare knowledge apps	Privacy-first deployment on internal data
DeepSeek (China)	DeepSeek-V2	Bilingual LLMs (English-Mandarin)	Localized for Chinese platforms	Search, productivity, virtual assistants	High Mandarin performance, open weights
Baidu	ERNIE Bot	Chinese NLP, cultural understanding	Used in Baidu search and smart services	Search, content filtering, knowledge bots	Optimized for domestic Chinese use cases
Tencent	Hunyuan	Multimodal Chinese AI	Deployed in WeChat and cloud services	Conversational AI, smart content	Integrated with Chinaâ€™s largest app ecosystem
Mistral	Mistral 7B, Mixtral	Efficient open-weight LLMs	Popular in lightweight apps and dev tools	DevOps, education, start-ups	Small, fast and transparent models
MosaicML	MPT-7B	Customizable foundation models	Adopted for private model training	Enterprise custom AI stacks	Optimization for training speed and control
TII (UAE)	Falcon	Open-weight, Arabic-centric LLMs	Deployed in government and research	Language translation, document AI	Leadership in Arabic AI capability

AI development is no longer confined to a few research labs, as is conspicuous in the table. It is dynamic, multi-regional and highly competitive. It is important for businesses as well as educators to appreciate the capabilities and orientations of the platforms for proper adoption, integration and policy formulation. It is important to understand that there is a particular philosophy and market focus for each platform, which highlights the importance of strategic alignment when choosing AI partners or solutions.

Reflection Prompt

As research institutions transform into policy-shaping AI labs, what questions should business leaders and educators ask themselves to remain responsibly innovative and relevant?

Evolution of AI in Business

Back-office automation is no longer the limit of AI; it has transformed into the nerve centre of contemporary business. AI was previously believed to be a cost-saving option for mundane tasks such as document classification and customer ticketing, but companies can now use it to improve value, agility and scale personalization. Its evolution in business resembles the digital maturity curve, progressing from initial caution to orchestrated widespread adoption.

Practically, AI has had an impact on all business verticals. The list includes but is not limited to marketing, where hyper-personalization is practised, in recruitment that is automated, predictive operations and intelligence in financial systems. There is a rapid change in these domains. Chapter 2 delves into these domain-specific transformations using real-world case studies to **provide clarity on how AI is applied in various functions.**

The adoption trajectory of AI can be best understood not as a binary (used or not used), but as a continuum – a strategic progression that reflects the depth, scope and intent of AI implementation. At one end are businesses that experiment with AI in silos, often in low-risk functions. At the other end are organizations that embed AI across decision-making, innovation pipelines and customer strategy. To help organizations assess where they are and where they could go, the author proposes an AI Adoption Continuum. This framework is explored in detail in Chapter 4.

This evolution is not linear – it is layered, strategic and increasingly central to how businesses create value in a data-driven economy. What's clear is that AI is no longer a technical add-on – it's a strategic asset. The question for businesses is no longer whether to adopt AI, but how far and how fast.

Chapter Summary

AI is no longer an abstract technological concept – it is a strategic business capability with real and immediate implications. This chapter laid the foundation by defining AI and differentiating it from related fields such as ML, DL and data science. Through a historical lens, we traced AI's evolution from philosophical roots and rule-based systems to today's advanced, multimodal models. We examined the core mechanisms of AI, including learning paradigms, neural networks and DL architectures, to understand how intelligence is built, scaled and applied.

The chapter also outlined the different types of AI – from narrow to super-intelligent – and introduced AI agentics, marking a transition from tools to semi-autonomous actors. Furthermore, the landscape of global AI platforms was explored, highlighting how organizations like OpenAI, Microsoft, Google DeepMind, Meta and others are shaping the business adoption of AI. Finally, we examined the adoption continuum, positioning AI not as a binary decision but as a journey from experimentation to enterprise-wide transformation.

Future Outlook

As AI becomes more agentic, multimodal and integrated into core functions, business leaders must not only adopt it – but also govern, scale and humanize it. The chapters ahead will delve deeper into applications across marketing, operations, CRM, ethics and analytics. Understanding AI's foundations now equips you to navigate its future – one where organizations will be judged not only by how they use AI, but by how responsibly and creatively they do so.

Discussion Questions

(1) How would you define AI in your own words, and how does your definition align with or differ from the formal definitions presented in the chapter?
(2) In what ways does understanding the distinction between AI, ML, DL and data science influence how businesses adopt technology?
(3) Which historical milestone in AI do you think had the greatest impact on business adoption – and why?
(4) Which type of AI (Narrow, General, Superintelligent, Agentic) is most relevant for your industry today? Which type might be relevant in 5–10 years?
(5) What are the strategic risks and rewards of integrating agentic AI into decision-making processes in business functions like marketing, HR or finance?
(6) Where would you place your current organization or industry on the AI Adoption Continuum introduced in this chapter? What would it take to move to the next level?

Reference

Zao-Sanders, M. (2025, April 9). How people are really using Gen AI in 2025. *Harvard Business Review.*

Further Readings

Avery, J., & Steenburgh, T. (2024, November–December). Should we deploy a Gen AI salesbot? *Harvard Business Review.* https://hbr.org/2024/11/case-study-should-we-deploy-a-gen-ai-salesbot

Baabdullah, A. M. (2023). The precursors of AI adoption in business: Towards an efficient decision-making and functional performance. *International Journal of Information Management*, *75*, 102745. https://doi.org/10.1016/j.ijinfomgt.2023.102745

Gupta, S., & Cespedes, F. (2025, March). How one company used AI to broaden its customer base. *Harvard Business Review.* https://hbr.org/2025/03/how-one-company-used-ai-to-broaden-its-customer-base

Ivey Publishing. (2025, April). *Starbucks deep brew: AI-powered customer experience.* Ivey Business School. https://www.iveypublishing.ca/s/product/starbucks-deep-brew-aipowered-customer-experience/01tOF000007Z2pJYAS

Maiti, M., Kayal, P., & Vujko, A. (2025). A study on ethical implications of artificial intelligence adoption in business: Challenges and best practices. *Future Business Journal*, *11*(1), 34. https://doi.org/10.1186/s43093-025-00462-5

OECD. (2025). *The adoption of artificial intelligence in firms.* OECD Publishing. https://doi.org/10.1787/f9ef33c3-en

Rahman, S., & Lim, M. (2024, May). How aggressively should a bank pursue AI? *Harvard Business Review.* https://hbr.org/2024/05/case-study-how-aggressively-should-a-bank-pursue-ai

Schwäke, J., Peters, A., Kanbach, D. K., & Kraus, S. (2024). The new normal: The status quo of AI adoption in SMEs. *Journal of Small Business Management*, *63*(3), 1297–1331. https://doi.org/10.1080/00472778.2024.2379999

Wharton AI and Analytics Initiative and GBK Collective. (2024). *Growing up: Navigating Gen AI's early years.* https://ai.wharton.upenn.edu/focus-areas/human-technology-interaction/2024-ai-adoption-report

Chapter 2

The Current Landscape of AI in Business

CEO: "So, we have AI. Are we future-ready?"

CTO: "We're not future proof because we have AI. We're future proof because we know how to use it."

Case Study: From Efficiency to Intelligence: Siemens' AI Journey

In 2018, Siemens, an industrial giant with 175 years of history, faced a problem common to many old-line companies: how to keep up with the digital world. Operating in energy, manufacturing, healthcare and infrastructure across more than 150 nations, the company was dealing with a vast and intricate network of assets, supply chains and product lifecycles. Efficiency gains from conventional practices had stabilized, while the expectations of customers for speed, precision and customization were increasing rapidly. Rather than taking incremental steps, Siemens took a courageous step in adopting artificial intelligence (AI) as the cornerstone of its digital transformation. The organization began to incorporate AI into factory machinery for predictive maintenance, deploying machine learning to streamline supply chains and leveraging generative AI in product development. Siemens started questioning how its entire business could operate smarter, quicker and more sustainably. This was not just about automation; it was about enabling humans and machines to work together in new, more productive ways. Today, Siemens saves millions annually with predictive maintenance, accelerated product innovation cycles and provides smarter solutions to customers worldwide. The Siemens narrative also points to a

(*Continued*)

AI and Business, 31–43

Published under exclusive licence by Emerald Publishing Limited
doi:10.1108/978-1-83708-888-120261002

(*Continued*)

greater truth: AI is not merely a technological tool, but it is a transformative driver for business. This chapter will demonstrate that the Siemens journey is not isolated, but one of a greater sea change happening across multiple industries.

Sources:

Siemens. (2024, January 8; 2023, September 15; 2024, January 9) https://press.siemens.com/global/en/pressrelease/siemens-accelerates-path-toward-ai-driven-industries-through-innovation-and

https://www.siemens.com/global/en/company/insights/leveraging-artificial-intelligence-in-a-sustainable-digital-enterprise.html

https://press.siemens.com/global/en/pressrelease/siemens-unveils-break-through-innovations-industrial-ai-and-digital-twin-technology-ces.

The relentless march of technology has ushered in numerous innovations, but few have the potential to redefine the game, reach deeply into the masses, and have both promise and concern like AI. AI was once confined to research labs and science fiction, but it has evolved to become a primary driver of efficiency, innovation and competitive advantage in business processes. We are at a turning point where understanding and using AI's practical applications is no longer just a goal for tech giants. It has become essential for organizations of all sizes and sectors working in today's highly competitive and data-rich landscape. This chapter serves as a preliminary guide, describing AI's transition into the mainstream of business, explaining why it is necessary to comprehend its true applications across disciplines, and outlining the steps we will undertake to offer actionable insights. It discusses how AI is presently applied across major business areas such as marketing, finance, operations and human resources. It also examines insights from top international business organizations that incorporated AI as a core operation. The aim is to provide a holistic picture of how AI plays a role in defining today's business environment. To most, AI still equates to automating routine work, but business organizations have utilized AI to unearth deep insights buried in massive datasets. AI is fundamentally changing how organizations create value, engage with customers, manage resources and develop their workforce. This chapter explores the various ways AI is being applied in different areas within modern businesses, showing its significant effects on efficiency, decision-making and competitive advantage.

AI as the Catalyst for Business Transformation

The AI business landscape is undergoing a revolutionary shift that is transforming the manner in which companies compete, operate and generate value across virtually every sector. Developments in technologies such as machine learning, deep learning, natural language processing (NLP), computer vision and robotics have helped AI come into mainstream business planning. From small start-ups to multinational corporations, businesses are leveraging AI to automate processes, personalize customer experiences, reduce costs, accelerate innovation and make data-driven decisions with unparalleled precision. At the core of this transformation is a surge in data and processing power, enabling AI systems to analyze and interpret massive amounts of data in real-time.

The use of AI is no longer a distant, futuristic dream; it is a fact occurring today, revolutionizing strategy, process and organizational culture. Organizations across all industries are employing AI to solve complex problems, seize new possibilities and deliver superior value to their stakeholders. This chapter examines how the capabilities of AI, ranging from machine learning and NLP to computer vision and predictive analytics, are being used to drive innovation and enhance performance in a business's core functions, such as marketing, finance, operations and human resources. This inquiry will establish particular applications and the accompanying mechanisms through which AI is reshaping the competitive landscape and elevating standards for organizational excellence.

Marketing

Precision, Personalization and Predictive Power

The marketing landscape has undergone a seismic shift, moving from mass communication to highly individualized engagement. AI is at the forefront of this transformation, enabling marketers to understand customer behaviour with unparalleled depth, craft hyper-personalised campaigns and predict future trends with remarkable accuracy. This section explores AI's pivotal role in personalized marketing campaigns and predictive analytics which are reshaping the role of marketing in the business:

Personalized Marketing Campaigns: Generic advertisements are quickly becoming a thing of the past. Today's consumers expect brands to understand their individual preferences, needs and shopping behaviour. AI-powered personalization enables companies to send customized messages, product suggestions, and offers to individual customers at the precise time via the most effective channels.

Customer Segmentation and Profiling: AI can process vast datasets of customer information, such as demographics, purchase history, browsing behaviour, social media activity and even emotional reactions, to develop micro customer segments. In contrast to conventional segmentation based on wide categories, AI detects subtle patterns and micro-segments that provide deeper insights into the motivations of customers. For example, a computer program could recognize a group of consumers who regularly visit hiking equipment but buy only during the holiday seasons, and send targeted advertisements at those very times. This rich profiling enables marketers to learn not only who their customers are, but also why they act the way they do.

Dynamic content and product suggestions: Online retailers such as Amazon and Netflix are classic examples of the strength of AI in suggestions. Collaborative filtering and AI-driven content-based recommendation systems scan user interests, past interactions and user behaviours similar to those of other users to recommend products, movies or articles. This goes beyond recommending just items to generating dynamic content for websites and emails. An AI system can edit web page layouts, present varying banner advertisements or modify email subject lines and copy in real-time according to the individual user's profile and existing browsing session, for optimum engagement and conversion. Envision an online apparel store where the home page reconfigures its product presentation dynamically to showcase sustainable fashion for one customer and high-end brands for another based on their previous interactions and expressed preferences.

Automated Customer Journey Orchestration: AI can orchestrate multi-touch customer journeys across email, social media, mobile apps and websites. It analyses how customers move through the sales funnel to determine the best points for intervention, like sending a reminder email after a cart abandonment or providing an incentive for a hesitant buyer. AI chatbots and virtual assistants offer real-time, one-on-one assistance, responding to questions, assisting customers with product selection and even completing transactions, all in a smooth and hassle-free customer experience 24/7. Not only does this improve customer satisfaction, but it also frees the human agents to deal with more complex issues.

Predictive Personalization: Beyond responding to past behaviour, AI can forecast future customer behaviour. By identifying churn, repeat buy offers or upgrade patterns, AI enables marketers to be proactive in engaging customers. For instance, if a customer is forecasted by an AI model to churn, then the model will launch a retention campaign with customized incentives ahead of the customer's decision to leave. This proactive strategy repositions marketing as a reactive reaction to customer behaviour into a predictive and preventative process.

Predictive Analytics in Marketing

Predictive analytics applies statistical algorithms and machine learning methods to predict future outcomes based on past data. In marketing, this capability is priceless to maximize campaigns, allocating budgets efficiently and adapting to market dynamics.

Lead Scoring and Qualification: Not all leads are created equal. AI-driven lead scoring models assess different characteristics of a lead (e.g., company size, industry, content engagement, site visits) to determine a score for their likelihood of conversion. This enables sales and marketing teams to focus on high-value leads, using resources more effectively and enhancing conversion rates. A high score may represent a "hot" lead that should be contacted for immediate sales, while a reduced score suggests nurturing using automated email campaigns.

Customer Lifetime Value (CLTV) Forecasting: Knowing the long-term value of a customer is important for sustainable growth. AI algorithms can forecast CLTV by analysing past purchase behaviour, the level of engagement and demographic data. The forecast is useful for marketers to determine high-value customers who should receive special attention. They can also optimize marketing spend by prioritizing it on acquiring and retaining customers who are most likely to bring high revenue during their lifetime. It moves from an individual transaction to a lasting customer relationship.

Campaign Optimization and Budget Allocation: AI can analyze the performance of previous marketing campaigns across multiple channels and determine which method returns the highest ROI. With knowledge of causal connections among marketing expenditure, channel mix, creative content and customer response, AI can suggest maximum budget allocation over different channels (e.g., social media, search ads, email) and optimize bids in real-time for digital advertising platforms. This will guarantee that marketing budgets are invested in the most effective activities, driving maximum reach and conversion.

Market Trend Predictions: AI can scan large external datasets-including economic signs, social media sentiment, news and competitor activities – to forecast upcoming market trends, changes in customer preference and potential disruptions. Businesses can then adjust their marketing strategies ahead of time, create new products or services that suit upcoming demand and gain a competitive advantage. For example, AI can identify increasing interest in eco-friendly packaging several months before it enters mainstream consumer demand, and then a company could place itself at the forefront in that space.

Finance: Mitigating Risk and Maximizing Returns

The finance industry, characterized by vast amounts of data, complex transactions and stringent regulations, has been an early adopter of AI. It's ability to process and analyze data at superhuman speeds makes it indispensable for tasks ranging from fraud detection to algorithmic trading, significantly enhancing security, efficiency and profitability. Below are some of the areas where AI has been transformative in bringing change and building organizational performance.

Fraud Detection

Financial fraud is a multi-billion-dollar problem worldwide, increasingly sophisticated in nature. AI and machine learning present an active and robust protection from such illegal schemes.

- Pattern Detection in Transactions: Conventional rule-based anti-fraud solutions are normally rigid and easily evaded by sophisticated fraudsters. AI, specifically supervised and unsupervised machine learning techniques, is best suited to detect subtle, complex and new patterns reflecting fraudulent behaviour in enormous financial transaction datasets. These tendencies may consist of unorthodox consumption patterns, out-of-pattern locations of transactions, accelerated series of transactions or departures from normal trends for an account. For instance, if a credit card that has typically been used for low-value, local purchases suddenly has a high-value cross-border transaction, an AI system can mark it immediately.

- Behavioural Analytics: In addition to basic transaction information, AI systems examine behavioural biometrics and user behaviour. These parameters cover things such as typing speed, mouse movements, login durations, the computer used and location on the network. A notable deviation from an individual's predetermined behavioural pattern will induce an alarm. If a valid user typically logs in from a certain range of IPs and at specific hours, an attempt to log in from a different location at an unusual time may be suspicious. This provides an incredibly strong layer of security that is hard for the fraudster to emulate.
- Real-time Anomaly Detection: The rapid speed at which transactions take place requires real-time fraud detection. AI systems can handle millions of transactions per second, detecting anomalies in the moment, before fraudulent transactions are finalized. Instant reaction is essential to credit card fraud, internet banking and e-commerce, where seconds can mean thousands of dollars in losses. Advanced deep learning frameworks, like autoencoders, are especially well-suited to learning regular transaction patterns and detecting anomalies without the need for explicit rule coding.
- Network Analysis: AI can map and analyze relationships between entities (accounts, individuals, merchants) and examine their connections to discover organized fraud networks. By graphing and examining these networks, AI can find clusters of suspicious activity, similar traits among fraudulent accounts, or individuals that are parties to numerous suspicious transactions, even when individual transactions look legitimate. This bird's-eye view is able to expose broader, coordinated fraud schemes.
- Adaptive Learning: Scammers keep changing their tactics. AI models are trained to learn and evolve in the long term. Whenever new fraud trends are detected and recognized (either by analysts or through semi-supervised learning), the AI model can be retrained or upgraded to identify these new strategies, maintaining its effectiveness against new threats. This cycle of continuous learning makes AI an extremely robust defence mechanism.

Algorithmic Trading

Algorithmic trading, or "algo-trading," involves making trades using computer algorithms at volumes and speeds impossible for human traders. AI refines these algorithms, creating more advanced strategies and higher returns. Below are several key uses of algorithmic trading:

- High-Frequency Trading (HFT): While HFT primarily depends on speed and low latency benefits in the first place, AI and machine learning algorithms are increasingly applied to process enormous streams of market data (price movements, order book levels, news sentiment) at microsecond speeds. These models have the ability to identify fleeting arbitrage opportunities, forecast short-term price action and complete trades quicker than the human eye, profiting from infinitesimal price variations. AI assists in optimizing order placement and routing for minimal market impact.
- Predictive Market Analysis: AI algorithms can examine past price history, trading volumes, economic metrics, news sentiment, social media and even satellite imagery (e.g., to forecast commodity production) to predict future market movements. In contrast with standard econometric models, AI has the ability to identify non-linear relationships and complex interactions among variables, producing precise predictions of asset prices, volatility and market direction. For instance, NLP AI can search news stories and social media for sentiment changes that could influence stock prices.
- Risk Management and Portfolio Optimization: AI models can more dynamically evaluate and manage portfolio risk. By simulating multiple market conditions and evaluating the correlations among assets in stressed situations, AI can maximize returns for a given risk level or minimize risk for a desired return. AI is also able to recognize hidden risks in a portfolio that may not be realized with conventional methods. AI can constantly monitor market environments and rebalance portfolios automatically whenever risk factors change, maintaining maximum risk-adjusted returns.
- Execution Efficiency: AI enables traders to execute large trade orders with little market effect. Instead of executing a big trade all at once, which could shift prices against them, AI algorithms can break orders into smaller pieces and execute them gradually, considering the liquidity, volatility and order book behaviour of the market. This "smart order routing" is designed to get the best possible execution price and reduce slippage.
- Sentiment Analysis for Trading: AI, especially NLP techniques, is increasingly applied to analyze news headlines, social media mentions and earnings call transcripts to measure market sentiment regarding individual companies or the general market. A sudden spike in negative sentiment regarding a company, as captured by AI, might activate a sell signal, while positive sentiment might be a buy signal. This offers a faster, complimentary data point for trading decisions than older-style fundamental analysis.

Operations: Streamlining Processes and Enhancing Efficiency

AI is revolutionizing operational efficiency by optimizing complex processes, predicting equipment failures and managing intricate supply chains. Its ability to process real-time data and make intelligent decisions is leading to significant cost savings, improved productivity and enhanced resilience. Below are some of the areas where AI has consistently supported and helped in building a seamless supply chain.

Supply Chain Optimization

Modern supply chains are global, complex and susceptible to numerous disruptions. AI provides the intelligence needed to manage these complexities, ensuring the smooth flow of goods and services from origin to consumption.

- **Demand Forecasting:** Accurate demand forecasting is the cornerstone of an efficient supply chain. AI models analyze historical sales data, promotional events, economic indicators, weather patterns, social media trends and even competitor actions to generate highly accurate demand predictions. Unlike traditional statistical methods, AI accounts for non-linear relationships and external variables, leading to reduced stock-outs and minimized overstocking. For instance, an AI can predict a surge in demand for winter apparel based on long-range weather predictions and social media conversations about impending cold snaps.
- **Inventory Management:** Leveraging demand forecasts, AI optimizes inventory levels across various warehouses and distribution centres. It determines optimal reorder points and quantities, considering lead times, carrying costs and potential obsolescence. AI can dynamically adjust inventory strategies in response to real-time changes in demand or supply, minimizing capital tied up in inventory while ensuring product availability. This prevents both costly overstock and lost sales due to shortages.
- **Logistics and Route Optimization:** AI algorithms determine the most efficient delivery routes for fleets of vehicles, considering factors such as traffic conditions, delivery windows, fuel costs, vehicle capacity and driver availability. This leads to reduced transportation costs, faster deliveries and lower carbon emissions. Furthermore, AI can optimize warehouse layouts, picking paths for order fulfilment, and even drone delivery routes, significantly improving throughput and efficiency within logistics hubs. Companies like UPS use AI to optimize routes daily, saving millions of miles and gallons of fuel.
- **Risk Management and Resilience:** Supply chains are vulnerable to disruptions from natural disasters, geopolitical events, supplier failures or sudden demand spikes. AI monitors global events in real-time, identifies potential risks and predicts their impact on the supply chain. By simulating various scenarios, AI recommends alternative suppliers, reroutes shipments or pre-position inventory to mitigate the impact of disruptions, building a more resilient supply chain. This proactive risk assessment helps companies avoid costly delays and reputational damage.
- **Supplier Relationship Management:** AI analyzes supplier performance data, including delivery times, quality control, pricing and compliance. This helps businesses identify reliable suppliers, negotiate better terms and proactively address potential issues with underperforming partners, strengthening the overall supply chain ecosystem. AI also facilitates onboarding new suppliers by rapidly assessing their capabilities and risks.

Predictive Maintenance

Predictive maintenance uses AI and machine learning to forecast when and how equipment might fail, enabling maintenance to be performed exactly when needed, rather than on a fixed schedule or after a breakdown.

- **Sensor Data Analysis:** Industrial equipment, vehicles and machinery are increasingly equipped with sensors that collect vast amounts of operational data: temperature, pressure, vibration, motor speed, current, acoustic signatures and more. AI algorithms analyze this continuous stream of sensor data in real-time. By learning the "normal" operating patterns of equipment, AI can detect subtle anomalies or deviations that indicate an impending malfunction or degradation.
- **Failure Prediction Models:** Machine learning models are trained on historical datasets that include both normal operations and data recorded before known equipment failures. AI learns the unique "signatures" of failure modes. For example, a slight increase in vibration frequency or a gradual rise in bearing temperature might precede a motor breakdown. Once trained, these models can predict the probability of failure for a given component or machine within a specific timeframe.
- **Optimized Maintenance Scheduling:** Armed with precise failure predictions, maintenance teams can transition from reactive (repairing after a breakdown) or preventive (fixed-schedule maintenance, which can be costly and unnecessary) approaches to a proactive, "just-in-time" strategy. AI determines the optimal time to schedule maintenance activities, minimizing downtime and costs. Instead of replacing a part every 10,000 hours, it's replaced only when the AI predicts it's nearing its end-of-life. This extends asset lifespan and reduces unplanned stoppages.
- **Root Cause Analysis:** When a failure does occur, AI assists in root cause analysis by examining historical sensor data and operational logs to identify the exact sequence of events or contributing factors that led to the breakdown. This helps engineers understand underlying problems and implement more effective preventive measures in the future.
- **Resource and Spare Parts Management:** Predictive maintenance allows for better planning of spare parts inventory and technician availability. Knowing which machines are likely to require service soon, companies can ensure the necessary parts are on hand and skilled personnel are scheduled, further reducing downtime and carrying costs for parts.
- **Safety Enhancement:** By preventing unexpected equipment failures, predictive maintenance significantly enhances workplace safety. It reduces the risk of accidents caused by sudden mechanical breakdowns, protecting workers and ensuring compliance with safety regulations. This is particularly critical in industries such as manufacturing, aviation and energy.

Human Resources: Optimizing Talent and Employee Experience

Talent Acquisition and Recruitment

AI automates and enhances the hiring processes, making them faster and more efficient:

- Resume Screening and Candidate Matching – AI-powered Applicant Tracking Systems (ATS) analyze resumes, match skills to job descriptions and rank candidates based on suitability.
- Chatbots for Recruitment – AI chatbots like Mya, Olivia, etc., engage candidates, answer FAQs, schedule interviews and provide updates.
- Bias Reduction – AI reduces unconscious bias by anonymizing resumes and focusing on skills rather than demographics.
- Predictive Hiring – AI assesses historical hiring data to predict candidate success and cultural fit.

Employee Onboarding and Engagement

AI personalizes onboarding and keeps employees engaged:

- Automated Onboarding Workflows – AI guides new hires through paperwork, training and introductions via chatbots and digital assistants.
- Personalized Learning Paths – AI recommends training programs based on employee roles, skill gaps and career aspirations.
- Sentiment Analysis – AI analyzes employee feedback (surveys, emails, chats) to gauge morale and identify concerns.

Performance Management and Career Development

AI enables data-driven performance insights and career growth:

- Continuous Feedback Tools – AI-powered platforms (e.g., 15Five, Lattice) analyze performance in real-time and suggest improvements.
- Skill Gap Analysis – AI identifies training needs by comparing employee skills with industry trends.
- Career Path Recommendations – AI suggests internal mobility opportunities based on skills and aspirations.

Employee Retention and Predictive Analytics

AI helps HR predict and reduce turnover.

- Attrition Risk Prediction – AI analyzes engagement surveys, performance data and behavioural patterns to flag employees at risk of leaving.

- Personalized Retention Strategies – AI recommends tailored interventions (e.g., promotions, mentorship) to retain top talent.

HR Operations and Workforce Planning

AI optimizes administrative tasks and strategic workforce decisions:

- Automated HR Queries – AI chatbots handle routine employee questions about payroll, leave policies and benefits.
- Workforce Forecasting – AI predicts future hiring needs based on business growth, turnover trends and market conditions.
- Diversity and Inclusion Analytics – AI tracks diversity metrics and suggests ways to improve inclusivity.

Enhancing Employee Experience With AI Assistants

- Virtual HR Assistants (e.g., Slack bots, Microsoft Viva) provide instant support for HR-related queries.
- AI-Powered Wellness Programmes – AI recommends mental health resources, fitness plans and stress management tools based on employee needs.

AI is revolutionizing HR by making talent management more efficient, data-driven and employee-centric. By automating repetitive tasks, enhancing decision-making, and personalizing employee experiences, AI helps organizations attract, retain and develop top talent while fostering a positive workplace culture.

Conclusion: The Path Forward for AI in Business

The pervasive adoption of AI across various functions of organizations like marketing, finance, operations and human resources functions signifies a fundamental shift in how businesses operate and strategize. AI is no longer a futuristic concept but a powerful suite of tools that enhances decision-making, automates complex processes and uncovers efficiencies previously unattainable. From crafting hyper-personalized marketing campaigns and fortifying financial systems against fraud to optimizing intricate supply chains and transforming talent management, AI's impact is undeniable and continues to expand.

The benefits of these applications are manifold: increased operational efficiency, significant cost reductions, superior customer experiences, more robust risk management and the ability to attract and retain top talent. However, the journey towards AI integration is not without its challenges. Ethical considerations, data privacy concerns, the shortage of skilled AI professionals, and the imperative to manage algorithmic bias remain critical areas of focus. Organizations must ensure that AI systems are developed and deployed responsibly, transparently and with human oversight to maximize their positive impact while mitigating potential risks.

As AI technologies continue to mature, their applications will become even more sophisticated and integrated, paving the way for truly intelligent enterprises that can adapt rapidly to change, innovate continuously and achieve unprecedented levels of performance. The businesses that embrace AI strategically, investing in both the technology and the talent required to leverage it effectively, will be best positioned to thrive in the complex and dynamic global economy of tomorrow. AI is not just a tool; it is a strategic imperative for navigating the future of business.

Discussion Questions

(1) Which business function – Marketing, Finance, Operations or HR – has seen the most significant transformation due to AI, and why?
(2) Ethical and unbiased use of AI in critical functions like hiring, credit scoring or personalized marketing? What governance measures are necessary?
(3) AI tools are increasingly used to predict customer behaviour and personalize experiences. To what extent does this enhance marketing effectiveness without compromising consumer privacy?
(4) In Finance, AI-driven automation (robo-advisors, fraud detection) is reducing human intervention. What are the implications of this shift for trust, accountability and regulation?
(5) To what extent can AI replace or augment human decision-making in HR, such as in recruitment, performance evaluation or employee engagement? Where should we draw the line?

References

Siemens. (2023, September 15). *Leveraging artificial intelligence in a sustainable digital enterprise*. Siemens Global. https://www.siemens.com/global/en/company/insights/leveraging-artificial-intelligence-in-a-sustainable-digital-enterprise.html

Siemens. (2024, January 8). *Siemens accelerates path toward AI-driven industries through innovation and partnerships*. Siemens Press. https://press.siemens.com/global/en/pressrelease/siemens-accelerates-path-toward-ai-driven-industries-through-innovation-and

Siemens. (2024, January 9). *Siemens unveils breakthrough innovations in industrial AI and digital twin technology at CES*. Siemens Press. https://press.siemens.com/global/en/pressrelease/siemens-unveils-breakthrough-innovations-industrial-ai-and-digital-twin-technology-ces

Further Readings

IBM. (2025). Boost productivity with AI agents. *IBM Solutions*. https://www.ibm.com/solutions/ai-agents

Renieris, E. M., Kiron, D., & Mills, S. (2024, October 29). A fragmented landscape is no excuse for global companies serious about responsible AI. *MIT Sloan Management Review*. https://sloanreview.mit.edu/article/a-fragmented-landscape-is-no-excuse-for-global-companies-serious-about-responsible-ai/

Modhy, K. (2024, November 13). *AI's role in business transformation: Overcoming challenges and driving growth*. MIT Sloan Management Review Middle East. https://www.mitsloanme.com/article/ais-role-in-business-transformation-overcoming-challenges-and-driving-growth/

World Economic Forum. (2025, January). *AI in action: Beyond experimentation to transform industry*. https://reports.weforum.org/docs/WEF_AI_in_Action_Beyond_Experimentation_to_Transform_Industry_2025.pdf

Wingate, D., Burns, B. L., & Barney, J. B. (2025, May 8). Why AI will not provide sustainable competitive advantage. *MIT Sloan Management Review*. https://sloanreview.mit.edu/article/why-ai-will-not-provide-sustainable-competitive-advantage/

McKinsey & Company. (2025, May 9). *Superagency in the workplace: Empowering people to unlock AI's full potential at work*. https://www.mckinsey.com/capabilities/mckinsey-digital/our-insights/superagency-in-the-workplace-empowering-people-to-unlock-ais-full-potential-at-work

Chui, M., & McCarthy, B. (2025, June 11). *The state of AI in 2025: How organizations are rewiring to capture value*. McKinsey & Company. https://www.mckinsey.com/capabilities/quantumblack/our-insights/the-state-of-ai

Chapter 3

The AI Ripple Effect: Transforming the BFSI

Data fuels the engine, but AI gives it breath.
If data is the oil, AI is the oxygen –
unseen but essential, sustaining the pulse of modern business.

Case Study: Mastercard – Pioneering Artificial Intelligence (AI) in Global Payments

Mastercard is one of the world's leading payment technology companies, operating in more than 210 countries and processing billions of transactions annually. In an industry where speed, security and trust are paramount, financial services firms face relentless pressure to fight fraud, enhance customer experiences and enable seamless commerce across both digital and physical channels. With the payments ecosystem expanding through e-commerce, contactless payments and fintech innovations, AI has emerged as an important driver of resilience and growth.

The Challenge

Mastercard needed to protect its vast global network from increasingly sophisticated fraud while minimizing false transaction declines that frustrated genuine customers. As payment volumes grew exponentially, traditional rule-based systems struggled to keep pace with the complexity and scale of fraud. Additionally, consumers and merchants demanded smoother, more personalized payment experiences without compromising security.

(*Continued*)

AI and Business, 45–60

doi:10.1108/978-1-83708-888-120261003

(*Continued*)

The Solution

Mastercard implemented an advanced AI-powered intelligence layer across its global payment network. These AI models continuously analyze transaction patterns to detect fraud in real time, allowing for rapid, automated decision-making. Simultaneously, Mastercard expanded AI applications beyond fraud prevention by introducing intelligent shopping assistants and payment tools that created a more intuitive and secure customer journey.

Implementation Strategy

AI deployment was phased, starting with parallel testing alongside existing fraud detection systems before transitioning to full-scale deployment. Mastercard built its AI capabilities on decades of transactional data, ensuring robust model training. The development was guided by ethical AI principles, which emphasize transparency, fairness and accountability. Teams across data science, cybersecurity and product development collaborated to integrate AI into Mastercard's core operations.

Business Impact

The AI systems significantly improved fraud detection rates while sharply reducing false declines, safeguarding billions of dollars' worth of transactions. Merchants benefited from fewer abandoned carts and smoother checkout experiences. Consumers gained access to personalized shopping tools and faster, more secure payments – helping Mastercard deepen trust and engagement across its global ecosystem.

Lessons

- When responsibly deployed, AI can simultaneously reduce risk and enhance the customer experience.
- Organizations with rich data ecosystems are well-positioned to lead AI innovation.
- Success in AI transformation requires not just technology but cross-functional alignment and ethical governance.

Questions to Think About

1. How can payment companies balance security with convenience in the age of AI-driven commerce?
2. What ethical considerations should guide AI deployment in sensitive industries like financial services?
3. How will AI-powered personalization redefine the relationship between payment companies, merchants and consumers?

Sources

1. https://www.mastercardservices.com/en/capabilities/mastercard-business-intelligence
2. https://www.mastercard.com/us/en/news-and-trends/press/2023/july/mastercard-leverages-its-ai-capabilities-to-fight-real-time-payment-scams.html
3. https://www.youtube.com/watch?v=817XQU0XfSA
4. https://www.mastercard.com/news/ap/en/perspectives/en/2025/from-fighting-fraud-to-fueling-personalization-ai-at-scale-is-redefining-how-commerce-works-online
5. https://www.businessinsider.com/sc/how-ai-at-scale-is-shaping-the-future-of-commerce

AI is changing how companies compete, operate and grow. In today's business climate, change is constant and increasing. Companies no longer propose to reinvent themselves through a few adaptive strategies once every couple of years. Still, they are looking to manage multiple business transformations and often overlapping transformations. AI is already established in all types of business, realizing the science-fiction reality of 10 years ago, in all kinds of business, including healthcare, finance and manufacturing, retail, logistics and education. AI has already demonstrated, long before the pandemic, its value as a solution to drive systemic change, either by automating back-end processes and number-crunching, but now applying in a way that is assisting more strategic decision-making, optimizing customer engagement, facilitating inquiry, generating product innovation and changing business models altogether. In health care, AI-based diagnostic software is enabling clinicians to better and earlier diagnose life-threatening illnesses when there is a greater chance for a cure. In the world of finance, algorithms build economic models and execute trillions of dollars in high-speed trading or personalized wealth management. Retail giants like Amazon rely primarily on AI to forecast the demand for a product, dynamically manage inventories asynchronously and provide personal recommendations for product purchases that drive customer activity, engagement and sales. In manufacturing, AI-based predictive maintenance reduces downtime and extends the life of expensive equipment. In farming, meanwhile, AI-driven drones and intelligent sensors optimize irrigation and crop monitoring, allowing farmers to grow more with less.

The AI Transformation: Revolutionizing Financial Markets and the Banking, Financial Services and Insurance (BFSI) Sector

The BFSI industry is at the forefront of AI adoption. With humongous data sets, intricate processes, regulatory requirements and fierce competition, BFSI organizations are adopting AI not just for incremental change but for disruptive change on their value chains. Ranging from hyper-personalized customer experiences to effective risk management and optimized operations, AI is transforming the face of finance. We explore the actual, high-impact use cases of AI in BFSI and present its disruptive impact through case studies.

Revolutionizing Customer Engagement and Personalization

Hyper-Personalized Banking and Wealth Management: AI analyzes transaction history, life events (inferred from spending patterns), risk tolerance questionnaires, market trends and even social sentiment to create highly individualized financial advice, product recommendations and portfolio management strategies. Some of the running examples of this are:

- **Robo Bank Advisors:** Platforms like Betterment and Wealth front use algorithms to automatically allocate, manage and rebalance investment portfolios based on individual goals and risk profiles, making sophisticated wealth management accessible.
- **Personalized Offers:** DBS uses AI to analyze customer data in real-time, offering tailored loan pre-approvals, credit card upgrades or savings products at the precise moment of relevance within their mobile apps.
- **Next-Best-Action (NBA):** AI engines predict the most valuable action for a customer service representative or chatbot to take next (e.g., offer a mortgage refinance after detecting large home improvement payments, suggest a higher-yield savings account when a large deposit is made).
- **Intelligent Conversational AI (Chatbots and Virtual Assistants):** Natural Language Processing (NLP) powered chatbots handle routine inquiries (balance checks, transaction history, payment due dates), resolve simple issues and escalate complex ones, providing 24/7 support. Advanced virtual assistants (VAs) engage in more complex, contextual conversations.

Case 1: Bank of America's Erica

Bank of America has integrated Erica, its AI-powered virtual financial assistant, into its banking platform to improve customer experience and simplify financial management. Accessible through the Bank of America mobile app, Erica uses AI, predictive analytics and NLP to deliver tailored banking support. Users are able to communicate with Erica through voice or text in order to conduct a range of activities, such as checking balances, viewing recent transactions, sending money, paying bills and even tracking credit scores. In addition to routine transactions, Erica offers proactive guidance by warning users about potential overdrafts, unusual spending or upcoming bills, allowing them to manage their finances better. The application also helps with budgeting by classifying expenses and providing tips on savings. Furthermore, Erica can also walk customers through elaborate processes such as disputing a transaction or locating nearby ATMs. By combining automation with tailored advice, Bank of America aims to make banking easier and more convenient for customers. Since its launch in 2018, Erica has managed to process millions of customer interactions, reducing the need for branch or call-centre assistance and showing the increasing presence of AI in contemporary banking. The continuous improvement in Erica's features is a testament to Bank of America's emphasis on innovation and customer-driven solutions for digital banking.

Source

https://newsroom.bankofamerica.com/content/newsroom/press-releases/2024/04/bofa-s-erica-surpasses-2-billion-interactions–helping-42-millio.html

Case 2: Capital One's Eno

Capital One developed Eno, its intelligent virtual assistant, to transform digital banking with personalized, real-time financial guidance. Eno interacts with customers via SMS, email and the Capital One mobile app, leveraging sophisticated natural language processing and machine learning to converse with customers. In contrast to conventional chatbots, Eno actively monitors accounts for suspicious activity, possible fraud or subscription fee adjustments, alerting customers to stay up to date. Eno can be accessed by customers to check balances, view transactions, make payments and even negotiate reduced rates for bills that recur regularly. A unique feature is Eno's ability to produce virtual card numbers for secure online purchases, thereby reducing the chances of fraud. Eno also offers insights on spending, monitors subscriptions and assists users in setting savings goals, simplifying financial management. Capital One continues to advance Eno's capabilities, like integrating it with smart home devices such as Amazon Alexa to enable voice-controlled banking. By merging security, convenience and proactive financial advice, Eno represents Capital One's dedication to innovation within the fintech industry. Its success indicates an increasing desire for AI-based tools that streamline banking while ensuring security and user engagement.

Source

https://www.capitalone.com/tech/machine-learning/capital-ones-intelligent-assistant-why-we-built-enos-nlp-tech-in-house/

Case 3: HSBC's Amy

HSBC has rolled out Amy, its virtual assistant powered by AI, in the hopes of improving customer service and simplifying banking processes. Accessible via HSBC's digital platforms, such as the bank's website and mobile apps, Amy leverages NLP and machine learning to respond in real time, 24/7, to customer inquiries. Amy assists with several banking-related queries, ranging from checking account balances and transaction history to the explanation of financial products such as loans, credit cards and mortgages. Unlike basic chatbots, Amy can handle sophisticated questions and guide users through processes like international money remittances, replacement of cards or fraud reporting. Amy offers 24/7 English, traditional and simplified Chinese-language assistance for tasks like verifying account balances, providing product and service information and locating an ATM in the vicinity. Amy has also been used within HSBC's internal processes to assist employees in locating banking policy and compliance information promptly. As part of the bank's overall digital transformation effort, Amy puts the focus on HSBC's dedication to adopting AI to create smarter, faster and more personalized banking.

Source

https://www.scmp.com/business/companies/article/2128179/hsbcs-amy-and-other-soon-be-released-ai-chatbots-are-about-change

Let us go through some practical applications of the use of AI in Banking and BFSI globally (see Table 3.1).

Predictive Customer Service and Churn Reduction

One of the most powerful applications of AI in banking is predictive customer care and churn prevention. Banks can now identify risk-taking customers who will churn and step in through behaviour analytics and machine learning. These algorithms draw on diverse sources such as transaction history, mobile app usage, call centre records and even social media activity. Tracking a decline in app usage behaviour, a steep decline in activity, zero transactions and negative interactions with customer support can be early warning signs of dissatisfaction. NLP is increasingly being used by banks to conduct emotion and tone analysis in voice to identify frustration long before true churn. HSBC's AI-powered churn prediction is a shining example. HSBC, with attrition rates at record highs among digitally aware millennials, employed machine learning algorithms to measure app usage as a proxy, observing logins, card usage and even

Table 3.1. AI-Powered Customer Engagement Solutions.

AI Application	Description	Example/Company	Benefit/Outcome
Personalized recommendations	AI analyzes customer data, preferences and behaviours to offer tailored financial products and advice.	DBS Bank, Moneyhub	Enhanced customer satisfaction, increased loyalty, proactive financial insights and debt reduction suggestions.
Chatbots & virtual assistants	AI-powered conversational agents provide instant, 24/7 support for routine inquiries and personalized guidance.	Bank of America's Erica, Morgan Stanley, Google Cloud	Handled over 2 billion client interactions, 2 million engagements daily, frees human agents for complex issues, personalized customer support
Sentiment analysis	AI analyzes unstructured data (e.g., calls, social media) to gauge customer sentiment and market trends.	TAZI's Voice of Customer Solution	Rapid analysis of customer communications, understanding sentiments and trends and continuous service improvement.

sophisticated loan payment, suggestive of disengagement. These 'at-risk' customers were being addressed with custom offers like fee waivers, cashback and fee rebates along with dedicated bank assistants. By being proactive and even introducing AI-driven UX enhancements, the bank decreased churn by 12% in one year and considerably enhanced customer satisfaction. Through this shift from reactive to predictive service models, banks not only gain loyalty but also protect long-term customer lifetime value.

Fortifying Risk Management and Security

Real-Time Fraud Detection and Prevention

Modern AI-based systems enable real-time fraud detection, identifying and preventing fraudulent transactions within milliseconds and help in minimizing potential harm. Rules-based techniques and batch processing dominated conventional fraud discovery, leaving windows of opportunity for deep-rooted fraudulent transactions. Conversely, AI-driven systems are based on high-end real-time data processing via deep learning techniques. The systems examine multi-dimensional streams of data such as user activity, transactional data, device data, geo-location and even network traffic to detect anomalies indicative of fraud. With time, AI models that update their information on a continuous basis learn reconstruction algorithms in the form of emerging tactics of cunning fraudsters, and they restrict improper red flags occasioned by innocent transactions, effectively calibrating systems within the banking sector, e-commerce and online payments. These preventive and real-time steps preclude possible losses, strengthen account security, reduce account takeovers, strengthen user confidence and save customers' trust by eliminating chances of losses in fraudulent attempts.

Case 1: PayPal: Fraud Detection Mechanism

PayPal, one of the world's largest digital payment leaders, has greatly enhanced its fraud detection ability by incorporating deep learning into its transaction monitoring infrastructure. With billions of transactions per year processed, PayPal uses neural networks to examine hundreds of real-time inputs such as device type, geolocation, network activity, user behaviour and transaction history, all within milliseconds. This AI-led method allows the platform to identify sophisticated fraud schemes that rule-based systems commonly fail to detect. This has helped the company minimize fraud-linked losses by more than 75% in some high-risk segments without compromising the customer experience. By constantly learning from changing data and evolving from new fraud strategies, PayPal's deep learning models not only provide enhanced security but also strategic value by fostering customer trust and business efficiency in a rapidly expanding digital economy.

Source

https://www.paypal.com/us/brc/article/payment-fraud-detection-machine-learning

Case 2: Mastercard's Decision Intelligence

Mastercard's Decision Intelligence is a state-of-the-art, AI-driven fraud prevention and detection solution that represents a major departure from conventional rule-based systems to contextual, data-driven decisioning. This technology employs sophisticated machine learning models to analyze the context of each transaction in real time, drawing upon a massive network of worldwide transaction knowledge. Instead of using fixed rules (such as flagging large transactions or out-of-pattern locations), Decision Intelligence weighs many dynamic factors, including purchase history, merchant category, spending patterns, time of day and device attributes, to determine the likelihood of fraud. One of the major advantages is the prevention of false declines, legitimate transactions incorrectly held back as suspicious, one of the biggest sources of frustration for customers and lost sales for businesses. By enhancing precision and being able to interpret the context of each transaction, Mastercard can identify and prevent more fraud while letting valid purchases flow through without hindrance. This not only increases security but also enhances customer experience and increases merchant approval rates, showing how AI can provide protection and performance in finance.

Source

https://www.forbes.com/sites/bernardmarr/2024/06/21/how-mastercard-uses-ai-strategically-a-case-study/

Advanced Credit Scoring and Underwriting

AI surpasses credit scoring models, such as FICO, utilizing alternative data like income flows in bank accounts, rental payment history, utilities paid, even education track history and professional credentials to determine creditworthiness. AI has incorporated sophisticated credit scoring and underwriting systems; this represents a substantial paradigm shift for the banking environment, employing machine learning, big data and predictive analytics to measure creditworthiness at unprecedented accuracy and speed as compared to traditional credit score models like FICO or Vantage. AI models can allow for a considerable range of alternative data sources, like rent history, utilities paid, social media usage, behaviours for products in a category to get a fuller and more inclusive measure. The neural network in AI can find faint correlations or trends in large datasets that human analysts would struggle to recognize, enabling more accurate predictions of borrower behaviour. Thus, lenders can utilize AI systems to expand credit access to the underserved segment of the population and effectively calculate the risk. For instance, a gig economy worker or a young professional with little credit would be seen as too high risk, but AI is able to give lenders access to additional data points in creating a borrower who is relatively low risk.

In addition to improving the underwriting process by reducing and accelerating the decision process, decreasing human bias and reducing operating costs, AI also reduces processing time in two ways: machine-learning algorithms will increase predictive power by incorporating evolving economic conditions and consumer behaviour, continually learning from data and improving with experience; and with NLP, it is possible to process unstructured data (employment histories and bank statements), so that income and sustainability of employment information supplied can be analyzed more effectively. AI allows instantaneous credit scoring, allowing lenders to make faster decisions during the application process and improving the borrower experience. Another advantage of AI is fraud prevention, as AI systems routinely identify discrepancies or deviant patterns in loan applications, thus lowering defaults. Let's look at some examples.

Case 1: Lemonade Insurance-Tech

Lemonade is an insurance-tech firm that disrupts the insurance sector through the application of AI, behavioural economics and a digital-first business model. It was established in 2015 and mainly operates in the United States and Europe. Lemonade offers renters, homeowners, pet, auto and life insurance with a completely digital, easy-to-use platform. In contrast to the legacy system-dependent, manually underwritten traditional insurers, Lemonade utilizes AI-powered chatbots to make policy buys, process claims and provide customer service within minutes, free of paperwork and extended approval processes.

One of the main innovations is Lemonade's business model, which has a flat-fee operation. Conventional insurers retain unclaimed premiums as profits, which introduces a conflict of interest when settling claims. The firm's AI-driven underwriting and claims platform, fuelled by machine learning algorithms, processes massive amounts of data, such as third-party files, Internet of Things (IoT) sensors and customer interactions, to calculate risk, dynamically price policies and flag suspicious claims in real-time. Its revolutionary model illustrates how AI and customer-first thinking can disrupt the insurance business, making it quicker, more equitable and more affordable.

Source

https://aimagazine.com/articles/lemonade-sets-world-record-with-2-second-ai-insurance-claim

Anti-Money Laundering (AML) and Know Your Customer (KYC)

AI has become an agent of transformation in reinforcing AML and KYC initiatives within the financial services domain. In AML, AI enables monitoring of high-volume transactions in real-time to detect suspicious patterns and anomalies. Machine learning algorithms identify patterns that could indicate money laundering and alert compliance teams to those transactions. By reducing false positives, which characterize legacy rule-based systems, AI allows compliance teams to focus on high-risk transactions. Deep network analysis can also uncover hidden relationships between accounts as well as intricacies of the laundering efforts. In KYC processes, AI facilitates faster customer onboarding through automated document verification via optical character recognition (OCR) and facial recognition to expedite the identity verification process and authenticate identity. AI also allows for continuous monitoring of customer activity to detect shifts in risk profiles and support enhanced due diligence. Along with improving operational efficiency and effectiveness, AI also improves compliance risk, as in the case of HSBC, which was able to utilize AI for fraud detection while reducing operational costs. Let's explore these examples further.

Case 1: HSBC Bank

The world's biggest bank, HSBC, was facing increasing regulatory pressure and reputational risk from a longstanding failure to detect and prevent money laundering activity. To remedy this, HSBC undertook a major revamp of its compliance architecture, placing AI and machine learning at the centre of its

(*Continued*)

(Continued)

AML strategy. HSBC's current AML systems were generating a vast number of alerts, the majority of which were false positives, resulting in inefficiency and significant investigative delays. Not only was this contributing to the cost of operations, but also allowing opportunities to identify real money laundering activity to be lost. In a bid to solve the issue, HSBC collaborated with Quantexa, a UK-based AI company and other technology partners to implement contextual monitoring systems. These systems moved beyond traditional transaction-level analysis by incorporating graph-based analytics and network intelligence to map out the connection between customers, accounts and transactions. Key elements of HSBC's AI deployment included:

- **Entity Resolution**: Using AI to consolidate disparate customer data and create unified profiles, even when identities were spread across various data sources.
- **Dynamic Risk Scoring**: Instead of using static rules, HSBC used AI to assign risk scores based on changing behaviour, peer comparisons and contextual data.
- **Machine Learning Models**: Historical cases were used to train models that could learn which patterns of activity were most likely to be linked to money laundering, significantly improving accuracy.

The compliance teams became more efficient, as they concentrated on true risks instead of false alerts, which amounted to a very large number. The efficiencies gained were substantial for operational sustainability and ultimately lowered compliance costs, while restoring regulator confidence. HSBC's AI-led approach is now considered to be 'best practice' in the banking sector as a result of modernizing AML systems.

Source

https://futuredigitalfinance.wbresearch.com/blog/hsbc-artificial-intelligence-strategy-to-beat-money-launderers

Driving Operational Efficiency and Automation

Intelligent Process Automation (IPA)/Cognitive Automation

In the BFSI sector, AI is leading the way to maximize operating efficiency as well as powering intelligent automation in core business operations. AI-driven solutions are enabling financial institutions to automate processes from front-end customer interaction to back-office processing, reducing expenses and improving accuracy. Virtual assistants and chatbots with NLP are processing repeat customer questions, loan status requests and service requests 24/7, reducing call centre volume and improving customer satisfaction. In the back office, Robotic Process Automation (RPA) coupled with AI is automating repetitive tasks such as data entry, KYC verification, transaction monitoring and claim processing, leading to faster turnaround times and reduced manual errors. In insurance, AI-driven algorithms are accelerating underwriting and claims assessment using document examination and pattern matching. Banks are applying AI in intelligent document processing, anti-fraud detection, compliance verification and even in internal audit procedures. By utilizing the application of AI in core processes, BFSI organizations are not only achieving massive cost savings and improved agility but also constructing scalable, customer-focused models that respond in real time to shifting markets and regulatory requirements.

Automated Claims Processing (Insurance)

Automated claims processing is among the most far-reaching uses of AI in the insurance sector. Historically, handling claims has been a time-consuming process that involves several steps: filing of claims, verification of documents, assessment of damage, fraud detection, estimation of settlements and payment authorization. This manual process tends to be slow, subject to errors and vulnerable to false claims, causing customer complaints and procedural inefficiencies. But AI-based systems are transforming this landscape by streamlining and speeding up the complete claims lifecycle, from first notice of loss (FNOL) to end-to-end settlement, while ensuring precision, transparency and cost-effectiveness. Some of the dimensions where AI is making crucial contributions in the Insurance claim processing segment are:

(1) Immediate Claim Registration and FNOL: AI chatbots and voice assistants allow customers to report an incident immediately using mobile applications or call centres. These systems gather required information, confirm policy coverage and start the claims process automatically.
(2) Document and Image Analysis: Machine learning models based on Computer Vision and OCR can read and pull relevant information from documents (invoices, driver's licence, medical records) and images (e.g., vandalized property or vehicle damage). This reduces manual effort and accelerates claim intake.
(3) Cost Estimation and Damage Assessment: In motor insurance, AI algorithms evaluate the severity of vehicle damage based on pictures uploaded by customers and estimate repair expenses based on historical data. In health or property insurance, AI cross-checks hospital bills, repair estimates or asset valuations against standard benchmarks to assess fair settlement values.
(4) Fraud Detection: AI models examine patterns, anomalies and past claim behaviour to identify potentially fraudulent claims. This allows insurers to minimize losses and shorten the time taken for manual investigation.

(5) Decision-Making and Payout: AI can automatically accept low-risk, legitimate claims and initiate payouts within hours or even minutes, without any human intervention. More risky or unclear cases are referred for human examination, enhancing efficiency without sacrificing control.

One of the most visible cases in the Indian insurance industry is ICICI Lombard. ICICI Lombard employs AI to expedite motor insurance claims by enabling customers to upload vehicle damage photographs. The AI calculates the damage and quotes repair costs. This has reduced the turnaround time from days to a few hours, significantly improving customer satisfaction.

Case Study: JPMorgan Chase's Contract Intelligence (COiN)

JPMorgan Chase, one of the world's largest financial institutions, manages an enormous volume of legal and commercial documentation, especially related to loans, derivatives and securities. Traditionally, reviewing these complex contracts was a labour-intensive process handled manually by legal teams and loan officers, requiring extensive time, resources and cross-functional coordination. The bank's legal and operations teams were spending **over 360,000 hours annually** reviewing and interpreting commercial loan agreements. These documents often contain dense legal language and require careful extraction of critical data points to ensure compliance, mitigate risks and uphold operational accuracy. Manual processing not only delayed transaction execution but also posed risks of **human error, inconsistency and compliance failures**, especially as the volume of contracts scaled.

In response to these inefficiencies, JPMorgan developed **COiN** – an AI-powered platform designed to automate the review and interpretation of legal documents. Built by the bank's internal tech team within its **Intelligent Solutions unit**, COiN uses a combination of:

- **NLP** to understand and interpret legal language,
- **OCR** to scan and digitize physical or scanned documents,
- **Machine Learning algorithms** to identify and extract key data points,
- **Private cloud infrastructure** for secure processing at scale.

Initially trained on commercial credit agreements, COiN can identify over 150 key contractual clauses and terms, including collateral details, termination conditions and covenant structures.

The impact of COiN has been both measurable and transformative:

- **Time Savings**: The platform performs document analysis in **seconds**, tasks that previously took **thousands of man-hours.**
- **Accuracy Improvement**: It delivers **near-zero error rates**, significantly reducing the risk of compliance issues and financial penalties.

- **Cost Efficiency**: Freed-up legal staff can now focus on complex advisory and strategic tasks, reducing reliance on external counsel and lowering legal spend.
- **Scalability**: COiN's architecture allows it to be scaled across other documentation-heavy areas, including **ISDA agreements, custodial contracts, and regulatory filings.**
- **Compliance**: Enhanced consistency and transparency in contract analysis help JPMorgan meet increasingly stringent global regulatory standards.

COiN exemplifies how **AI is not just about automating routine tasks, but about fundamentally rethinking how complex workflows can be transformed**. It aligns with JPMorgan's broader digital strategy to modernize its operations, reduce friction and build intelligent systems that offer a competitive edge. The success of COiN has set a precedent for other BFSI institutions to invest in AI for legal, compliance and operational excellence.

Source

https://medium.com/arahmedraza/how-jpmorgan-uses-ai-to-save-360-000-legal-hours-a-year-6e94d58a557b

Future Outlook

Looking ahead, AI's influence will deepen across sectors, driving both opportunities and responsibilities. Key trends shaping the future include:

- Expansion of AI-powered autonomous finance, ethical credit scoring using alternative data and real-time compliance solutions.
- Growth of immersive shopping experiences (e.g., virtual try-ons), autonomous supply chains and AI-led sustainable retail practices.
- Wider adoption of AI in personalized medicine, predictive diagnostics and virtual health ecosystems – balanced by stricter governance on data privacy and clinical transparency.
- Integration of AI tutors, adaptive assessments and real-world learning simulations – creating inclusive, lifelong learning environments supported by responsible AI use.

Across all sectors, the convergence of AI with cloud computing, IoT and emerging fields like quantum computing will redefine business agility and customer experience. Yet, success will depend on ethical AI adoption, continuous learning and human–machine collaboration.

Data is the fuel, but AI is the breath of modern business – vital, invisible and life-giving. The future will not be built by algorithms alone, but by people who harness them with purpose, responsibility and vision.

Discussion Questions

(1) How can AI be ethically and responsibly integrated into frontline healthcare systems, particularly in low-resource settings?
(2) To what extent should patients and clinicians trust, AI models in making critical diagnostic or treatment decisions?
(3) Can AI replace human clinicians for first-level medical issue handling, or should it only play a supportive role?
(4) What role does AI play in transforming personalized treatment and drug discovery, and what are the associated risks?
(5) Who should be held accountable when an AI-driven system leads to a medical error – the developer, hospital or clinician?
(6) How can continuous learning and model updates be managed in AI systems to keep pace with evolving medical knowledge and diseases?

Further Readings

Biswas, S., Carson, B., Chung, V., Singh, S., & Thomas, R. (2020). *AI-bank of the future: Can banks meet the AI challenge?* McKinsey & Company.

Grewal, D., Guha, A., & Becker, M. (2024). AI is changing the world: For better or for worse? *Journal of Macromarketing*, *44*(4), 870–882.

https://www.ey.com/en_gr/insights/financial-services/how-artificial-intelligence-is-reshaping-the-financial-services-industry

Kasula, V. K. (2023). AI-driven banking: A review on transforming the financial sector. *World Journal of Advanced Research and Reviews*, *20*(02), 1461–1465.

Rashid, A. B., & Kausik, M. A. K. (2024). AI revolutionizing industries worldwide: A comprehensive overview of its diverse applications. *Hybrid Advances*, *7*, 100277.

Chapter 4

AI in Healthcare: Paradigm Shift in Modern Healthcare

'The Listening Machine'

By the time we speak, it's heard us breathe –
A whisper caught beneath the scan.
It learns from data, not from doubt,
To help where human hands began.

It doesn't cure, it doesn't feel,
Yet patterns pulse beneath its gaze –
A code of care, a silent guide,
To light the dark in healing's maze.

CASE: Google DeepMind and Moorfields Eye Hospital – Artificial Intelligence (AI) for Eye Disease Diagnosis

Moorfields Eye Hospital, based in London, is one of the world's leading centres for ophthalmic treatment, research and education. Partnering with Google DeepMind (now part of Google DeepMind Health), a collaboration began in 2016 aimed at improving the diagnosis and treatment of eye diseases using AI, particularly deep learning models.

(*Continued*)

AI and Business, 61–71

doi:10.1108/978-1-83708-888-120261004

(*Continued*)

Eye diseases such as age-related macular degeneration (AMD) and diabetic retinopathy are among the leading causes of blindness globally. Early and accurate detection is crucial but challenging due to:

- **Long waiting times** for eye scans to be analyzed by specialists.
- **Shortage of trained ophthalmologists.**
- **Variability in diagnosis** based on human interpretation.
- **The complexity of retinal scans**, particularly Optical Coherence Tomography (OCT) scans.

DeepMind developed a deep learning system capable of analyzing 3D OCT eye scans to detect over 50 different retinal conditions. The AI system was trained using anonymized scans and corresponding diagnoses from Moorfields' patient records. It was capable of detecting multiple conditions in a single scan. It could also recommend the urgency of referral (urgent, semi-urgent or routine). The system used a two-part structure that includes a segmentation model that highlights abnormal regions in scans and a classification model that provides diagnosis probabilities.

The results were impressive: the AI system matched or exceeded the performance of world-leading retina specialists in diagnostic accuracy. It showed a 94–99% accuracy range across different eye conditions. Its triage recommendation accuracy also showed a high level of agreement with clinical decisions. Importantly, the system can fasten the review process by helping prioritize patients at risk of rapid vision loss.

The system is not yet in routine clinical use but represents a breakthrough in how AI can support and scale ophthalmic care. The success of this system has prompted further studies into using AI for diagnostic assistance, screening and workflow optimization in eye hospitals.

Source: (Keane, 2024)

AI is at the centre of a transformative healthcare ecosystem comprising doctors, patients and hospitals. AI is the connecting point between doctors and patients to deliver services and transfer information through the healthcare value chain. For doctors, AI supports them in obtaining the most accurate diagnosis, improves clinical workflow and enhances decision-making through advanced data analytics and predictive models. For patients, AI supports personalized care, early disease detection, virtual health assistants and access to healthcare. For hospitals, AI supports operational efficiency ranging from resource planning and patient triage to asset management via predictive maintenance and improved risk control. This AI-powered ecosystem fosters a patient-centric healthcare experience through a proactive, systems-based approach and moves us into precision medicine. AI will be pivotal as we intersect at these points of connection to improve healthcare delivery and outcomes, as it offers more options and efficiencies in our healthcare value chain. AI is revolutionizing healthcare through improving diagnostics, treatment and operating efficiency. By tapping the power of machine learning, Natural Language Processing (NLP) and deep learning, AI can process large volumes of data and derive patterns and predictions with unprecedented precision. The chapter discusses these uses in case studies and prognostications.

AI in Medical Diagnostics

Early Disease Detection

AI is revolutionizing the early detection of disease by identifying conditions faster, more accurately and often before symptoms develop. Diagnosing conditions is time-consuming and can vary based on a clinician's training level. The most impactful contributions of AI are in the early detection of **chronic and life-threatening diseases**, such as cancer, cardiovascular disorders, diabetes and neurodegenerative conditions like Alzheimer's and Parkinson's disease. For instance, AI algorithms trained on large datasets of mammograms can detect early-stage breast cancer with an accuracy comparable to, or sometimes exceeding, that of experienced radiologists. Google Health's AI system demonstrated remarkable results in identifying breast cancer from screening mammograms, reducing false positives and false negatives more effectively than human readers in certain studies. Similarly, in cardiology, AI models can analyze electrocardiograms (ECGs), echocardiograms and wearable device data to detect subtle patterns associated with atrial fibrillation, arrhythmias or early signs of heart failure – well before symptoms become clinically evident.

AI is instrumental in genomics and proteomics, particularly to identify certain biomarkers, which can foretell increased risk for a disease, well ahead of any clinical symptoms. AI also assists with designing personalized medicine – preventive strategies that encapsulate an individual's genetic predisposition and lifestyle choices. Another promising area is the role of AI in public health surveillance and epidemiology, improving early detection of disease outbreaks and emerging health challenges. AI, among other representational data sources, will ingest social media feeds, health care utilization data and environmental data sources to analyze diseases that might exhibit unusual patterns and, in turn, inform early warning signals about the emergence of illnesses such as influenza, dengue fever or the next pandemic. The integration of health data and data science has shown promising results, but still faces considerable challenges.

AI cannot replace diagnosis, but should be viewed as an effective facilitator of proactive, pre-emptive acts of care. With the opportunity to evaluate patient-specific risks or conditions as they occur before any serious deterioration takes places, both clinicians and patients can act. The application of AI for early disease detection is an essential transformation from reactive medicine to proactive, predictive personalized and precision-based healthcare that has the potential to help improve health outcomes, decrease overall healthcare costs and most importantly, save lives.

Case Study: Paige.AI – Prostate Cancer Diagnosis

Paige.AI, a company spun out of Memorial Sloan Kettering Cancer Centre, developed an AI-based pathology platform, which received FDA approval to detect prostate cancer in biopsy samples in 2021. Trained on more than 44,000 slides, the Paige Prostate system performed with a sensitivity of over 95% and helped pathologists make cancer assessments with both greater validity and efficiency. This was one of the first AI-based pathology tools to receive clinical approval for use in practice. It was a significant achievement in the development and use of digital pathology.

Source: The Paige Prostate Suite: Assistive Artificial Intelligence for Prostate Cancer Diagnosis: Emerging Health Technologies [Internet]. Ottawa (ON): Canadian Agency for Drugs and Technologies in Health; September 2024. Available from Canadian Agency for Drugs and Technologies in Health (2024).

AI in Treatment Personalization and Drug Discovery

Treatment personalization refers to the adaptation of medical treatment tailoring medical care to an individual's unique characteristics, such as genetic profile, lifestyle and disease progression. AI has the power to transform precision medicine by leveraging enormous datasets (genomic, clinical, imaging and lifestyle) to form individualized treatment recommendations. Potential contributions of AI to patient treatment are provided below:

- **Predictive Modelling:** AI can predict the likelihood that a patient will respond to a specific treatment based on prior data, allow physicians to avoid ineffective therapies and minimize adverse drug effects.
- **Clinical Decision Support Systems (CDSS):** These systems assist physicians with selecting treatment options by considering patient data and the latest clinical understanding and research. IBM Watson for Oncology (now discontinued) was a pioneering example in this domain.
- **Real-Time Monitoring and Adjustment:** AI-enabled wearable devices or health apps can monitor vital signs and drug adherence, and suggest timely interventions. For chronic conditions like diabetes or hypertension, AI can adjust medication doses dynamically.

Case Study: Tempus Using AI for Precision Oncology and Treatment Personalization

Tempus, a Chicago-based health technology company founded in 2015 by Eric Lefkofsky (co-founder of Groupon), aims to build the world's largest library of clinical and molecular data to enable physicians to deliver personalized cancer care. Tempus leverages AI, machine learning and big data analytics to draw insights from complex healthcare data and translate them into actionable clinical decisions.

In traditional oncology practice, there are several key challenges such as fragmented patient data, slow genomic analysis and a lack of personalized treatment pathways. Tempus aims to overcome these challenges by unifying clinical and molecular data using AI, thus enabling evidence-based and personalized treatment decisions (HyScaler, 2024). Tempus addresses these challenges in three key areas:

Clinical Data Structuring Using AI (NLP and Machine Learning)

Tempus uses NLP to extract clinical data from unstructured sources like physician notes, pathology reports and discharge summaries. For example, NLP algorithms can identify tumour stage, biomarker status, treatment history and comorbidities from disparate EHR systems. This allows Tempus to convert fragmented and textual clinical records into structured, searchable and analyzable datasets.

Genomic Sequencing and Molecular Profiling

Tempus operates a state-of-the-art lab that conducts:

- DNA sequencing (e.g., 648-gene panels);
- RNA sequencing;
- whole exome and transcriptome sequencing.

These genomic tests help in identifying mutations, copy number alterations, gene fusions and expression profiles that can influence treatment choices. AI models then interpret these genomic alterations in the context of clinical evidence.

Clinical Decision Support

Tempus's AI platform compares a patient's clinical and molecular profile with a vast database of other cancer patients to suggest (Fig. 4.1):

- targeted therapies (FDA-approved or off-label);
- immunotherapies;
- relevant clinical trials;
- potential adverse drug interactions or resistance patterns

(*Continued*)

(*Continued*)

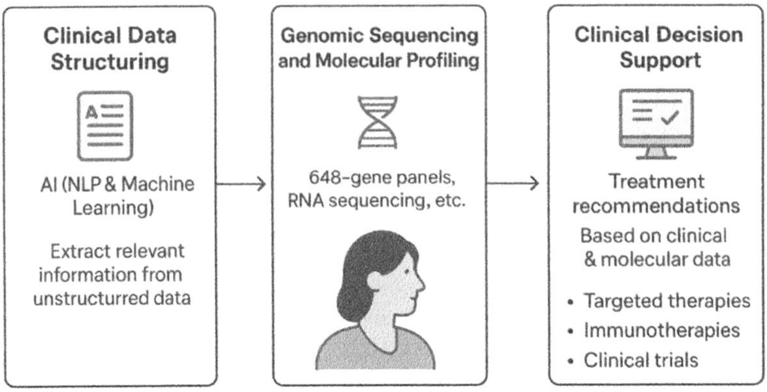

Fig. 4.1. Case of Tempus Using AI and Data in Treatment Personalization. *Source:* Author created.

Doctors receive this in a customized clinical report to guide personalized treatment plans. Tempus represents the real-world convergence of AI, big data and molecular medicine. By building a learning healthcare system, it continuously improves its algorithms as more data is processed. Its approach is shifting cancer care from generalized protocols to hyper-personalized, data-driven interventions, potentially applicable across other diseases such as neurological disorders and infectious diseases.

Drug Discovery: Accelerating and Optimizing Development

The traditional drug discovery process is long, expensive and has a high failure rate, often taking over a decade and billions of dollars to bring a new drug to market. AI is streamlining this process by optimizing each phase, from target identification to lead optimization and clinical trials. Some of the prominent contributions of AI in drug discovery are in the area of:

AI significantly contributes to drug Discovery. The traditional drug discovery process is long, expensive and has a high failure rate, often taking over a decade and billions of dollars to bring a new drug to market. AI is streamlining this process by optimizing each phase, from target identification to lead optimization and clinical trials.

- **Target Identification and Validation:** AI analyzes biological data to identify novel drug targets (e.g., proteins, genes) linked to a disease. Machine learning can reveal unknown pathways or biomarkers with therapeutic potential.

- **Molecular Screening and Design:** AI models can predict the activity of millions of compounds, enabling **virtual screening** of drug candidates much faster than traditional lab-based methods. Generative AI models can also design new molecules with desired properties.
- **Drug Repurposing:** AI can identify new uses for existing drugs by analyzing molecular mechanisms and clinical data. This was evident during the COVID-19 pandemic, where AI suggested drugs like remdesivir for repurposing.
- **Optimizing Clinical Trials:** AI helps design smarter trials by selecting optimal patient populations, predicting trial outcomes and identifying early warning signs of failure, saving both time and cost.

AI-Powered Symptom Checkers and Medical Chatbots

In the evolving landscape of healthcare, AI is becoming indispensable in the initial stages of medical care, where early detection, triage and timely interventions are critical. First-level medical issues – such as common infections, mild chronic symptoms, seasonal illnesses and mental health concerns – are typically the first points of contact for most patients. AI technologies are now helping streamline this process by offering rapid, data-driven and accessible support to both patients and healthcare providers. AI symptom checkers and health chatbots are designed to act as the digital frontlines of patient engagement. These tools employ NLP and clinical knowledge graphs to simulate a conversation with the patient, analyze symptoms and provide initial assessments.

Users/patients describe their symptoms through a conversational interface (text or voice), and the chatbot asks follow-up questions using branching logic. Based on the input, it provides a probabilistic list of possible conditions, self-care advice or recommendations to seek medical attention. A prominent case to discuss is that of Ada Health.

Case Study: Ada Health: AI at the Frontline of Patient Care

Ada Health was created in 2011 by a multidisciplinary team including geneticist Dr. Claire Novorol, AI specialist Prof. Martin Hirsch and entrepreneur Daniel Nathrath. The focus on Ada was to establish a clinical decision support system, Ada DX, for healthcare professionals to assist in diagnosing complex and rare diseases using Bayesian probabilistic reasoning. In 2016, Ada decided to transform into a consumer-facing AI chatbot that was related to healthcare and addressed the growing necessity to reach the general public with easily accessible health information, as well as an

(*Continued*)

(*Continued*)

acknowledgement that past strategies were not successful. The outcome of Ada's transformation was in the form of the Ada Symptom Assessment App to for which usage, a user would enter symptoms as input that would return a probabilistic health assessment, triage recommendation and details about potential health conditions (Pennsylvania State University, 2023).

Ada's AI engine is built on over a decade of research and is backed by a clinician-curated medical knowledge base. The platform uses Bayesian networks to dynamically generate relevant follow-up questions based on users' responses and demographics, creating a personalized, conversational interface. After assessment, Ada provides a clinical triage level, indicating whether the user needs urgent care, should consult a doctor or can manage symptoms at home. This AI-led early triage not only supports self-care but also significantly reduces unnecessary clinical visits, easing pressure on the healthcare infrastructure.

Ada Health's AI application addresses three critical issues in modern healthcare:

- Access to Primary Care: In regions with a shortage of clinicians or long wait times, Ada offers a scalable alternative for initial medical guidance.
- Empowering Patients: By democratizing access to medical insights, Ada helps patients become active participants in their health journey, enhancing health literacy and engagement.
- Reducing System Burden: Hospitals and clinics benefit from reduced overload at the primary care level, as Ada helps divert non-urgent cases and supports pre-visit documentation.

The most interesting part of the platform is its business model. Ada operates through a freemium model and also licenses its platform to health systems, insurance providers and pharmaceutical companies. Notable partners include:

- Samsung and Bayer (investors and integration partners);
- Novartis and Pfizer (clinical support and care journeys);
- AXA and Sutter Health (enterprise clients);
- Gates Foundation (global health initiatives).

These collaborations demonstrate the role of AI not just as a diagnostic tool but also as a platform for care navigation, remote monitoring and health system integration. Ada is evolving into a 'personal health operating system', aiming to integrate data from sensors, lab results and genomic profiles. This could usher in a new phase of personalized preventive care, where AI continuously guides individuals based on a unified health data profile, redefining the role of technology in lifelong health management.

Chapter Summary

This chapter explores the transformative role of AI in modern healthcare, emphasizing its profound implications for diagnostics, treatment, operations and patient engagement. Through compelling real-world case studies – from DeepMind's eye disease detection to Ada Health's symptom checker – the chapter illustrates how AI is transitioning healthcare from reactive to proactive systems.

The narrative begins by unpacking how AI-powered diagnostics are revolutionizing early disease detection, enabling identification of conditions like cancer, cardiovascular diseases and neurodegenerative disorders at stages where interventions can be most effective. By leveraging vast datasets – medical imaging, genomics and wearable data – AI can spot subtle patterns undetectable by the human eye. This shift is particularly evident in oncology, cardiology and pathology, as seen in the case of Paige. AI's prostate cancer diagnosis platform.

Next, the chapter dives into AI's contributions to treatment personalization. It showcases how technologies like Tempus are enabling precision oncology by integrating clinical data, genomic sequencing and predictive models. These insights help physicians tailor therapies to individual patient profiles, potentially increasing efficacy and reducing adverse effects. AI's role in drug discovery is also examined, with emphasis on how it accelerates target identification, molecular design and clinical trial optimization – dramatically reducing cost and time-to-market.

Equally important is AI's impact on operational efficiency and patient experience. Chatbots and virtual triage systems, like Ada Health, are reshaping first-level healthcare access, particularly in underserved regions. These tools offer scalable, real-time support while easing the burden on primary care providers.

Throughout, the chapter underscores a recurring theme: AI is not replacing healthcare professionals, but augmenting their capabilities. It enables more accurate, faster and personalized care, ultimately improving health outcomes. At the same time, it highlights the ethical, logistical and infrastructural challenges that must be addressed for widespread adoption.

Future Outlook

As AI continues to mature, its role in healthcare will expand from isolated tools to integral components of learning health systems. Several key trends are likely to shape the future:

- AI will increasingly become embedded within hospital information systems, enabling seamless data sharing across departments and institutions.
- Wearables and remote sensors will feed continuous streams of data, allowing real-time diagnostics, monitoring and personalized interventions outside traditional clinical settings.
- AI chatbots, remote diagnostics and mobile apps will extend quality care to remote and low-resource environments, potentially reducing global health disparities.

- Medical professionals will need to evolve into AI-literate practitioners – capable of interpreting machine-generated insights while preserving the human touch in caregiving.
- As AI systems gain autonomy, robust policies around accountability, data privacy and algorithmic transparency will be critical to maintain public trust.
- The convergence of AI with genomics, neuroscience, behavioural science and environmental data will unlock new frontiers in personalized and preventive medicine.

In essence, AI will not just treat illness but help redesign healthcare delivery models to be more anticipatory, inclusive and efficient.

Discussion Questions

(1) How does AI shift the healthcare model from reactive to proactive?
(2) What are the opportunities and challenges in using AI for treatment personalization?
(3) In what ways can AI help overcome barriers to healthcare access in underserved populations?
(4) What ethical dilemmas arise when AI becomes a frontline actor in medical decision-making?
(5) How can clinicians maintain their decision-making autonomy while benefiting from AI support systems?
(6) What kind of new roles and skills will healthcare professionals need as AI becomes more integrated into clinical workflows?
(7) What limitations remain in AI's ability to replicate or understand human nuances in healthcare delivery?
(8) How can hospitals and healthcare systems prepare for responsible AI adoption?

References

Canadian Agency for Drugs and Technologies in Health. (2024). *The Paige Prostate Suite: Assistive artificial intelligence for prostate cancer diagnosis* (CADTH Horizon Scan, Report No. EH0123). https://www.ncbi.nlm.nih.gov/books/NBK608438/

HyScaler. (2024). *Transforming healthcare with Tempus AI: A comprehensive overview*. https://hyscaler.com/insights/tempus-ai-powered-precision-medicine/

Keane, P. (2024). *Moorfields and DeepMind: Bringing A.I. closer to the eye clinic*. NIHR Moorfields Biomedical Research Centre. https://moorfieldsbrc.nihr.ac.uk/case-study/deepmind-research-report/

Pennsylvania State University. (2023). *Artificial intelligence: Lesson 6.2 - Ada Health*. LEAP for PIT. https://sites.psu.edu/leapforpit/artificial-intelligence/ada-health/

Further Readings

American Hospital Association. (2025, February 11). *Early disease detection: 3 tech trends to watch.* https://www.aha.org/aha-center-health-innovation-market-scan/2025-02-11-early-disease-detection-3-tech-trends-watch

Chen, J., Li, X., & Wang, Y. (2025). Leveraging AI for early detection, treatment, and disease prevention in community health settings: A scoping review. *Frontiers in Public Health*, *13*, Article 12236417. https://pmc.ncbi.nlm.nih.gov/articles/PMC12236417/

Information Technology and Innovation Foundation. (2024, November 15). *Harnessing AI to accelerate innovation in the biopharmaceutical industry.* https://itif.org/publications/2024/11/15/harnessing-ai-to-accelerate-innovation-in-the-biopharmaceutical-industry/

IoT World Magazine. (2024, October 28). *10 examples of AI in personalized medicine: Case studies from London, UK, Europe, US, and Asia.* https://iotworldmagazine.com/2024/10/28/2540/10-examples-of-ai-in-personalized-medicine-case-studies-from-london-uk-europe-us-and-asia-in-20250-examples-of-ai-in-personalized-medicine-case-studies-from-london-uk-europe-us-and-asia-in-2

Keragon. (2025, April 24). *Top 6 AI chatbots in healthcare in 2025.* https://www.keragon.com/blog/ai-chatbots-in-healthcare

Paul, D., Sanap, G., Shenoy, S., Kalyane, D., Kalia, K., & Tekade, R. K. (2025). Artificial intelligence revolution in drug discovery: A paradigm shift in pharmaceutical research and development. *International Journal of Pharmaceutics*, *685*, Article 123626. https://www.sciencedirect.com/science/article/pii/S037857325006 26X

Rajpurkar, P., Chen, E., Banerjee, O., & Topol, E. J. (2025). Transforming diagnosis through artificial intelligence. *npj Digital Medicine*, *8*(1), Article 14. https://www.nature.com/articles/s41746-025-01460-1

Scilife. (2025, February 20). AI in the pharmaceutical industry: Innovations and challenges. https://www.scilife.io/blog/ai-pharma-innovation-challenges

Semigran, H. L., Linder, J. A., Gidengil, C., & Mehrotra, A. (2024). Self-diagnosis through AI-enabled chatbot-based symptom checkers: A systematic review. *JMIR Medical Informatics*, *9*(4), e26315. https://pmc.ncbi.nlm.nih.gov/articles/PMC8075525/

Shojaeian, N., Li, Z., Kaurav, R. P. S., & Salem, A. A. M. (2022). Theory of mind among Swedish children with ASD, Down syndrome and typically developing group. *Journal of Autism and Developmental Disorders*, *52*(11), 4774–4782.

World Economic Forum. (2025, August 13). *7 ways AI is transforming healthcare.* https://www.weforum.org/stories/2025/08/ai-transforming-global-health/

Chapter 5

AI in Retail: Redefining the Future of Commerce

'The Mirror Aisle'

In every shelf a signal lives,
In every cart, a trail.
Not just things we buy or try –
But rhythms in the sale.

A camera sees what cash once missed,
A code now greets your name.
The aisles have learned to talk and think –
And yet, the core's the same.

The smile, the ask, the checkout beep –
Still here but now refined.
Where AI walks the store with us,
And learns the way we buy.

AI and Business, 73–87

doi:10.1108/978-1-83708-888-120261005

Case Study: Walmart's AI-Driven Transformation Across Retail Touchpoints

Walmart Inc., founded in 1962 and headquartered in Bentonville, Arkansas, USA, is the world's largest retailer with over 10,500 stores in more than 20 countries. Known for its everyday low-price strategy, Walmart has built its empire on scale, efficient supply chain logistics and aggressive pricing. However, the rising tide of digital transformation and competition from e-commerce giants, like Amazon, has pushed Walmart to embrace artificial intelligence (AI) as a strategic lever to maintain its leadership in retail.

Walmart's decision to integrate AI stems from multiple converging challenges and opportunities:

- Increasing customer expectations for seamless, personalized experiences.
- Evolving competition from e-commerce and digitally native brands.
- Operational inefficiencies in inventory, labour management and logistics.
- The need for real-time, data-driven decision-making.

What Were the Concerns and What Operations Did Walmart Revive?

Concern 1: Inefficiencies in forecasting often led to either excess inventory or stockouts, particularly in high-demand periods like holidays.

AI Solution: Walmart implemented machine learning models that analyze historical sales, local weather, regional events and even social media sentiment to predict product demand with high accuracy. AI tools developed in-house and through partnerships.

Result:

- 30% increase in inventory accuracy.
- Significant reduction in food waste from perishables.
- Faster restocking and automated replenishment.

Concern 2: Manual tracking of shelf inventory and planogram compliance was time-consuming and error-prone.

AI Solution: Deployment of shelf-scanning robots (Bossa Nova Robotics) and computer vision systems, like IRIS, to identify stockouts, misplaced products and pricing errors in real-time.

Results:

- 75% reduction in out-of-stock incidents.
- Enhanced shelf compliance and merchandising.
- Freed up store associates to focus on customer service.

Concern 3: Long queues and inefficient checkout processes were leading to cart abandonment.

AI Solution: Implementation of 'Scan & Go' checkout system that uses computer vision and mobile apps for self-checkout. AI algorithms monitor items to prevent fraud or mis-scans.

Results:

- 20% faster checkout times.
- Pilots showed increased average basket size.
- Reduction in labour costs.

Concern 4: Static pricing led to lost opportunities during high or low demand cycles.

AI Strategy: AI models analyze competitor pricing, customer behaviour and inventory levels to dynamically adjust prices. Real-time repricing is integrated with both online and offline systems.

Results:

- Increased price competitiveness.
- Improved profit margins.
- Better alignment with customer expectations.

Concern 5: Lack of relevant product suggestions, leading to low conversion rates online.

AI Implementation: Personalized recommendation engines based on browsing history, purchase patterns and contextual data (e.g., weather or location). A new feature, 'Text to Shop' AI chatbot, integrates with customers' existing shopping lists and preferences.

Result:

- Higher conversion and click-through rates.
- Increased customer retention and satisfaction.
- Growth in Average Order Value (AOV).

Walmart has not paused here; it is exploring advanced AI applications in:

- autonomous delivery using AI-driven drones and self-driving trucks;
- predictive maintenance of store equipment;
- augmented reality (AR) for virtual product trials;
- generative AI for automated content creation and chatbot support.

Walmart aims to use AI not just for operational gains but also to deliver superior customer value and build an intelligent, adaptive retail ecosystem.

Case Discussion Questions

1. Which AI application has had the most transformative impact on Walmart's retail operations? Justify your answer.
2. What are the major risks associated with Walmart's AI strategy? How can they be mitigated?

(*Continued*)

(*Continued*)

3. If you were a competitor, how would you respond to Walmart's AI investments?
4. What ethical considerations should guide the use of AI in retail?
5. Propose a new AI application Walmart could implement in the next five years.

Source

https://www.sap.com/resources/ai-in-retail

The retail sector has always been very dynamic, evolving due to changing consumer buying habits, technological advancements and globalization of buying and supply chains. With the amount of data being generated and the ability to analyze, the retail sector is leveraging AI to transform the entire value chain, freeing up human resources to make better-informed decisions, automate many lower-value daily operations and scale highly individualized and personalized customer experiences. The retail industry is entering a major period of disruption, where modern consumers are much more tech-savvy than previous generations and demand frictionless, personalized and highly convenient shopping experiences across every channel. This shift in consumer expectations, in addition to the highly competitive and growing e-commerce sector, has made it necessary for retailers to adopt AI, not merely to gain advantages but as a necessity. This section examines the multifaceted ways in which AI is transforming the retail landscape, highlighting real-world applications, practical outcomes and the challenges associated with integrating AI. The discussion draws from leading case studies to illustrate how global retailers are leveraging AI to gain a competitive edge and reimagine the future of commerce.

AI's Foundational Role in Transforming Retail

Overall, the ability for AI to transform retailers can be simplified into three areas: improved customer experience, improved sales and reduced operational costs. Although AI can be disruptive, it allows retailers to make better and faster decisions and respond more quickly to market changes, ensuring long-term success. AI is changing the retail industry by enabling businesses to automate processes, all while being able to innovate and anticipate and meet ever-changing expectations of modern consumers. Its ways of impacting the retail space are all-encompassing – all industries and elements of the sector impact customer experience, sales growth and cost reduction. With that as a precursor, we can get to AI and explore how AI influences the customer experience and sales growth, which leads to reduced operational costs.

How AI Fundamentally Impacts Customer Experience, Sales Growth and Cost Reduction

AI's impact on retail is not merely additive; it is transformative, creating a synergistic effect across various business functions.

Enhanced Customer Experience: AI enables delivering exceptionally personalized shopping experiences. By studying large amounts of purchase history, browsing history and stated preferences, AI systems can offer personalized product recommendations, personalized marketing messages and personalized offers. This very high level of personalization increases overall customer satisfaction, increases average spend and encourages customer lifetime value and loyalty. Additionally, AI creates a more 'human' experience in retail by letting AI handle repetitive and manual tasks so that humans can focus on higher-value roles, such as complex problem-solving or creating human relationships with customers. Retailers benefit from this by allowing staff to interact with customers at critical moments in their journey or experience, which is hard to achieve and scale.

Increase Sales: AI plays an important role optimizing and personalizing the buying journey; both of these improvements are linked to increased sales through higher customer conversion rates. AI-based recommendation engines are very influential in suggesting relevant products and lead to higher conversion rates. Personalization in marketing pulled together through AI-based analysis often generates an extra up to 40% in revenue for retailers compared to without AI personalization. The automation of actionable drives to personalized recommendations and content engages shopping customers may generate higher basket size and revenue.

Reduced Costs: AI streamlines numerous key processes, resulting in substantial reductions in operational costs. For example, AI-driven predictive analytics enable highly detailed demand forecasting, which in turn optimizes inventory levels. This capability allows retailers to carry less stock, cutting inventory costs by avoiding overstocking, while simultaneously minimizing the risk of empty shelves and reducing revenue loss due to stockouts. Beyond inventory, AI-based route planning for delivery logistics helps reduce transportation costs and fuel consumption by optimizing delivery paths and adapting to changing traffic conditions.

AI-enabled customer experience, greater sales and lower costs are three aspects of retail that are important to realize are interdependent and mutually reinforcing dimensions of retail trade. For instance, better customer experience through personal recommendations typically improves sales (conversion) rates. Retailers that have proactively adopted applications of AI are in a much better position to establish a relationship with customers more efficiently and operate with greater effectiveness, which are vital elements for succeeding in the AI-enabled environment of today. This is a significant transformation that takes place, going from a variety of silo connected functions to an ecosystem that is interconnected and a more intelligent retailer.

Applications of AI Across the Retail Value Chain

In order to understand the contribution of AI in retail, it is essential that we look at AI's influence on the entire retail value chain, from enhancing the initial customer interaction to optimizing complex back-end operations and ensuring security.

Elevating Customer Experience and Engagement

AI is fundamentally reshaping how retailers interact with and serve their customers, creating more personalized, convenient and engaging shopping journeys.

Hyper-Personalization and Recommendation Engines: AI-based systems carefully analyze large amounts of data, including previous purchases, browsing behaviour and indicated preferences, to provide highly personalized product recommendations and cross-selling opportunities. This also extends to personalized marketing messages that are relevant to each customer. For example, when a customer visits an online shopping site, it displays personalized product recommendations based on what the customer purchased previously, then sends a promo/e-mail marketing message. Similarly, Amazon, being the leader in this aspect, personalizes each customer's home page by developing a customer profile that is continuously optimized and uses AI-based analytics in real-time to suggest activities (i.e. based on the customer purchase history, customer preferences, customer wish lists, stuff in their customers' cart, etc.). This is an effective way to improve customer satisfaction and generate incremental revenue for organizations

24/7 Customer Service and Conversational AI (Chatbots, Virtual Assistants): AI's role in customer service is revolutionary, giving retailers the ability to provide faster, more effective and lower-cost service. Virtual assistants, often powered by generative AI, allow customers to 'talk' to a chatbot that can answer questions, offer information on product options and features, and maybe even help make a purchase. By using a chatbot, retailers are able to assist customers 24*7, if they have concerns or questions, regardless of the time they are shopping online and can take advantage of support. Taco Bell's ordering process features TacoBot, an AI chatbot that allows customer to order using their phone or computer with either text or voice commands. Sephora has developed many interesting services, including a chatbot with a 'Reservation Assistant' and 'Colour Match' for easy access to relevant services. You may visit https://www.sephora.com/beauty/foundation-shade-finder to explore the Sephora's shade match services.

Frictionless Shopping, Checkout, and In-Store Technologies: AI has already begun to streamline the in-store experience through frictionless interactions and automated processes. Examples of this include cashier-less checkout systems without human cashiers, smart self-checkouts and video analytics that are able to identify products without barcodes and/or even missing barcodes. Amazon Go stores are filled with cameras, sensors and AI algorithms that track products that a customer picks up and charges customers automatically when they leave the store, reflecting no cashier and no checkout lines. Moving outside of checkout, populated AI smart shelves with sensors and RFID functionality can track product levels in real-time and help stores avoid stockouts while also managing replenishments. Robots and AI are also being deployed in stores to help conduct tasks from inventory management to stocking shelves, assisting customers to find products and providing information on product features. AI-enabled digital price tags allow real-time price changes and dynamic displays of product information to improve not only operational efficiency but also customer decision-making.

Virtual Try-on, AR and Visual Search: AR-powered virtual try-ons are transforming the online and in-person shopping experience, giving customers the ability to see products, from apparel to eyewear and cosmetics to furniture, in their own space or their own hands before they make a purchase decision. Ranging from furniture visualization to makeup assistance or finding a perfect eyewear, brands are using AR technology to improve return rates and customer satisfaction and confidence in their buying decisions. According to Bar (2023), AI-powered visual discovery tools are also enhancing the way customers search for and discover products. Rather than relying on text search, customers can now find products simply by uploading images, making it a more intuitive and efficient experience. For example, Lowe's uses visual search to match photos that customers take of home decor products to similar items in its catalogue.

Optimizing Operations and Supply Chain Efficiency

The efficiency of the retail value chain defines the success of a retailer. And AI's impact on the back-end of retail operations is equally transformative, driving efficiencies, reducing waste, and improving overall profitability. Some of the contributing factors in optimizing retail operations are listed below:

Advanced Demand Forecasting and Merchandising: The use of AI systems for demand forecasting is reshaping the process. Analyzing historical sales data, market fluctuations, seasonality and 'environment' factors, like weather, the use of AI systems enables much better forecasts. As per a recent article by Sifted (2024), improved forecasting streamlines important decisions such as pricing, product ordering and product placement, enabling retailers to strike an optimal balance between assortment depth and assortment diversification. For example, Amazon exploits AI-based demand forecasting to fine-tune their production schedules and quantities.

Intelligent Inventory Management and Automated Replenishment: AI optimizes inventory spend to limit how much stock is carried but avoids empty shelves, leading to significant savings. Furthermore, predictive analytics and the real-time monitoring of stock status through cameras/vision systems and sensors provide retailers with automated reordering and restocking alerts when low on stock. Lowe's has mounted small cameras on shelving and streamed real-time information about stock status (Edwards, 2022). When the stock is low, the AI notifies staff about restocking opportunities.

Dynamic Pricing and Promotional Optimization: AI empowers retailers to adjust prices in real-time, maximizing profitability while remaining competitive. Prices can dynamically change based on factors such as demand, stock levels, competitor pricing, time of year or even specific customer buying behaviour. This facilitates personalized deals and optimizes promotional campaigns to boost customer loyalty and maximize impact. According to Gomes (2024), an AI-powered system can recommend effective price ranges for every product in a catalogue, considering strategic parameters like sales goals, target margins, supply predictions and estimated product availability. Zara, for instance, is noted for leveraging AI for dynamic pricing to ensure its products are competitively priced based on customer demand and seasonality.

Streamlined Delivery Logistics and Warehouse Automation: AI significantly enhances supply chain efficiency from production to final delivery, reducing errors and improving overall operational effectiveness. AI-based route planning is a key component, reducing transportation costs, improving delivery times and cutting fuel consumption by optimizing routes and adapting to changing traffic conditions. Automated picking and packing, such as Ocado's AI-powered robotic arms, enable rapid fulfilment, completing a 50-item order in just minutes.

Predictive Maintenance and Quality Control: AI is also being applied to ensure the reliability of equipment and the quality of products. Through the use of sensors, AI can identify mechanical failures in manufacturing plants before they occur, enabling proactive maintenance and preventing costly downtime. Furthermore, AI-powered quality inspections help maintain high product quality standards.

Enhancing Security and Fraud Prevention

AI plays an increasingly critical role in retail security, protecting both businesses and customers from fraudulent activities and theft. Retail shrinkage being a critical concern for retailers, AI comes to the rescue.

Real-time Transaction Monitoring and Loss Prevention: Retailers leverage AI-powered analytics to monitor transactions for unusual activity, effectively detecting and preventing fraud. AI-enabled biometrics provide secure customer authentication, further reducing the risk of unauthorized transactions. In physical stores, AI-based surveillance systems are capable of identifying suspicious behaviour and alerting staff in real-time, thereby preventing losses from theft. This includes sophisticated object detection, motion analytics at self-checkout and the use of digital sensors to mitigate product loss and theft in near-real time. The fraud prevention market is experiencing significant growth, underscoring AI's critical role as an investment area for retailers seeking to protect revenue while maintaining a seamless customer experience.

The widespread adoption and success of AI in retail are best illustrated through concrete examples of prominent retailers leveraging these technologies to achieve their business objectives. The following Table 5.1 highlights some key players and their specific AI applications.

Table 5.1. Prominent Retailers and Their AI Use Cases.

Retailer	Specific AI Use Case	Brief Description/Impact
Amazon	Personalized recommendations, demand forecasting, cashierless stores	Customizes homepages, optimizes warehouse stock for 400M + products, enables 'Just Walk Out' shopping.
Walmart	Route optimization, inventory management, demand forecasting	Saved 30M driver miles, tracks real-time inventory, and predicts product demand efficiently.
Sephora	Chatbots, virtual try-on	Offers reservation assistant, colour match, and AR makeup try-ons; increased online sales by 45%.
Lowe's	AI chatbots, visual search, inventory monitoring	Guides DIY projects, matches photos to products, uses cameras for real-time shelf stock alerts.
Zara	Dynamic pricing, supply chain optimization	Adjusts prices and production based on demand and seasonality.
IKEA	AR try-on	'IKEA Place' app allows visualizing furniture in homes, reducing return rates by over 30%.
H&M	Chatbots, visual search	Assists customers with styling, product discovery via image uploads.
Taco Bell	Chatbots for ordering	'TacoBot' streamlines order placement via text/voice.
Starbucks	Loyalty programs	Uses AI (Deep Brew) to personalize promotions and increase customer retention by 15%.
Levi Strauss	Demand sensing	Analyzes consumer demand signals to predict product needs by geography.
Ocado	Automated picking and packing	AI-powered robotic arms complete 50-item orders in minutes.
FedEx	Real-time vehicle tracking	'FedEx Surround' provides predictive delay alerts and ensures timely deliveries.

Source: Based on secondary data available across open sources/company websites.

The Future of AI in Retail: Emerging Trends and Strategic Outlook

The future of AI in retail suggests that we are heading towards a future that is increasingly intelligent, autonomous and integrated, where technology functions as the operating system rather than simply a tool for commerce. Generative AI is expected to continue to advance rapidly and further revolutionize retail by automating content creation, optimizing advertisement placements, enhancing customer targeting through predictive analytics and generating hyper-personalized marketing content, realistic virtual prototypes of products and accelerated product design timelines. Additionally, Multimodal AI, which can aggregate analyses on several different data types (not just sales data, but also supplier communications, consumer sentiment, and product visuals), will provide businesses with substantially higher levels of insight needed to drive responsible inventory and marketing strategies as well as allow for a more collective understanding of market dynamics and consumers preferences.

The Evolution of AI Agents and Autonomous Systems

The retail landscape of the future will see new, highly sophisticated AI agents that go far beyond today's basic chatbot systems. These AI agents are turning into the 'new digital front-line workers', leading users to the right products, answering complex user questions and ultimately pushing personalized product recommendations through every customer journey stage. We are currently at the early stages of the evolution of AI agents, beginning with the ability to interpret and analyze user data, which is rapidly transitioning to the agents making their own decisions and executing actions, enhancing operational efficiency. This will result in the emergence of autonomous supply networks.

Integration With Metaverse Retail and Immersive Experiences

AI is a vital enabler for the developing concept of Metaverse retail, which involves the combination of virtual reality (VR), AR and other immersive technologies in the retail experience. This combination creates moments when the lines between online and offline retail become blurry and allows for highly engaging and interactive experiences. The future will hold many more virtual storefronts and immersive experiences (e.g., fashion shows, product launches), as well as consumer-created virtual products within the metaverse. AI will power personalization and accessibility in these immersive spaces, providing virtual try-on experiences that allow customers to visualize the product in 3D spaces through smartphones or AR glasses before purchase. Brands like Sephora, Gucci and Nike have entered the metaverse, allowing customers to interact with their products in entirely new ways.

AI's Role in Driving Sustainable Retail Practices

AI will optimize supply chains to reduce waste, lower emissions and align with broader sustainability goals. Specific applications include improved inventory planning and order accuracy that help supermarkets achieve substantial reductions in food waste, saving millions in expired product costs. AI-powered energy management systems can significantly reduce store electricity consumption, lowering both utility costs and carbon footprints. Furthermore, AI-driven logistics improvements, such as optimized route planning, directly lead to reductions in CO2 emissions, contributing to global climate impact efforts. At the consumer level, AI can help assess overconsumption trends and patterns, thus making consumers aware of the maladaptive behaviour they are moving towards.

Strategic Recommendations for Successful AI Implementation and Scaling

(1) To effectively adapt to this changing environment and to maximize the benefits of AI, retailers have to identify and be responsive in a tactical, phased manner.

(2) Begin with Small Pilots: Begin with a single department or single store implementation of AI solutions. This will allow retailers to evaluate the new technology's impact, evaluate performance and see how sustainable improvements occurred in one area and, only after a careful and deliberate process, begin to implement and scale gradually across the enterprise.

(3) Value Employee Engagement and Adoption: Make a conscious effort to upskill existing employees to become fast and proficient with the new products to be implemented. This should also include allaying fears of job loss through coaching or training to see how AI technologies can help them focus on higher value tasks. The more team effort put into implementation, the more successful it will be.

(4) Engage Specialists: Given the complex nature of AI, engaging AI solution providers who specialize in retail means engaging experts who can provide tailored specialist solutions and maintenance into the future.

(5) Demonstrate Ethical AI: The appropriate first step is to commit to ethical AI. To follow, they could ensure clear transparencies in any AI systems adopted, collaborate and actively pursue work to mitigate algorithmic bias, and place the highest priority on ensuring that data security is undertaken.

(6) Invest in Robust Data Infrastructure and Governance: High-quality, accessible data are the backbone of effective AI. Retail leaders should invest in robust data infrastructure and governance frameworks to ensure data are clean, accurate and readily available across all departments. Implementing a unified data management system helps centralize data, making it easier to feed into AI models and fostering a culture of data literacy within the organization.

(7) Develop a Clear AI Strategy and Roadmap: Avoid fragmented efforts by establishing a comprehensive AI roadmap. This involves clearly defining how AI will support overarching business objectives, identifying areas where AI can deliver the most value, setting measurable goals and creating a phased implementation plan. Treating AI as an integral part of a broader digital transformation initiative, rather than an isolated experiment, is key to realizing its full potential.

Charting a Course for Intelligent Commerce

AI is truly changing the way retailers do business at all levels, from accurately predicting customer tastes to managing inventory with unmatched precision. By digesting and making sense of tremendous amounts of information and using it to produce intelligent alternatives, AI transforms the entire shopping management process in retailing as well as shopper–brand experiences. AI is also not just a distant concept, it's a competitive necessity that releases new efficiencies and areas of growth that will reshape retailing.

Significant evidence identifies a partnership effect where AI is advancing together with businesses and consumers. AI leads retailers to an optimized supply chain, more robust return on investment for marketing and better decision-making capabilities. At the same time, AI helps shoppers with enhanced product discovery, personalized journeys and speedier checkouts. However, the successful adoption of AI will depend on a strategic plan, sound data governance, ongoing investment and up-skilling of their workforce, and commitment to the ethical and transparent treatment of consumers. These approaches will help retailers safeguard their futures, as well as allow continuous innovation in the increasingly intelligent and inter-dependent business environment that retail is becoming.

Chapter Summary

Chapter 5 explores how AI is redefining the future of retail by acting as a powerful force across the entire commerce value chain – from consumer-facing innovation to backend efficiency. As consumer expectations shift towards personalization, convenience and seamless interaction, AI enables retailers to respond with data-driven agility and precision.

The chapter begins by contextualizing the evolving nature of modern retail, driven by the convergence of digital transformation, increasing competition from e-commerce players and changing buyer behaviour. AI emerges as the strategic enabler to navigate this complexity. Three foundational pillars of AI's impact are introduced:

- Enhanced customer experience through hyper-personalization, chatbots and virtual try-ons.
- Sales growth via recommendation systems, predictive marketing and dynamic promotions.
- Cost optimization through intelligent supply chains, demand forecasting and autonomous checkout.

The chapter then dives into specific applications of AI across retail functions, highlighting innovations in inventory automation, visual search, smart shelves, cashier-less stores and dynamic pricing strategies. These use cases are supported by detailed examples from global leaders like Amazon, Walmart, Sephora and IKEA, making the conceptual framework deeply practical.

Furthermore, the chapter examines emerging trends such as generative AI, multimodal AI and AI-powered immersive retail experiences (e.g., metaverse integration). The narrative concludes with strategic recommendations for successful AI adoption, emphasizing pilot-first approaches, employee upskilling, ethical AI governance and data infrastructure readiness.

Ultimately, the chapter positions AI not just as a technological upgrade but as a transformational lens through which the very nature of retail is being reimagined – from transactional commerce to intelligent, interconnected and personalized consumer ecosystems.

Future Outlook

Looking ahead, the retail industry is set to become an intelligent commerce ecosystem, where AI no longer supports but drives decision-making, product creation and customer relationships. Key trends and forward-looking developments include:

- Content creation – from product descriptions to marketing copy and customer queries – will be increasingly handled by generative models, reducing cost and time while ensuring brand consistency.
- The next generation of AI will process not just transactional data but integrate visual inputs, social sentiment, supplier logs and voice interactions into holistic business intelligence.
- Virtual agents will go beyond answering FAQs to executing tasks like product configuration, real-time repricing and even initiating reorder cycles, redefining retail roles.
- AI will shape the backbone of immersive commerce experiences. From avatar-led consultations to AI-generated virtual store layouts, customer interaction will be redefined.
- Retailers will rely on AI for sustainable practices, including waste reduction, carbon optimization in logistics and monitoring consumption patterns, to promote responsible shopping.

- As AI touches more aspects of consumer life, accountability, algorithmic fairness and privacy protection will move from compliance checklists to brand differentiators.
- Human roles will shift towards managing customer empathy, creative strategy and system oversight. Retailers who reskill their teams to work alongside AI will unlock greater value.

AI's influence will not just modernize retail operations but usher in a new era of responsive, responsible and immersive commerce, where retailers must innovate not just to compete but to remain relevant.

Discussion Questions

(1) How is AI transforming customer experience in retail, both online and in-store?
(2) Can AI-driven personalization risk cross the line into consumer privacy invasion? What are some examples of how retailers are using AI for hyper-personalized marketing? Is it always effective?
(3) Is AI adoption more impactful in online retail than in physical stores? Why or why not?
(4) How are physical stores using AI to stay competitive in an increasingly digital marketplace?
(5) Will AI in retail lead to job loss or job transformation? How should retailers prepare their workforce?

References

Bar, R. (2023). Case study: Lowe's Visual Search, mobile web. *The Medium*. https://rebeccabardesign.medium.com/case-study-lowes-visual-search-mobile-web-d5e236631609. Accessed on December 22, 2024.

Edwards, C. (2022, September 22). *Reinventing retail: Lowe's teams with NVIDIA and magic leap to create interactive store digital twins*. https://resources.nvidia.com/en-us-omniverse-industrial-digital-twins/lowes-retail-digital. Accessed on February 12, 2025.

Gomes, G. (2024, October 24). AI for retail: How Zara leads in fast fashion innovation. *CTO Magazine*. https://ctomagazine.com/zara-innovation-ai-for-retail/. Accessed on December 30, 2024.

How Amazon is using AI to become the fastest supply chain in the world. (2024). Sifted. https://sifted.com/resources/how-amazon-is-using-ai-to-become-the-fastest-supply-chain-in-the-world/. Accessed on 2025.

Further Readings

Cao, L. (2021). Artificial intelligence in retail: Applications and value creation logics. *International Journal of Retail & Distribution Management*, *49*(7), 958–976.

Gupta, A. S., & Mukherjee, J. (2025). Framework for adoption of generative AI for information search of retail products and services. *International Journal of Retail & Distribution Management*, *53*(2), 165–181.

Petrescu, M., Krishen, A. S., Gironda, J. T., & Fergurson, J. R. (2024). Exploring AI technology and consumer behavior in retail interactions. *Journal of Consumer Behaviour*, *23*(6), 3132–3151.

Sagar, S. (2024). The impact of digital transformation on retail management and consumer behavior. *Journal of Business and Management*, *26*(1), 06–14.

Chapter 6

Reimagining Education: The AI Revolution in Learning

> Education is not the filling of a pail, but the lighting of a fire – with AI, the flame can learn to shape itself.

Case Study: Transforming Math Learning With Artificial Intelligence (AI) – Carnegie Learning's MATHia

To illustrate the practical application and impact of AI in education, this section examines Carnegie Learning's MATHia, an intelligent tutoring system that has significantly transformed math education for middle and high school students. Carnegie Learning's MATHia is an intelligent math tutoring system specifically designed for middle and high school students. At its core, MATHia is powered by Artificial Intelligence that dynamically adapts to individual learning paths, providing real-time feedback and adjusting to skill levels as students' progress. The system is meticulously engineered to mimic the personalized guidance a human tutor would offer, providing a scalable solution for individualized instruction. Its core functionality includes offering step-by-step assistance, continuously tracking student progress and proving particularly effective in complex subjects like mathematics. Each time students engage with MATHia, their data is constantly recorded and assessed, allowing the software to programmatically adapt to their mastery level, ensuring a truly personalized learning experience.

Source: Sloan, (2024).

AI and Business, 89–106

doi:10.1108/978-1-83708-888-120261006

Let's explore the case in detail and understand MATHia's impact on Student Progress and learning outcomes.

MATHia's adaptive capabilities ensure that learners access content at the correct challenging level, and in the right way to target the learners' learning gap and learning rate. These personalized learning paths are designed to improve the learning experience by delivering meaningful, targeted remediation while tracking student progress. An important part of the way MATHia provides an impact is through the data it can provide educators about their students. When using MATHia educators receive instantaneous, durable and actionable insights into their students' use of MATHia through MATHia Class Reports and Student Reports. MATHia reports include data surrounding the number of active students, average usage minutes per student per week, average syllabus completion and average APLSE performance and success indicators. This detailed data is invaluable for teachers because it allows them to think about student learning and adjust their teaching when appropriate. By being able to observe this data, educators can develop a true individualized data-driven personalized learning path and move away from traditional generalized learning and move towards the benefits of personalized learning. Although specific research reports on student achievement that can be solely attributed to Carnegie Learning's MATHia were not referenced in the information you provided, it is assured that pilot studies use findings demonstrated MATHia's tools were designed to improve academic performance of students who engaged with the tool by increasing engagement of students using intelligent tutoring systems (or ITS) like an intelligent tutor such as MATHia.

As it relates to MATHia, simply having the functionality of 'constantly recording and measuring' student data and thus event-driven adapting to student mastery levels, coupled with the fact that MATHia provides very detailed reports on usage, completion and performance, is already a huge leap towards a true data-driven pedagogy. Enabling educators to 'continually assess this progress and use that information to create personalized, data-driven learning plans allows educators to not just move from more traditional, periodic assessments to continuous, actionable feedback of student learning. Educators can now revolutionize their understanding of student needs and how they meaningfully change the way they teach, and education will be much more actionable and responsive. It should be clear, then, that we can make a meaningful impact in creating dashboards and user-friendly ways to enhance and maximize what we get to see and analyze in terms of the outflows of so much data we have captured to better inform them what to do with their student data.

Moreover, as an ITS that 'simulates a human tutor,' offering customized instruction, MATHia exemplifies the cascading possibilities of a 'scalable tutor' model. Provided through a software platform, PSD delivery provides tailored, one-on-one pedagogical support, scaled in a way that humans cannot provide individually or worse, it would be a far costlier endeavour with human tutors alone. This model supports the broader potential of AI to democratize education. Success in models like MATHia demonstrates AI's capacity to narrow the education gap by providing high-quality, individualized academic support and instructional support available to a significantly greater audience of students without regard to socioeconomic background or geographical barriers. This scalable tutor model may change both remedial and advanced learning, while promoting more equitable outcomes for students by providing individualized support to all students.

Lessons Learnt for Effective AI Integration

The implementation of Carnegie Learning's MATHia offers several valuable lessons for effective AI integration in education:

- Power of Personalization at Scale: MATHia demonstrates that AI can effectively deliver highly personalized and adaptive instruction, particularly in subjects requiring mastery of foundational concepts. This capability makes high-quality, individualized tutoring accessible to a broader student population than traditional methods allow.
- Actionable Data for Instructors: The system highlights the crucial role of real-time, granular data collection and reporting. This empowers educators to monitor student progress, identify struggling learners immediately, and intervene effectively, transforming teaching into a more precise, data-informed practice. Key Takeaways from Carnegie Learning's MATHia for AI Integration in Education:
- Power of Personalization at Scale: MATHia is an example of how AI can offer high levels of personalization and adaptive instruction, especially in subject areas requiring mastery of foundational concepts. This personalization provides high-quality, individualized tutoring to a larger population of students than ever before.
- Actionable Data for Educators: The learning system leverages the importance of collecting and reporting real-time, detailed data. Thus, aiding the instructor in tracking student progress, discovering struggling learners right away, and providing effective intervention, in effect, scaling up teaching as a precision, data-based practice.
- Augmentation, Not Replacement: MATHia is an example of how AI will augment the role of the instructor and never replace them. AI will supplement teaching by providing detailed reports and freeing up time from repetitive tasks that will allow educators to make better human decisions about pedagogy for individual students. The key takeaway is not that AI does not replace the instructor's role but that it increases accuracy and capacity on tasks related to educating individual students. AI is a copilot.

AI and Education

AI is not a far-off reality; it is a reality here and now and is shaping more and more how educational knowledge is taught, learnt and managed worldwide. Within education, Artificial Intelligence may be using machines that show simulated human intelligence, using programming to perform tasks that require human cognition, including understanding natural language, recognizing complex patterns, solving complex problems and making informed decisions. The advent of AI in the education sector signifies a major shift of the paradigm, not simply a technological upgrade that aims to change the learning environments and instructional practices enhanced by technology. AI appears to be allowing very effective levels of personalized learning, efficiency in administrative activities, increased access and vast opportunities to build students and educators capability. Yet, this major change comes with many different considerations on data privacy, bias in algorithms, academic integrity and the importance of AI literacy for all stakeholders.

In practice, AI in educational contexts are being utilized to help support personalized learning experiences, automate administrative work and promote content that is interactive and entertaining. There is also a distinguishing perspective that technology/AI artefacts will augment, and not replace, what is fundamentally possible with human educators and learners. The pervasive and accelerating adoption of AI makes it unequivocally clear that this technology is 'here to stay.' Consequently, educational institutions face a strategic imperative to proactively determine how to leverage AI positively to enhance their offerings. A core objective of education is to equip students to contribute meaningfully to society. Integrating current AI technology is not merely a matter of convenience; it represents a significant opportunity to elevate both teaching methodologies and learning experiences, ultimately providing students with the 'best, most relevant education possible.'

Additionally, the rapid growth anticipated in the AI in education sector, likely to outpace the overall EdTech sector, indicates a pull-back of the market altogether. This is not merely an increased spend on existing education technologies, but a sign that AI has opened a whole new category of educational tools and services. This extent of projected market growth suggests that AI is an integral factor in future innovations and investments in EdTech. This would suggest that an intensely competitive environment will result, where institutions (and possibly EdTech companies) will put strategic efforts into partnerships with or developing AI solutions to gain relative competitive advantage in attracting students to their institutions, retaining faculty or delivering an experience to students that surpasses previous delivery of education.

We examine the disruptive nature of AI's applications throughout the education sector. The effects of Artificial Intelligence cover all types of education, from intensely personalized learning for individual students to considerably changing the operational and effective efficiencies of institutions. This section describes the range of significant applications causing this sector-wide disruption.

Personalized Learning and Adaptive Systems

AI will play a major role in transitioning the educational process to a more personalized, efficient and effective experience for all types of learners. AI-based adaptive learning technologies adjust the educational material based on students' individual needs, pace and learning style, which has demonstrated improved educational performance. Adaptive learning platforms analyze individual student performance data and learning patterns, modifying content difficulty and providing targeted resources or additional support in real time. This allows students who are struggling to receive support, and students who can move on without delay.

Intelligent Tutoring Systems are a premier example in this area. These AI systems provide one-on-one, personalized instruction that meets and follows the learning path for each student. It's breaking the mould of human tutoring, with instant feedback, step-by-step support and always tracking progress. Research shows that ITS can tremendously improve learning and student engagement. With the ability to analyze learning patterns, student data and learning progress, AI can help teachers quickly identify when a student doesn't understand a concept, quickly put in place an intervention, and adjust their teaching strategies and materials based on student understanding and progress. In addition, the degree of focus on personalization – an ability to adapt to each student's 'pace, style and struggles,' deliver 'one-on-one instruction' and assess 'emotional state and well-being,' indicates a level of individualization that can rarely be done at scale. This capability has been described as 'hyper-personalization,' which represents a break from the standardized, 'one-size-fits-all' education model. The progress indicates that students will not be going through a fixed curriculum at a fixed pace but will instead have individualized learning experiences – with personalized content and help evolving in real-time for maximum effect. The implications of this evolution suggest that the time-fixed curriculum and set pace will inevitably become a thing of the past as AI systems can receptively adjust to a learner's individual journey.

Enhancing Teaching and Learning Curve

AI considerably enhances the teaching and learning process in numerous ways. Dynamic content creation and curation tools utilize AI to develop a multitude of learning materials such as customized content, comprehensive lesson plans, accurate rubrics, comprehensive assessments, stimulating discussion prompts and engaging presentations with only simple keywords or prompts. Those tools help create interactive lessons that meet the intended learning objectives and enhance students' engagement. Some of the AI platforms that are broadly used by students and teachers include Canva Magic Write, Curipod, Eduaide, Magic School AI and many more. Additionally, AI can help teachers save a lot of time by finding relevant quality learning resources for their work. The number of such platforms is growing each and every day, adding to the record that AI platforms are acts of building supports for the stakeholders. There are few evident areas where AI builds a support are:

- ***Immersive learning*** is another space where AI significantly enhances the learning experience through technologies like virtual reality (VR) and augmented reality (AR). These technologies can help simulate realistic everywhere anywhere there is experiential learning happening, allowing learners to re-enact significant historical events or inquiring into scientific phenomena. These immersive happenings greatly enhance the scope of the theoretical knowledge available which is built upon, improve understanding and increase retention rates by a magnitude over traditional methods of instruction. An example of this includes Google Expeditions, which allows virtual tours and field trips, taking students places around the world without them having to travel there in person.
- ***Automated grading and feedback systems*** are a substantial efficiency gain. Using AI can automate the grading process and deliver feedback on an immediate and on-going basis to all students, with consistent detail on aspects such as grammar and style, and structure, meaning students can quick understand their potential performance and effectively remediate them for improvement. While automated grading is commonplace, specifically with objective scoring methods such as multiple-choice questions, ongoing developments will see AI tool being used to also assess subjective written responses as well. This really is a rich area of tools developed, and some of the more predominant titles associated with them would be such tools as: Grammarly, Turnitin and ClassCompanion.
- ***Curriculum development and alignment*** is one other meaningful area where AI support is needed. AI can help instructional designers in developing customized curricula that meet the individual needs of students, capitalizing on their unique strengths or weaknesses. In addition, it can ensure lesson plans are designed to meet the needs of curriculum guidelines and learning objectives while also operating 'test' educational materials where it can simulate student actions to identify potential points of confusion. Finally, AI is enhancing student creativity and their ability to solve problems by generating new ideas, promoting multiple perspectives and enabling students to use AI collaboratively to address real issues, which is influencing their role in knowledge as they move from passive consumers to active creators.

Streamlining Administrative and Operational Efficiency

One big advantage of AI in education is that it can reduce the administrative and operational work; freeing teachers from unnecessary, but important work, that has taken up a large portion of educators' time. AI can automate standard tasks as attendance tracking, assessment, crafting and writing progress reports, running reports, managing student data, etc. Automating a greater number of these tasks is beneficial because it allows instructors to perform their first functions: teaching; working with students on an individualized level and pursuing substantive teaching endeavours.

Artificial Intelligence can also assist with decision-making, at an institutional level. Educational AI can accumulate and analyze large data sets and provide rich insights that capitalize those data sets for enhanced decision-making and support of student learning in designing policies and developing policies for additional purposes. In implementing artificial intelligence, institutions could anticipate enrolment trends and focus forward-moving areas of student support, developing data sets of evidence-driven and intentional student resources with greater ease. Student support and communication has also significantly improved by artificial intelligence. AI-defined chatbots are more plentiful; giving students on-demand support of academic and administrative questions, thus advancing student service and operational efficiency as a whole (Table 6.1).

Challenges and Ethical Considerations

Despite its immense potential to revolutionize education, the integration of Artificial Intelligence presents a complex array of challenges, particularly concerning data governance, fairness, academic integrity and human readiness. Proactively addressing these issues is crucial for responsible and effective adoption.

Data Privacy and Security

AI undoubtedly relies on students' past information, which includes personal characteristics, educational history, behavioural data and digital footprint, amplifying the threats of surveillance, discrimination and the risks that come from educational technology (EdTech) vendors encroaching. Student data is also highly sensitive and therefore requires more intensive privacy measures and security protocols. Another concern is the 'black box' problem, or transparency of how AI uses personal information usually results in reduced individual rights around their information. The speed at which AI is developing also opens up a gap of cyber risks, and many may not be currently factored by common practices. AI, also increases the attack surface for schools and increases the avenues for bad actors to come into the school system and increases their vulnerabilities and opportunities to compromise the school system or network. It lowers the barrier of entry for bad actors to develop and inject malware into the school system and increases the level of sophistication, which can enable phishing using automated impersonation and profiling of individuals and disrupted denied service through malicious DDoS (Distributed Denial of Service) attacks.

To lessen this enormous weight of risks, several steps must be taken. Institutions must strive for informed consent and transparency by communicating to students and parents what data are collected, where it will live and for what purposes it will be used. Schools must adhere to laws such as the Family Educational Rights and Privacy Act (FERPA) and the General Data Protection Regulation (GDPR), both of which require that schools obtain written consent to share data and are responsible for record retention. Effective data

Table 6.1. Key AI Applications and Their Educational Impact.

Application Area	Specific AI Tools/Methods	Primary Impact/Benefit	Example Tools/Platforms
Personalized learning	Intelligent tutoring systems (ITS), adaptive learning platforms	Tailored instruction, improved student engagement, real-time adaptation	Khanmigo, Carnegie Learning's MATHia, DreamBox, Smart Sparrow
Enhancing teaching and learning	Generative AI for content, immersive learning (VR/AR), automated grading and feedback systems, AI question generators	Dynamic content creation, deeper comprehension, time savings for educators, immediate feedback, fostering creativity	MagicSchool, Eduaide, Google Expeditions, Grammarly, Turnitin, ClassCompanion
Streamlining administration	AI-powered chatbots, predictive analytics, automation of routine tasks	Reduced workload for educators, enhanced decision-making, improved student support, operational efficiency	Mainstay, SchoolAI
Fostering accessibility	Real-time captioning and transcription, assistive technologies, language translation tools	Increased inclusivity, customized experiences for diverse learners, breaking language barriers	Microsoft Immersive Reader, Microsoft Seeing AI, Dysolve

Source: Compilation of multiple open-source information retrieved from secondary data sources.

minimization and anonymization strategies include collecting less data and pseudonymizing or anonymizing student data prior to utilizing AI tools to process the data. Security is paramount: retaining data securely, utilizing encryption, secure logins, limiting access based on the role of the user and regular security audits/assessments are necessary. Automation tools can assist with data security, for example, AI-enabled automated redaction tools can recognize sensitive information about students, and can assist with storage/sharing compliance with privacy legislation. Institutions should also appropriately vet the AI platforms and vendors they are using to ensure information is passed securely, with information made public by the user stored transparently, and operating in compliance with privacy laws.

Algorithmic Bias and Fairness

Bias in AI algorithms raises serious ethical considerations when the results produced by a particular AI system are unfair or biased because of something related to the data it learns from, or the AI programming it begins with (there might just not be enough variables). This can happen if the training data does not include a multitude of views, if the system is poorly designed, or if the training data itself actually embeds societal privilege or inequity in its baseline data. Examples of bias include grading systems that are inadvertently favourable to students from specific backgrounds, or admission decisions that intentionally or unintentionally keep some groups of people from getting in or learning tools that work better for some groups of people than others. How an AI system is designed and how it works often reflects the values or positions of the designer and the data it is trained with, and it may reinforce existing inequity and discrimination, or even widen it.

Mitigation strategies for algorithmic bias include many methods. The chief among them is ensuring that the data collected is diverse and representative. Essentially this means that datasets should represent the diversity of the full population served, considering factors like age, gender, race and socioeconomic background. Processing data beforehand through a variety of methods can help mitigate bias. For instance, data can be prepared prior to using an algorithm through cleaning, normalizing, standardizing, anonymizing, resampling or reweighting. Careful selection and design of algorithms, as well, is important because some AI algorithms are more likely to result in biased data than others, even though there are many bias-free options available as well. In choosing the right algorithm, we want to incorporate fairness constraints during training and while using fairness-aware algorithms. Human oversight and review are a crucial aspect, and we can adopt a 'human-in-the-loop' approach, which ensures there is human judgement of AI outputs, including a correction of flawed decisions being made by AI. Transparency and explainability is part of ensuring there is trust in the AI system. Organizations should be transparent about how their AI systems are functioning: including data, algorithms and decision-making processes so users will understand and be provided appropriate context to challenge outcomes. Continuous monitoring and auditing outputs obtained from AI for bias (and other potential issues) is good practice, and they should complete periodic audits of the AI system. Also, collaboration with diverse teams of people (data scientists, subject matter experts, end-users, etc.) to identify potential bias in algorithmically driven AI systems is also a significant approach.

Academic Integrity and Over-Reliance on AI

The emergence of AI presents new and intricate challenges to academic integrity, opening important concerns about plagiarism and the originality of student work. Students are increasingly employing AI tools for various forms of academic dishonesty including, but certainly not limited to, writing entire essays, finding solutions to homework, responding to exam questions, choosing existing content, rephrasing before submitting to check for plagiarism, and writing code for programming courses. Beyond direct rule-breaking, many students may unknowingly become overly reliant on AI for answers and completing tasks, thus stunting the development of critical thinking and problem-solving skills necessary for academic success and any future career. A particularly concerning case featured researchers embedding hidden AI prompts in academic papers to generate content and manipulate AI reviewers into generating positive evaluations for paper acceptance. As a result, the paper represents a significant breach of integrity within the academic publishing ecosystem.

Mitigation strategies are essential when integrating AI and addressing integrity concerns. Institutions should establish and communicate comprehensive policies regarding the use of AI, establishing responsible versus irresponsible use (e.g., using AI to cheat) and establishing acceptable use. It is important to use integration/disruption of AI as a teachable moment, thinking through the implications of ethics, value in original work, and focusing on evaluating, analyzing and editing AI responses versus memorization of content. Citation and attribution requirements should stipulate that all work identifies any input used and acknowledges AI's contribution, and records the prompt used, along with the AI's exact response. Educational institutions should also reconsider assessments so that content easily generated by AI is not focused on that level, and instead, looks to deeper learning tasks, critical thinking, and uniquely human skills. Comprehensive instructor training is also needed to arm instructors with a holistic understanding of AI's capacities and limitations and allow them to create assignments that can potentially leverage AI positively while mitigating the risk of misuse.

Instructor Readiness and AI Literacy

A major concern with the incorporation of AI is whether or not educators are sufficiently prepared and confident in their use of new technology. There are many instances where instructors feel pressured to use AI tools without understanding how they work, and they may feel uncomfortable when faced with the pressure to use new technology. Therefore, educators need training in a timely manner and to be educated about what appropriate use of AI looks like in delivering classrooms and curriculum design. To address the concern of Instructor readiness, professional development and upskilling of teachers is vital. Training will need to take into account the appropriate use of AI tools, demonstrate how AI can meet different learner needs and show how AI can help accelerate learning. The overall goal is to develop comprehensive AI literacy, which includes baseline AI concept knowledge, theoretical proficiency in using AI tools, ethical knowledge and collaborative thinking, to develop their comfort and confidence in the evolving space. By giving teachers usable examples and practical training, instructors can walk away with a new way of thinking and concrete strategies to effectively engage in AI-enabled instructional practices.

Infrastructure, Cost and Equitable Access

Although AI tools are becoming progressively more accessible, the high cost of acquiring advanced systems and difficulties with maintenance may restrict widespread usage in some educational institutions and classrooms. Financial and logistical barriers may result in AI potentially aggravating gaps of inequity, especially if students do not access AI-powered learning tools, if students or institutions do not have reliable broadband internet connections, and if students or institutions do not utilize culturally responsive AI tools. Eventually, to prepare for an AI future, educational institutions will need to make substantial capital investments in the underlying infrastructure to provide AI technologies broadly to students and instructors.

There is an alarming degree of individual AI usage occurring in an educational system where the overall level of institutional and systemic global AI strategies (or lack thereof), support, and clear recommendations about AI usage are in various stages of development and/or disagreement. The level of AI adoption of systems like ChatGPT by students and instructors prior to the establishment of stronger ethical policies, frameworks and supports is concerning. Individual AI usage is likely occurring in ungoverned environments, and this pre-emptive usage has the potential to contribute to heightened concerns about data privacy, algorithmic bias and academic integrity. The experience students have embedding hidden AI prompts in academic writings is a powerful example of academic integrity's nascent challenges amidst an unplanned and reactive integration of AI tools. When educational systems are forced into uncredentialed AI integration, it will accumulate an ethical debt. The immediate benefits of AI are being pursued without fully addressing the systemic risks, which could lead to significant long-term consequences such as reputational damage, legal liabilities (e.g., data breaches, discrimination lawsuits), and a fundamental erosion of trust among students, parents and the broader community. The urgency is not merely to implement AI, but to govern its implementation responsibly and proactively address the ethical gaps that have emerged from its rapid, unguided adoption.

Strategic Plan for AI Integration in Education

A successful and sustainable integration of Artificial Intelligence into the educational framework necessitates a phased, thoughtful and human-centric approach. This section outlines a strategic roadmap for institutions to navigate the complexities of AI adoption, from initial assessment and vision setting to scaled implementation and continuous improvement.

Phase 1: Assessment and Vision Setting

The first step of any AI integration effort is conducting a needs assessment. This will start with evaluating the needs of the student audience and determining what exactly AI will do to improve learning outcomes and mitigate existing education issues. The needs assessment step ensures that the technology solution is responsive to a determined need versus simply adopting technology for technology's sake. Once needs are assessed, the next step is developing a well-defined and explicit AI strategy that supports the educational goals and core values of the institution. Also important at this step is developing a policy scope. This will involve identifying specifically what kind of things the AI policy will operationalize, such as procurement solutions where AI tools will be purchased as a result, practical directions for educator use and boundaries around how students will interact with AI technology. Finally, as with any policy development process, it is crucial to create opportunities to have discussions and engage multiple stakeholders including educators who are actively using AI and who have experience with technology use, students who have a thought process that is inherently different than those producing policy, parents/caregivers who have insight on safety and privacy issues, and administrators who will have an important role in ensuring policy compliance. Engaging multiple stakeholders as a decision-making group sets direction, clarifies particular concerns and builds group consensus to develop responsible usage of AI.

Phase 2: Pilot Implementation and Capacity Building

Once the vision and initial policies are established, the next stage is using AI in practice and building institutional capacity. This includes thoughtful consideration of AI buying and selection. Institutions should aim to develop a consistent vetting process to evaluate and select AI tools, requiring criteria such as alignment with district values and educational goals, adequate data privacy and security supports, misuse prevention measures, compliance with appropriate regulations and means to train educators. Focusing on products designed for educational contexts can help ensure appropriateness, security and quality provision.

Teacher education and AI proficiency and understanding should be the primary focus of this stage. Institutions must establish comprehensive professional learning opportunities addressing how to use AI tools effectively, how AI might be used to support diverse learners, and how AI can augment learning. These opportunities should have a strong emphasis on building a basic understanding of AI principles, competency in using AI tools, ethical considerations and a collaborative disposition required to appreciate the emerging field of Artificial Intelligence. At the same time, launching smaller-scale pilot programs around AI-enabled instructional practices provides the institutions an opportunity to trial their efficacy and to glean impressions from classroom educators about practices that show promise prior to scaling.

Emphasizing the human dimension of education during the pilots (and beyond) is key. This entails making sure learners continue to do the cognitive heavy lifting and active learning, and maintaining meaningful relationships among learners and instructors. Augmenting human capacity should be the intent of the AI, rather than diminishing it. In addition, we want to support the learners in considering a critical engagement with notifications assigned by AI, where learners learn to reflect back to the AI and evaluate proposed feedback in a potentially critical manner, leading to a set of more active learning activities. This is the point; we all understand that we want to respond to people's requests for help with developing guidelines for the responsible use of AI in formal academics. To be it be ethically sound, this would mean that developing and clearly articulating guidelines for use in ethics, plagiarism and circumstances where it's ready to be adopted would be important to process, so that students and the faculty use similar expectations.

The emphasis on various features of strategic planning to include comprehensive needs assessments, consideration of diverse stakeholders, professional development and AI literacy for educators, and most importantly, consideration to remain 'human' in teaching and learning suggests that there was a recurring principle in the thinking. The pattern suggests that adopting AI successfully is more than adopting a technology – it is fundamentally a human process. Therefore, to have an effective AI strategy in education – the human element has to be first and foremost. This means prioritizing significant investment in human capital – equipping educators with the knowledge and confidence to leverage AI, fostering students' critical engagement with AI and designing policies that augment human capabilities rather than seeking to replace them. The overarching objective is to ensure that technology serves pedagogical goals and human connection, rather than technology dictating the educational experience. This approach is vital for mitigating risks of alienation and ensuring that the unique value of human interaction in learning remains central.

Phase 3: Scaled Adoption and Continuous Improvement

The last stage is to scale successful efforts and create a system for continuous improvement. Universities and colleges should be able to map out an ambitious plan on how to expand AI integrations at a scalable level across the larger institution, in consideration of the positive results and feedback from pilot programs. Continuous monitoring and auditing must accompany institutional expansion and improvement efforts. Regular AI audits that allow you to continually evaluate the use of AI and monitor for biases and discriminatory outcomes by implementation are critical. If you discover any bias, you need to take action immediately.

It's important to understand that AI technologies are evolving rapidly and any institutional policies are going to need to adapt to these rapid transitions, which requires continuous policy review and updates that must occur on a regular basis – better annually – to capture rapid technological advances, new best practices and shifting expectations from the community. The 'ETHICAL Principles AI Framework' is meant to be flexible and adaptable, which denotes urgency. Also, while these efforts are ongoing, you should keep encouraging AI literacy development at every level of the institution, for students, faculty, staff and administrators, questioning, critiquing, being creative and being flexible to deepen their understanding of AI. Ensuring equitable access remains a paramount consideration. Institutions must actively work to ensure that AI tools are accessible to users with diverse needs and abilities, providing alternative options for those who cannot or choose not to use AI. This includes addressing fundamental issues such as access to technology, reliable broadband and culturally responsive AI tools. Finally, the strategic plan must continuously emphasize and design learning experiences that promote critical thinking, the careful evaluation of AI-generated content, and the development of the nuanced skills needed to navigate and thrive in an AI-infused world.

The theme of the pacing and the evolution of AI technology is woven throughout the strategic plan and the calls to 'evolve with it' outlined through regular reviews and updates (ideally annually), and the building of frameworks to prioritize 'flexible and adaptable' governance signals an important realization. This theme suggests that establishing policies one-time is woefully insufficient for the nature of AI. Education systems must embrace an agile and iterative governance framework for AI. There must be ongoing feedback loops from all members of an educational institution about AI stewardship, methods to make quick changes or situational policy adaptations, and conversations and dialogue that support and support movement with the changing landscape of opportunities from AI capabilities, new ethical concerns, and considerations around accepted practices in educational spaces. The 'AI policy' will then become less of a static document and more of a 'living' framework of addressing these operational and ethical concerns, founded on iterative experience, which is essential to maintaining relevance, effectiveness and trust in an evolving technological space (Fig. 6.1).

The Future of Education in an AI-Driven World

The trajectory of Artificial Intelligence suggests a future where education will be profoundly transformed, necessitating an evolution in the roles of both students and educators, an increasing emphasis on human-AI collaboration and a long-term vision for a truly AI-augmented educational ecosystem.

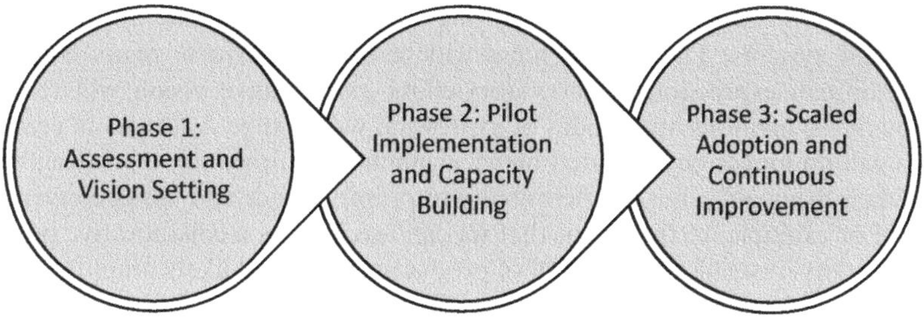

Fig. 6.1. Strategic Plan for Integrating AI Into the Education Sector. *Source:* Authors Own Work.

Evolving Roles of Students and Educators

For students, the future of learning will involve a fundamental shift in how their capabilities are evaluated. Learners may no longer be primarily assessed on their ability to recall information or apply pre-defined frameworks, but rather on their capacity to effectively collaborate with intelligent machines, interpret complex insights generated by AI and define novel problems worth solving. This transition signifies a move from being passive consumers of technology to becoming active creators with AI, leveraging its power for meaningful problem-solving. Consequently, education must increasingly emphasize 'learning how to learn and how to adapt.' Students will require robust skills in critically evaluating content for accuracy – especially given that current AI tools are not always reliable for fact-checking – and editing and refining AI-generated content to ensure quality and relevance.

For educators, the narrative is one of augmentation, not replacement. AI is not poised to replace instructors, who make countless critical decisions daily and play an essential, irreplaceable role in both education and the broader community. The unique elements of teaching, empathy, mentorship and the ability to inspire remain indispensable. Instead, instructors will evolve into strategic facilitators, becoming the 'architects of how AI is integrated into pedagogy.' AI will streamline their workloads, significantly reduce time spent on managerial tasks, and free up more hours for direct teaching and deeper student engagement. This shift will enable educators to encourage a greater focus on deeper learning among students, moving away from a primary emphasis on memorization.

The Emphasis on Human-AI Collaboration and Higher-Order Skills

Education in the future will increasingly be a dynamic partnership between humans and artificial intelligence (AI). Cognitive agents that are capable of more sophisticated and nuanced intellectual work (e.g., writing software, solving new problems) will become 'co-learners' with students and professionals, making 'learning' a process of guiding, auditing and augmenting the work of these intelligent systems. Though machines will be able to perform many cognitive tasks, human expressions of art, storytelling and creative vision will remain, although the methods and modes of expression will change. Learners in creative fields will no longer be evaluated on their manual manipulation of materials, or even their originality, but on their ability to prompt, guide and use generative AI tools. For example, to the extent that we can teach AI as a collaborative partner for creativity, instead of just a tool of productivity, AI will likely amplify human creativity and productivity. Thus, we will naturally gravitate towards deeper learning as a focus in classrooms, rather than sustained focus on memorization.

The recurring recognition that AI exists to relieve educators of administrative and rote-based tasks suggests an incredible potential for the 're-humanization' of education. The automation of the more mechanistic and data-heavy portion of teaching enables the education system to stress its already human dimensions more than ever before. The future of education may involve a genuine shift to more personalized, relationship-based and creativity-enhanced learning. The machine or data-driven tasks are handled by AI, and the human work can remain on the critical thinking, emotional intelligence and complex problem-solving parts, and the unique teacher–student relationship. This suggests that the education system could be undergoing a new cultural and methodological change where the value of human interaction and the inherently unique human attributes can take precedence while enabling a more satisfying and meaningful educational experience.

Chapter Summary

Chapter 6 offers a comprehensive examination of how AI is reshaping the education landscape – transforming how learning is delivered, personalized and assessed. It explores the technological, pedagogical and institutional changes that AI brings, while emphasizing the balance between innovation and ethics.

The chapter opens with a foundational understanding of how AI is influencing learning pathways, highlighting tools such as ITS, adaptive learning platforms and dynamic feedback engines. These innovations enable hyper-personalized learning experiences, allowing students to progress at their own pace and according to their unique strengths and challenges. Carnegie Learning's MATHia, for example, exemplifies this shift by offering tailored, data-driven instruction at scale.

Beyond instruction, the chapter maps the expanding role of AI in enhancing teaching itself. From automated grading and content generation to immersive virtual environments, educators are now equipped with tools that extend their creative and instructional reach. The narrative highlights a dual benefit: improved student outcomes and reduced teacher burnout. Operational and administrative efficiencies are another major area of impact. Chatbots, analytics dashboards and automation systems are streamlining processes like attendance, reporting and student support, enabling institutions to function more efficiently and responsively.

Yet, the chapter does not shy away from challenges. It thoughtfully addresses critical issues of data privacy, algorithmic bias, academic integrity and the urgent need for AI literacy among educators and learners alike. Importantly, it outlines the risks of over-reliance, infrastructure inequality and premature deployment without adequate governance.

Finally, the chapter offers a three-phase roadmap for AI integration in educational institutions – starting from vision and pilot implementation to scaled adoption. It advocates for a human-centred approach, where technology serves pedagogy, not the other way around.

Future Outlook

The future of education, as shaped by AI, is not just about smarter tools – but smarter systems, smarter collaboration and smarter learning. Several key directions are anticipated:

- Human–AI Collaboration Becomes the Norm.
- Deeper Learning, Not Just Faster Learning.
- Assessment Will Be Rethought.
- Cultural and Ethical Agility Will Be Crucial.
- AI Literacy Will Be as Fundamental as Reading.
- Equity Will Determine Success.
- Education Will Become a Living, Adaptive System.

AI is not merely improving how we teach and learn – it is redefining what it means to teach and learn. The path forward must be guided not just by algorithms and automation, but by vision, values and an unshakable commitment to the human purpose of education.

Discussion Questions

(1) How is AI changing the role of teachers in the classroom? Is it a support tool or a replacement risk?
(2) Can AI personalize learning without compromising standardization and curriculum goals?
(3) In what ways can AI improve learning outcomes for students with diverse needs and backgrounds?
(4) Will AI bridge or widen the digital divide in education? Who is left out of AI-powered learning?
(5) How can we ensure that AI tools used in education are inclusive and culturally sensitive?
(6) Will generative AI change how we define academic integrity and originality in student work?

Reference

Sloan, K. (2024, July 23). *How does MATHia use AI?* Carnegie Learning. https://www.carnegielearning.com/blog/mathia-ai

Further Readings

Fengchun, M., & Wayne, H. (2024). *Guidance for generative AI in education and research*. UNESCO. https://unesdoc.unesco.org/ark:/48223/pf0000386693

Ferreira, K., Ryan, C. T., & Mehta, S. (2023). ReUp education: Can AI help learners return to college? (Case No. 624007-PDF-ENG). *Harvard Business School Publishing*. https://store.hbr.org/product/reup-education-can-ai-help-learners-return-to-college/624007

Hashmi, N., & Bal, A. S. (2024). Generative AI in higher education and beyond. *Business Horizons*. Harvard Business School Publishing. https://store.hbr.org/product/generative-ai-in-higher-education-and-beyond/BH1280

Horvath, J. C. (2024, July 16). The limits of GenAI educators. *Harvard Business Review*. https://hbr.org/2024/07/the-limits-of-genai-educators

Rouhiainen, L. (2019, October 14). How AI and data could personalize higher education. *Harvard Business Review*. https://hbr.org/2019/10/how-ai-and-data-could-personalize-higher-education

Chapter 7

Implementing AI in Your Business

AI Is Not a Project. It is a Business Muscle.

AI isn't a tool you implement – it is a capability you build.

It doesn't end with a chatbot or a dashboard.

It begins when you stop asking "Where can we use AI?"

And start asking "What can we now do that we couldn't before?"

The future belongs to those who don't just adopt AI –

but embed it into how they think, decide, and grow.

Act fast. Learn faster. Scale responsibly.

Because in the age of AI, waiting is the ***most expensive*** decision of all.

Case Study: Commonwealth Bank of Australia (CBA) – Turning Data Into Daily Decisions

When Matt Comyn took the helm as CEO of the CBA, he faced a landscape familiar to many legacy institutions: immense customer expectations, fragmented data systems and emerging fintech threats that were moving faster and smarter. For a 100-year-old bank, it was time to act – not with incremental upgrades, but with transformative ambition.

CBA embarked on one of the most ambitious Artificial Intelligence (AI) transformations in the global banking sector. At the heart of its strategy was a bold bet: to move the entire enterprise data infrastructure to the cloud, build

(*Continued*)

AI and Business, 107–136

Published under exclusive licence by Emerald Publishing Limited
doi:10.1108/978-1-83708-888-120261007

(*Continued*)

intelligent systems capable of making millions of micro-decisions daily and achieve it all in under two years.

By partnering with AWS, the bank migrated over 157 billion data points and more than 61,000 data pipelines to the cloud. But the real breakthrough wasn't the scale of the migration – it was what came next. CBA operationalized over 2,000 machine learning models, which now make 55 million decisions daily. From fraud detection to personalized customer insights, these models help the bank predict, respond and serve in real time.

One standout initiative was the creation of a 'Customer Engagement Engine' in collaboration with H2O.ai. This platform personalizes financial advice, detects potential scams and offers customers timely nudges – such as reminders about subscription renewals or suggesting savings strategies – based on behavioural and transactional data. As a result, CBA reported significant reductions in fraud losses and higher customer engagement metrics.

This AI-first approach is not just about efficiency – it is about trust. With real-time alerts, proactive financial coaching and hyper-personalized experiences, the bank is not merely digitizing transactions – it is redesigning relationships. Ethical safeguards, data governance protocols and human oversight are built into every model to ensure responsible AI use.

What's remarkable is the pace. Within 18 months, CBA transformed itself from a traditional financial institution to a tech-forward AI-driven enterprise. It is now a global benchmark for how legacy institutions can reinvent themselves – not by chasing trends, but by placing AI at the core of their operating model.

As CBA's journey shows, AI implementation isn't a question of *if* or *when*. It is about *how fast* and *how well*. And for businesses in any sector, it is a lesson in courage, execution and vision.

CBA's AI Transformation Journey – From Legacy Bank to AI Leader

Phase	Action Taken	Impact
Cloud migration	Migrated 157B+ data points and 61K+ pipelines to AWS Cloud	Enabled scalable, real-time analytics and AI model training
Model deployment	2,000+ AI models making 55M+ daily decisions	Automated fraud detection, personalization, operations
Engagement engine	Partnered with H2O.ai to deliver tailored, real-time interactions	Improved customer satisfaction, proactive financial advice

(Continued)

Phase	Action Taken	Impact
Fraud detection	Real-time scam alerts, behavioural insights	Significant reduction in financial fraud
Cultural shift	Embedded AI governance and cross-functional AI squads	Fostered trust, ethical AI, and fast organizational learning

Key Takeaways From CBA's AI Playbook

- AI is not an add-on; it is a system-wide transformation.
- Data readiness is the foundation – quality, pipelines and cloud architecture matter.
- Customer-centricity wins: AI should enhance trust, not just efficiency.
- AI is not a destination, but a capability to be continuously evolved.

Questions to Think About

- Which customer or business challenge in your organization could benefit from automated, data-driven decision-making?
- Is your data infrastructure prepared to support real-time AI applications?
- How can AI enhance – not just automate – your customer experience?
- What governance or ethical safeguards will your business need if AI starts making decisions at scale?
- Are you ready to lead or be disrupted by AI-native competitors?

Note: ***This story was developed by the author based on publicly available academic and industry sources. It is intended for educational purposes and may simplify or generalize certain aspects for clarity.***

The Australian (2025); Commonwealth Bank of Australia (2025); Worrall (2024); Lakhani et al. (2021).

AI is no longer a futuristic aspiration – it has become a present-day necessity. However, despite widespread interest, many businesses struggle with the practicalities of implementation. This chapter serves as a pragmatic guide to implementing AI in your business – one decision, one process and one system at a time. We move beyond conceptual discussion and into the nuts and bolts of integrating AI within your operations. From aligning AI initiatives with strategic business goals to selecting tools, preparing data infrastructure and scaling successful pilots, this chapter offers a structured, step-by-step framework supported by real-world examples.

Turning Ambition Into Action

AI holds immense promise, but unlocking its value depends entirely on execution. Across industries, AI is revolutionizing how businesses operate, make decisions, serve customers and innovate. From personalized customer experiences to predictive maintenance, AI applications have matured from experimental technologies to mission-critical capabilities. However, a gap remains. Many businesses recognize AI's potential but stumble when trying to move from aspiration to action.

Why AI Implementation Is a Business Imperative Now

The urgency to implement AI stems from three converging realities:

- **Data abundance:** Organizations are inundated with data but lack the tools or skills to convert it into insights and actions. AI thrives on data and transforms it into strategic value at speed and scale.
- **Customer expectations:** In an era of instant gratification, AI enables personalization, real-time responses and contextual decision-making that today's customers increasingly expect.
- **Competitive pressure:** Early adopters of AI are already pulling ahead. Those who wait risk being outpaced by more agile, AI-native competitors.

As depicted in Fig. 7.1, the urgency to adopt AI stems from more than technological enthusiasm – it is a strategic response to evolving business realities. The exponential growth of data has created untapped opportunities for insight and automation. At the same time, consumers now expect hyper-personalized, instantaneous experiences across every touchpoint. Meanwhile, AI-first competitors are setting new standards for efficiency and innovation. The intersection of these forces represents a turning point – businesses that act decisively will shape the future, while those that hesitate may fall irreversibly behind.

Whether it is automating repetitive processes, improving forecasting or enhancing customer engagement, AI offers measurable gains in efficiency, accuracy and innovation. However, these benefits do not emerge on their own – they must be planned, tested and embedded into core systems and cultures.

From Hype to How: A Phased, Practical Approach

This chapter is designed to help leaders navigate the AI implementation journey with clarity and confidence. Rather than presenting AI as a monolithic transformation, this chapter breaks it down into actionable phases that can be adapted to any business size or maturity level. You will learn how to:

- Align AI initiatives with business strategy.
- Identify and prioritize use cases.
- Choose the right tools and partners.

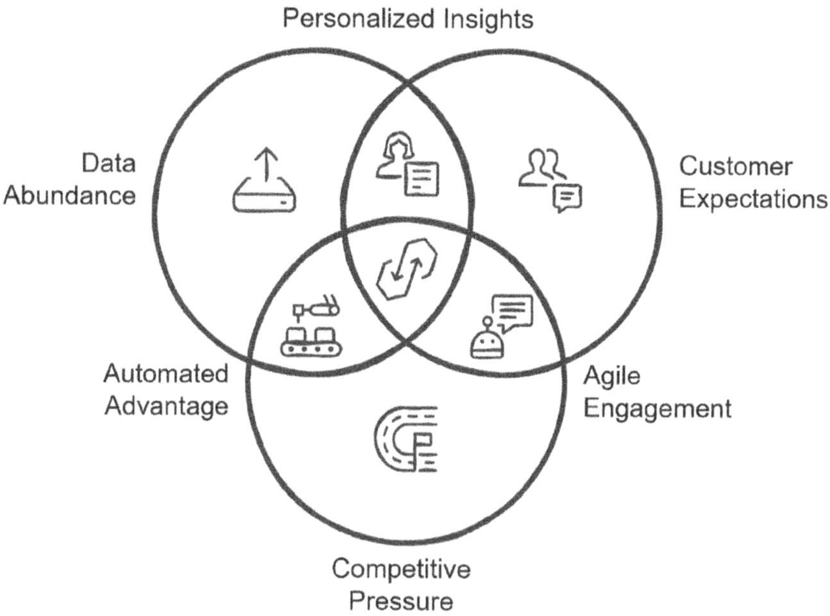

Fig. 7.1. The Sweet Spot of AI Implementation.

- Build the necessary data infrastructure.
- Pilot, test and iterate solutions.
- Scale and govern AI responsibly

The approach balances speed with stability, and innovation with integration, ensuring that AI evolves purposefully rather than disrupting blindly.

What Leaders Need to Know?

AI implementation is not an IT project – it is a business transformation. It requires executive sponsorship, cross-functional collaboration and a culture of experimentation. Leaders must ask the right questions, invest in the right capabilities and design AI initiatives around business outcomes, not just technological fascination. As businesses prepare to integrate AI across functions, leaders must move beyond delegating the task to IT teams or data scientists. Implementing AI successfully requires a holistic, strategic approach – anchored in clarity of purpose, cross-functional alignment and cultural readiness. Here are five critical considerations for leaders navigating the AI journey:

(1) **AI Is a Business Strategy, Not Just a Tech Upgrade:** AI is not another software installation – it reshapes how decisions are made, how teams function and how value is created. Leaders must ensure that AI efforts are

clearly aligned with business objectives, whether that means reducing costs, increasing revenue, improving customer satisfaction or gaining competitive advantage. Without this alignment, AI risks becoming an expensive experiment with limited impact.

(2) **You Don't Need to Know the Code, But You Must Understand the Logic:** Executives are not expected to become data scientists, but they must grasp AI's capabilities and limitations. This includes understanding what kinds of problems AI is good at solving (e.g., classification, prediction, automation), recognizing data quality issues and being able to ask critical questions about outcomes, fairness and explainability. Leaders must act as informed decision-makers – not passive observers.

(3) **Data Is a Strategic Asset – Treat It Accordingly:** Without quality data, AI initiatives will fail. Leaders must champion a data-first mindset: invest in cleaning legacy data, unify data silos and create governance structures that balance access with privacy and compliance. They should also be aware that AI readiness isn't just about quantity of data, but its relevance, structure and ethical use.

(4) **AI Adoption Is as Much About People as It Is About Technology:** Fear of job loss, mistrust of 'black box' systems and skill gaps can undermine even the best AI deployments. Leaders must prepare their teams through transparent communication, continuous training and by creating new roles (e.g., AI translators, ethics officers) that bridge the gap between technology and domain expertise. Empowerment, not replacement, should be the narrative.

(5) **Start Small, Scale Smart:** AI maturity does not happen overnight. Leaders should begin with narrowly defined use cases that demonstrate quick wins and build organizational confidence. These pilot projects act as a learning lab for broader scaling. As success builds, AI capabilities can be embedded more deeply across functions. The key is to avoid paralysis by complexity and focus on delivering measurable value in each phase.

AI implementation is not a departmental initiative – it is a leadership priority. It requires vision, discipline and a willingness to rethink how work is done. For leaders, the question is not 'Should we adopt AI?' but 'How can we embed AI to accelerate our mission responsibly?' The companies that lead with curiosity, competence and courage will shape not just their future – but the future of their industries.

Each level of the pyramid (Fig. 7.2) represents a core leadership responsibility that must be addressed for AI to move from potential to performance. At its base is Business Strategy Alignment – AI must serve a clear purpose rooted in business outcomes. From there, leaders need a functional understanding of AI logic, followed by a commitment to treat data as a strategic resource. Equally essential is a people-first approach that addresses organizational readiness, cultural change and skill development. Only when these foundations are in place can businesses truly start small and scale smart, ensuring AI grows responsibly and sustainably within the organization.

More importantly, leaders must prepare their organizations to integrate AI, not just deploy it. That means rethinking workflows, updating policies, managing risks and upskilling teams.

AI Leadership Readiness Checklist

Use this checklist to assess whether your leadership team is prepared to lead a successful AI implementation.

Leadership Priority	Reflection Question	Check
AI as a business strategy	Is AI tied to clear business outcomes (revenue, CX, etc.)?	□
Understanding the logic, not just the code	Can we explain what AI does and why it matters?	□
Data as a strategic asset	Do we have clean, connected and compliant data systems?	□
People-centred change	Are we addressing team reskilling and cultural adaptation?	□
Start small, scale smart	Do we have a pilot-first mindset and a clear scale plan?	□

Tip: If you're not checking at least four of these boxes, revisit your AI strategy alignment before moving forward.

Aligning AI With Business Objectives

The Strategic Starting Point

The first and most critical step in implementing AI is ensuring that it is aligned with the overarching goals of the business. Too often, organizations fall into the trap of exploring AI simply because competitors are doing it, or because leadership feels pressured to 'do something digital.' But AI is not a destination; it is a lever. And like any lever, its effectiveness depends entirely on where it is placed and what it is meant to move.

Fig. 7.2. AI Implementation Strategy Pyramid.

Defining What Success Looks Like

Before any tools are selected or models are trained, businesses must first answer a deceptively simple question: What does success look like to us? Is it any or combination or all of the following:

- Accelerated growth in new markets?
- Reduction in operational costs?
- Improved customer retention?
- Shorter product development cycles?
- Higher employee productivity?

Each of these goals may be served by different AI strategies and require different capabilities. Clarity at this stage determines everything downstream – from the type of data you need to the kind of talent you must recruit or upskill.

AI as a Value Driver, Not a Vanity Project

AI must be embedded into value-generating objectives, not treated as a separate initiative. Consider aligning AI with one of the following strategic pillars:

(1) **Revenue Growth:** AI can power product recommendations, targeted marketing, pricing optimization and sales forecasting to increase topline revenue.
(2) **Cost Optimization:** Robotic Process Automation (RPA), predictive maintenance and AI-assisted demand planning can streamline operations and reduce waste.
(3) **Customer Experience:** Chatbots, sentiment analysis, hyper-personalization and real-time service routing enhance how customers perceive and interact with your brand.
(4) **Innovation:** AI can be used for research, trend detection and new product development through simulations and synthetic data.
(5) **Risk Management:** Fraud detection, compliance monitoring and scenario planning models help mitigate operational and financial risks.

Case Story: Coca-Cola – AI for Product Innovation

Coca-Cola is leveraging AI to stay competitive in an increasingly health-conscious and diversified beverage market. Through its Freestyle machines – AI-enabled drink dispensers that allow users to mix hundreds of combinations – Coca-Cola collects consumer preference data in real time. These data feed directly into product development. For instance, Coca-Cola Cherry Sprite was launched based on flavour combinations that users were consistently choosing on Freestyle machines.

Beyond hardware, Coca-Cola also uses AI for predictive analytics in inventory management and image recognition in marketing, analyzing how its products are displayed in stores globally. All these applications tie directly into their growth, innovation and brand consistency goals – making AI a driver of both creativity and consistency.

Source:

https://www.coca-colacompany.com/media-center/coca-cola-creations-imagines-year-3000-futuristic-flavor-ai-powered-experience
https://digitaldefynd.com/IQ/ways-coca-cola-uses-artificial-intelligence/

Case Story: Axis Bank – AI for Customer Engagement

India's Axis Bank has strategically embedded AI into its customer relationship infrastructure to increase both responsiveness and relevance. Through its AI-based chatbot 'AXAA', the bank automates responses to millions of queries, reducing call centre dependency and improving turnaround times. But more importantly, AI is also used in personalizing financial advice, detecting churn risk and optimizing campaign timing.

(*Continued*)

(*Continued*)

By aligning AI with its customer-centricity strategy, Axis Bank is not only saving operational costs but also improving customer satisfaction – reflected in its Net Promoter Score (NPS). The bank doesn't treat AI as a cost-centre tool, but as a strategic enabler for customer loyalty and trust.

Sources:

https://analyticsindiamag.com/ai-features/the-tech-behind-axis-banks-multilingual-voice-bot/
https://www.axisbank.com/bank-smart/axis-aha/features
https://bankingfrontiers.com/axis-bank-introduces-humanoid-axaa/

Strategic Alignment in Practice: A 4-Step Roadmap

Strategic alignment is the most important aspect to consider when determining whether AI fits organizational functions and priorities. To ensure strategic alignment, organizations can follow this four-step process (Fig. 7.3):

Step 1: Clarify Business Priorities

Work with C-level leadership to distil 2–3 core business goals where AI could make a tangible difference. These must be metrics-driven and relevant to the bottom line.

Step 2: Map AI Capabilities to Use Cases

Once priorities are clear, identify the corresponding AI use cases. For example:

- Reducing customer churn → predictive modelling.
- Enhancing customer service → NLP-driven chatbots.
- Improving inventory accuracy → demand forecasting models.

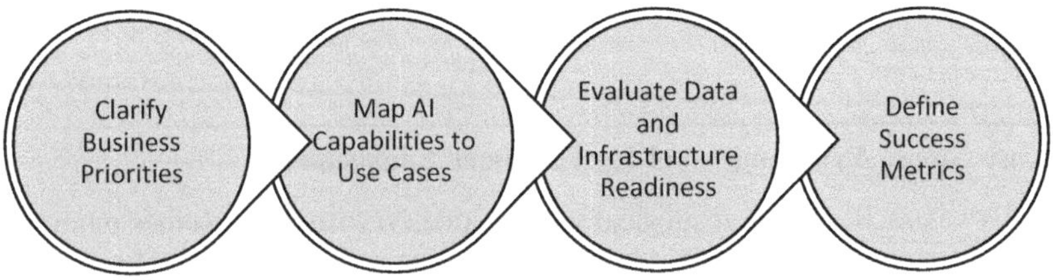

Fig. 7.3. A 4-Step Roadmap for Strategic Alignment in Practice.

Step 3: Evaluate Data and Infrastructure Readiness

Assess whether the organization has the data, infrastructure and skills needed to support the chosen use cases. If not, plan parallel investments to close the gap.

Step 4: Define Success Metrics

Tie every AI initiative to specific business KPIs (Key Performance Indicators) (e.g., increase in conversion rate, reduction in downtime, CSAT improvement). Make AI accountable – not just interesting.

Leadership Insight: The Role of the Executive Sponsor

Strategic alignment also requires executive alignment. Each major AI initiative should have a senior leader as a sponsor – someone who ensures the project stays connected to business outcomes and does not drift into technical abstraction. The role of this sponsor is to shield the AI team from shifting priorities, secure necessary resources and ensure organizational alignment.

This Table 7.1 serves as a practical decision tool for business leaders and managers seeking to align AI initiatives with tangible business outcomes. Each row links a strategic objective (such as revenue growth or risk management) to a relevant AI use case, supported by its core goal and primary domain of application. Importantly, the table also clarifies where leadership responsibility lies – whether in strategic visioning (top management), operational planning and execution (middle management) or frontline adoption (lower management and technical teams). This structure helps organizations not only choose the right AI solutions, but also prepare the internal stakeholders needed to drive success. It is recommended that readers use this table to assess their organizational priorities, identify low-risk pilot opportunities and assign ownership across appropriate levels of the management hierarchy.

Identifying AI Use Cases Across Business Functions

From Curiosity to Clarity: Where Should AI Begin?

Identifying the right use cases is the bridge between AI potential and AI performance. Many organizations stumble by launching AI projects in areas with low data maturity, unclear business relevance or limited stakeholder ownership. To avoid this, leaders must focus on high-impact, high-feasibility use cases – the sweet spot where pain points, data and workflows intersect.

Three Criteria for Spotting AI Opportunities

To narrow down potential areas for AI deployment, use the following three-lens approach:

Table 7.1. Strategic AI Use Case Mapping With Goals, Applications and Managerial Responsibility.

Strategic Business Objective	AI Use Case	Primary Goal	Business Suitability/Primary Application	Management Role Focus
Revenue growth	Dynamic pricing	Maximize revenue through real-time price adjustment.	E-commerce, retail, travel and hospitality	Top (strategy), middle (pricing), tech teams
	Product recommendations	Boost cross-sell and up-sell.	Online retail, OTT platforms, Banking (cross-selling products)	Middle (campaign), lower (execution)
	Sales forecasting	Improve planning and inventory management.	Manufacturing, FMCG, B2B sales	Top (forecasting), middle (planning)
Cost optimization	RPA	Automate repetitive admin tasks.	Finance, HR, procurement, compliance	Middle (deployment), lower (task execution)
	Predictive maintenance	Reduce downtime, save maintenance costs.	Manufacturing, transport, utilities	Top (investment), middle (ops), tech
	Demand planning	Align production with market needs.	Retail, manufacturing, logistics	Top (supply chain), middle (scheduling)
Customer experience	Chatbots	Provide 24/7 support at scale.	Customer service, BFSI, telecom	Middle (service), lower (support training)
	Sentiment analysis	Understand customer mood and adjust messaging.	Marketing, customer success, political campaigns	Top (strategy), middle (analysis)
	Personalized support	Improve satisfaction with tailored help.	Healthcare, banking, education	Middle (design), lower (delivery)

Innovation	Trend detection	Spot market shifts and emerging behaviours.	Fashion, media, consumer tech	Top (vision), middle (research)
	Synthetic data	Augment training data for new products.	Startups, R&D labs, regulated industries	Tech teams, middle (R&D), top (compliance)
	Prototyping	Rapidly test new ideas.	Design, product, automotive	Middle (innovation), lower (designers)
Risk management	Fraud detection	Identify and block anomalies in transactions.	BFSI, E-commerce, insurance	Tech teams, compliance, lower (ops)
	Scenario planning	Prepare for uncertain future events.	Strategy units, energy, public sector	Top (policy), middle (modelling)
	Compliance alerts	Detect breaches and trigger actions.	BFSI, healthcare, telecom	Top (audit), middle (monitoring)

Pain-Point Analysis

Start by asking, where are we losing time, money or customer goodwill? This may be a function with:

- repeated customer complaints;
- high error rates or rework;
- manual-intensive processes;
- inconsistent performance.

AI thrives in environments where complexity is high but patterns exist. If a function generates volumes of repeated decisions (e.g., claims processing, customer classification, inventory restocking), it is ripe for automation or augmentation.

Data Availability and Quality

No data, no AI. Functional areas that naturally generate and store structured or semi-structured data (such as CRM logs, ERP entries or sensor data) offer a head start. However, it is not just about having data – *it is about having the right kind of data*:

- Labelled and cleaned historical records.
- Sufficient volume and consistency.
- Timely access and ethical use clearance.

If a function scores high on data readiness, it should move up the implementation roadmap.

Repetition With Variance

Tasks that are repetitive but contain intelligent variance (e.g., understanding different customer intents or adjusting supply based on shifting demand) are strong candidates for AI. These workflows are often too complex for simple automation but too inefficient for human-only handling. AI fits well here – detecting patterns, making predictions and suggesting optimized actions.

Function-Wise AI Use Cases

AI's real power lies in its adaptability across business functions. Yet not all functions are equally suited to immediate AI deployment. Some face urgent pain points with ample data – ideal candidates for early AI pilots. Others may struggle with low data maturity or unclear problem definitions. To guide prioritization, the following matrix provides a function-by-function breakdown based on three key dimensions: business pain points, data readiness and AI suitability. Each row highlights practical use cases, contextual challenges and the strategic role of AI in driving measurable outcomes.

This matrix (Table 7.2) serves as a practical tool for identifying where AI can create the most immediate and measurable value across business functions. By evaluating each area against three critical dimensions – pain points, data availability and AI suitability – it helps decision-makers prioritize initiatives that are both impactful and feasible. High-scoring functions like operations, marketing and customer service often have well-defined problems, abundant data and high automation potential – making them ideal starting points. Functions with moderate or evolving readiness, such as HR or legal, may benefit from phased experimentation or targeted investments in data infrastructure. Readers are encouraged to use this matrix not only to launch pilot projects but also to develop a roadmap for broader AI maturity across the organization. It is particularly valuable during strategic planning or digital transformation assessments, where resource allocation must align with both business urgency and technical capability.

This 2 × 2 matrix (Fig. 7.4) helps identify which business functions are best suited for AI deployment, based on the urgency of operational pain points and the availability of usable data.

The matrix categorizes functions into four strategic quadrants, guiding decision-makers on where to initiate or defer AI efforts. Functions that experience high pain and have rich data availability – such as operations and customer service – fall in the top-right quadrant and are ideal candidates for immediate AI implementation. In contrast, areas with high pain but low data readiness may require targeted data infrastructure investments before any AI solution can be effective. The bottom-left quadrant, where both pain and data availability are low, suggests deprioritization, while the bottom-right quadrant calls for monitoring functions that are data-rich but not yet urgent. This framework ensures that AI investments are aligned with both business value and technical feasibility.

The Goldilocks Zone for AI Projects

Not every AI project is worth pursuing immediately. Some projects are overly ambitious – demanding vast data, complex domain expertise or regulatory clarity that does not yet exist. Others are too simplistic or low-impact, offering little return on investment. What organizations need is a strategic 'sweet spot' for AI experimentation: the Goldilocks Zone – where projects are not too big, not too small, but just right to deliver value and build momentum. The Goldilocks Zone is defined by the intersection of four critical dimensions:

(1) **Strategic Value:** The project must align with business goals – whether that's cost savings, customer satisfaction, risk reduction or growth. Strategic fit ensures executive interest and resource support.

Table 7.2. AI Fit Matrix Across Functions.

Business Function	Key Pain Points	Data Availability	Potential AI Use Cases	AI Suitability	Readiness Notes
Marketing	Low ROI from campaigns; poor personalization	High (clickstream, CRM, social)	Customer segmentation, ad targeting, sentiment analysis	Very high	Data-rich + strategic visibility
Sales	Pipeline uncertainty, lead mismanagement	Medium (CRM, sales logs)	Lead scoring, forecasting, next-best action	High	CRM data useable, needs label quality
Customer service	High response time, ticket overload	High (chat logs, feedback)	Chatbots, routing, ticket triage	Very high	Fast impact via automation
Operations	Stockouts, maintenance downtime	Very high (sensor, ERP)	Demand forecasting, predictive maintenance	Very high	Strong foundation in structured data
Finance	Manual tasks, fraud risk	High (transactions, reports)	Fraud detection, auto-reconciliation, planning	High	Strong fit for pattern-based models
HR	Bias in hiring, attrition, disengagement	Medium-low (CVs, surveys)	Resume screening, attrition prediction	Moderate	Emerging use cases; privacy concerns
Legal/ Compliance	Contract backlogs, review overload	Medium (contracts, logs)	Policy monitoring, clause extraction	Moderate	NLP potential, but needs clean text
Procurement	Supplier inconsistency, pricing variance	Medium (invoices, vendor data)	Vendor risk scoring, spend analytics	Moderate	High benefit, but often siloed data

IT/Security	Alert fatigue, breach risks	High (logs, event data)	Threat detection, anomaly detection	High	Good for anomaly-focused ML models
R&D/ Innovation	Long cycles, trend miss	Medium (market data, trials)	Trend spotting, synthetic data generation	Moderate	High impact; data may be external

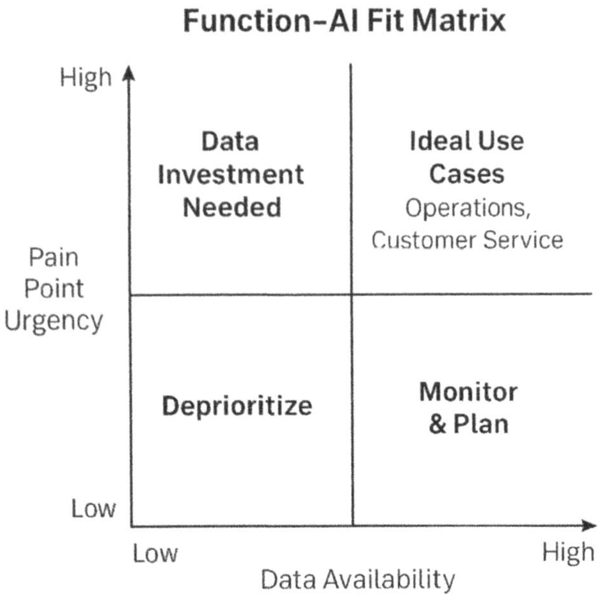

Fig. 7.4. Prioritizing AI Implementation Based on Function Readiness and Pain.

(O)-
perational Pain: AI should solve a clear and persistent pain point – one that slows the business down or leads to significant inefficiencies. This creates urgency and stakeholder buy-in.

(3) **Data Readiness:** Even the best idea fails without usable data. The project should involve data that is accessible, of reasonable quality, and ethically usable. It need not be perfect, but must be 'good enough' for an initial proof of concept.

(4) **Implementation Feasibility:** The technical and cultural feasibility of deploying AI matters. Consider existing infrastructure, team skill levels, vendor partnerships and change management maturity.

Why the Goldilocks Zone Matters

Projects in the Goldilocks Zone help organizations build internal momentum, prove the business case and refine their AI delivery muscle. They avoid the common pitfalls of AI strategy – like starting with moonshots, overengineering solutions or chasing use cases without business backing.

Projects that fall within the Goldilocks Zone (Fig. 7.5) are well-positioned for success because they are grounded in business relevance, solve a pressing need

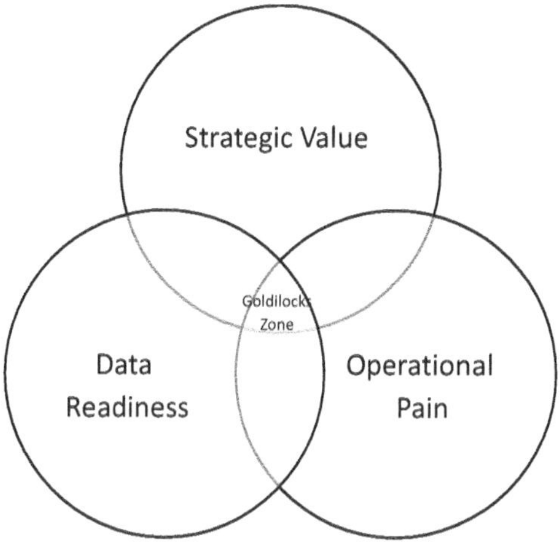

Fig. 7.5. The Goldilocks Zone for AI Projects.

and have access to usable data. Unlike high-risk moonshots or low-impact experiments, these initiatives are 'just right' – offering a balance of feasibility and strategic importance. This visual helps guide project selection by ensuring that AI efforts start where the conditions are most favourable for measurable impact and organizational buy-in. Use it as a diagnostic reference during AI planning workshops, prioritization meetings or technology roadmapping sessions.

> **Implementation Tip**
>
> Start with 2–3 high-impact, low-barrier pilots across different functions. These will create internal momentum, test your data and model maturity, and offer proof-points for scaling AI further.

Choosing the Right Tools, Vendors or Build Options

Once your organization has identified the right use cases for AI, the next big decision is how to implement them. Should you build your own solution? Should you buy an off-the-shelf tool? Or should you partner with a vendor? Each path offers trade-offs in terms of cost, speed, control and long-term adaptability.

Build vs. Buy: A Strategic Trade-Off

Build (In-House): Ideal when your use case is highly specific, offers competitive differentiation or when data security and IP ownership are critical. However, building requires time, skilled AI talent and robust infrastructure.

Buy (Off-the-Shelf): Best suited for widely available solutions like chatbots, recommendation engines or sentiment analysis. These tools offer fast deployment and scalability, but may limit customization.

Many businesses also adopt a hybrid model – *buying core capabilities and customizing them incrementally.*

Key Factors to Evaluate

Selecting the right AI solution – whether built or bought – requires thoughtful evaluation of several operational, technical and strategic considerations. These factors help ensure the chosen tool not only solves today's problem but also scales with tomorrow's needs.

(1) **Integration with Legacy Systems:** No AI tool functions in a vacuum. The solution must integrate seamlessly with existing systems – such as CRM, ERP or proprietary databases – without causing workflow disruptions or requiring excessive middleware. Custom-built solutions can be tailored for integration, while off-the-shelf tools often rely on standardized Application Programming Interfaces (APIs), which may have limitations.
Important to ask: Is our current IT infrastructure compatible with the proposed AI solution?

(2) **Scalability and Vendor Support:** AI tools must grow with the business. Can the tool support a growing user base, increased data volume and evolving use cases? Additionally, vendor support – including training, documentation and SLA-backed issue resolution – is critical to long-term success, particularly for smaller firms.
Important to ask: Does the vendor provide reliable support, product updates and customization pathways?

(3) **Explainability and Transparency:** Regulators, internal stakeholders and customers increasingly demand transparent AI decisions. For critical use cases like credit scoring or medical triage, explainable AI is non-negotiable. Off-the-shelf tools may lack model-level transparency, while custom builds allow full control over explainability mechanisms.
Important to ask: Can we confidently explain how the AI reached its decision?

(4) **Time-to-Value:** Off-the-shelf tools offer rapid deployment, enabling faster time-to-value – an essential consideration in fast-moving markets. On the other hand, building in-house often requires months of design, training and testing before the tool can go live.
Important to ask: Do we need a solution quickly, or can we afford a longer development timeline?

(5) **Cost and ROI Potential:** Building AI solutions requires significant upfront investment in talent, infrastructure and model development. However, it offers long-term cost advantages if scaled successfully. Bought solutions may have recurring licensing costs and limited ROI unless fully utilized.
Important to ask: Is the projected ROI worth the total cost of ownership?

(6) Talent Availability: In-house development is only feasible if the organization has access to skilled AI engineers, data scientists and MLOps professionals. Smaller firms or those new to AI may benefit from vendor tools that abstract technical complexity.
Important to ask: Do we have the right internal talent to build and maintain this solution?

Apply the AI Investment Lens

Organizations can use the following comparison table as a diagnostic tool when considering whether to build or buy their AI capabilities. The table summarizes key evaluation factors and their typical implications across the two options.

This table (Table 7.3) helps business and technology leaders evaluate the suitability of in-house development versus third-party solutions across critical decision dimensions. Use this table in planning sessions with your IT and business teams to determine which approach aligns with your timeline, budget and strategic priorities. For organizations new to AI, it may be practical to start with vendor solutions in low-risk areas and gradually build custom capabilities in core business functions where AI offers competitive advantage.

Building Data and Tech Infrastructure

AI is only as effective as the infrastructure that supports it. Without the right data foundations and technical architecture, even the most advanced models will fail to deliver value. Building a robust, scalable and ethical data and tech infrastructure is not just a technical task – it is a strategic necessity.

Data Strategy Comes First

Before any AI system is trained, a business must have a clear data strategy in place. This includes:

- Availability: Do we have the right kind of data – structured, unstructured, real-time – that reflects our business needs?
- Cleanliness: Is the data consistent, accurate and free of duplication or noise?
- Accessibility: Can relevant teams access data securely and efficiently, without bottlenecks or compliance violations?

Table 7.3. Build vs. Buy – Strategic Comparison of AI Implementation Approaches.

Factor	Build (In-House)	Buy (Off-the-Shelf)
Speed to deploy	Slower (4–12 months)	Faster (1–8 weeks)
Customization level	High – tailored to exact needs	Limited – fits common use cases
Initial cost	High – infrastructure, hiring, development time	Medium – licence and integration fees
Long-term cost	Lower per use if scaled well	Ongoing subscription and upgrade fees
Data security	Full control over data pipelines	Depends on vendor policies
Integration ease	Full control; requires internal IT coordination	API-based; may have compatibility constraints
Model transparency	High – explainability can be built-in	Varies – often a black box
Talent requirement	High – skilled AI and data engineering needed	Low – business users can operate
Vendor dependence	None	High – tied to vendor roadmap and service levels
Scalability	Highly scalable if designed well	Limited by vendor's scale options and pricing
Innovation potential	High – fosters internal experimentation	Low – constrained by vendor feature set

Data silos remain one of the biggest blockers in AI adoption. Breaking these down requires both technology (e.g., centralized data lakes) and culture (data-sharing policies, cross-team trust).

Checklist: *Does your organization treat data as a strategic asset or an operational leftover?*

Key Components of AI-Ready Infrastructure

To support scalable AI initiatives, certain technical building blocks are essential:

- ***Cloud Storage & Data Lakes:*** Centralized, scalable storage (like AWS S3, Google Cloud Storage or Azure Blob) allows data from multiple sources – CRM, POS, mobile apps – to be pooled and queried efficiently. Data lakes can accommodate structured and unstructured formats, making them AI-friendly.
- ***APIs and Integration Layers:*** APIs allow different systems – internal and external – to communicate. An API-first approach ensures modularity, reusability and real-time connectivity with analytics, third-party tools and ML models.
- ***Data Pipelines:*** ETL/ELT pipelines automate the flow of data from source systems to analysis or modelling environments. Tools like Apache Airflow, Talend or Azure Data Factory help ingest, transform and validate data continuously, reducing manual handling and error rates.
- ***Model Deployment and MLOps:*** Once a model is trained, it must be deployed and monitored in production. MLOps platforms (e.g., MLflow, Kubeflow, Amazon SageMaker) enable versioning, A/B testing, rollback and retraining – ensuring that AI doesn't become a one-time experiment.

Fig. 7.6 emphasizes the structured, linear progression required to operationalize AI. It begins with diverse data inputs collected from customer interactions, mobile applications or point-of-sale systems – that are then cleansed and structured via ETL pipelines. Once consolidated into a cloud-based data lake, the data is accessible for training AI models that are deployed into production environments. Finally, these models power a range of business applications –

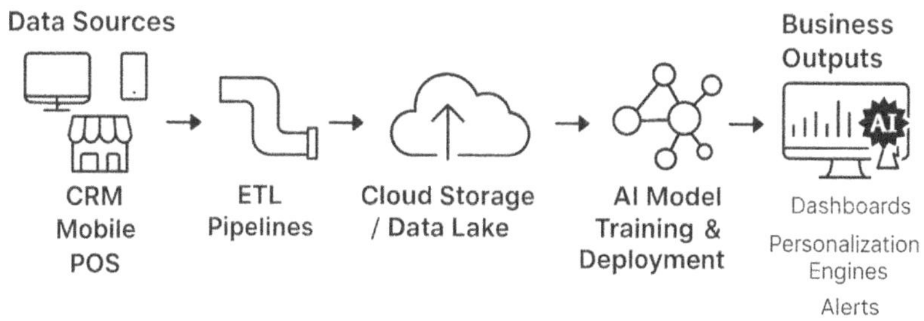

Fig. 7.6. End-to-End AI Infrastructure Flow.

from real-time dashboards to automated alerts and recommendation engines. Each stage is not only technically critical but also strategically linked to the organization's ability to scale AI effectively and ethically.

Cross-Functional Collaboration Is Non-Negotiable

AI success is not the job of the data science or IT team alone. It requires tight collaboration between:

- IT: Ensures secure, scalable infrastructure.
- Business/Domain Teams: Provide use-case clarity, label data and validate outputs.
- Legal/Compliance: Ensure governance, consent and adherence to local data laws.

This triangular collaboration should be embedded into the project structure from day one. One successful approach is forming AI pods – small cross-functional teams assigned to each use case or business unit, following agile sprints for iteration.

Data Governance, Ethics and Privacy by Design

Modern AI systems cannot be built first and 'made ethical' later. Governance must be embedded from the ground up:

- Consent-first collection: Always collect data with user consent and a clear value exchange.
- Data minimization: Don't collect more than needed.
- Access control: Role-based data access prevents misuse and ensures auditability.
- Bias checks and fairness audits: Regularly assess AI outputs for discriminatory patterns or unintended impacts.

Frameworks like the EU's AI Act, India's DPDP Act and industry-specific regulations (e.g., HIPAA, GDPR) must inform every technical decision – from storage location to model explainability.

Quick Tip: Appoint a Data Steward or AI Ethics Lead on every high-impact project to ensure compliance and consumer trust.

Case Story: Starbucks' Loyalty App Data Strategy

Starbucks is a powerful example of how infrastructure can drive AI success. The company's loyalty app collects millions of customer transactions across geographies in real-time. These data are fed into a cloud-based analytics engine to:

- Recommend personalized offers.
- Optimize product placement by region.
- Predict inventory demand at the store level.

What makes Starbucks stand out isn't just the volume of data – but how well it is integrated, secured and activated for decision-making. The infrastructure spans mobile apps, cloud services, real-time APIs and in-store POS – all stitched together seamlessly.

Running Pilot Projects and Proof of Concept (PoC)

Transitioning from strategy to implementation in AI requires more than ambition – it requires structured experimentation. Pilot projects and PoC initiatives offer organizations a low-risk, high-learning environment to explore AI solutions before investing at scale. Done right, these early-stage projects provide clarity, confidence and crucial course corrections.

Start Small, Learn Fast

In AI, perfect is often the enemy of progress. Pilots are designed not to deliver full-scale impact but to test a narrowly scoped use case under real-world conditions. Their primary function is to validate assumptions, surface hidden challenges and gather user feedback. The mantra here is simple: ***start small, fail fast, learn quickly***.

Organizations benefit most when they begin with a focused goal – one process, one use case, one team. This limited scope allows rapid development, faster iteration and a clear view of whether the AI system can deliver value in practice.

A good pilot teaches something important, whether the outcome is success or failure.

Defining Success Before Deployment

The effectiveness of a pilot hinges on clearly defined success criteria. Too often, AI pilots are launched without measurable goals, leading to confusion over what constitutes 'success.' These criteria must encompass both technical performance and business impact. On the technical side, metrics might include accuracy (e.g., precision, recall), latency, uptime and model confidence. On the business side, focus on metrics such as cost reduction, process efficiency, lead conversion rate or customer satisfaction scores.

Success is not binary. It is perfectly valid to discover that a solution may work well in some scenarios but not others, or the data infrastructure may need improvement before scaling. The key is that success is measurable and aligned with business priorities.

Pilots should be judged not only by performance, but also by what they reveal.

Who Owns the Pilot?

AI pilots are rarely successful when owned solely by the IT or data science team. They must be jointly owned by a cross-functional team that includes:

- Business owners who define the problem and interpret outcomes in context.
- Technical experts who build, tune and monitor the model.
- IT or engineering, who ensure integration with existing systems and manage deployment.

Some organizations form 'AI pods' – small, agile teams with representation from each function, empowered to run short sprints, evaluate results and adjust quickly. These teams benefit from using agile boards, shared logs and quick feedback cycles. Ownership also means accountability. Assigning a named business sponsor ensures the pilot remains grounded in organizational needs rather than technical novelty.

Tools for Tracking Progress

Running an AI pilot is not a one-time task but a learning process. Having the right tools in place supports iterative development and ensures transparency. Common tools include:

- Agile boards (e.g., Jira, Trello) for task tracking and visibility.
- Experimentation logs to document iterations, assumptions and outcomes.
- Collaboration platforms (e.g., Confluence, Slack) to enable real-time communication and knowledge sharing.
- A/B testing frameworks for comparing AI-driven and traditional approaches.
- Feedback tools to capture internal and user responses.

These tools not only support the pilot but also create a trail of evidence, critical for scaling, auditing and sharing learnings internally.

Case Story: Piloting an AI Chatbot for Lead Capture

A mid-sized B2B company wanted to improve the number and quality of inbound leads through its website. Rather than overhaul the entire customer journey, the team launched a simple AI chatbot pilot on one landing page.

Scope:

- Limited to answering FAQs and scheduling demos for one product line.
- Integrated with CRM for automatic lead logging.

Technology:

- Off-the-shelf chatbot builder with NLP features and drag-and-drop workflows.

Pilot Timeline:

- Two weeks for setup and content training.
- Two weeks live on site with A/B testing against the existing form.

Measured Outcomes:

- 22% increase in demo bookings from the chatbot-enabled page.
- 15% lower bounce rate.
- Positive feedback from sales team on lead relevance.
- Clear documentation of chatbot interactions for improvement.

Based on these results, the business case for full rollout was approved within three weeks. The chatbot was later scaled to all product pages and integrated with additional backend systems.

This example illustrates that a pilot doesn't need complexity – ***it needs clarity, scope control and measurable outcomes.***

Fig. 7.7 illustrates the cyclical nature of AI pilot execution, emphasizing four key stages – starting small, running a focused pilot, defining clear success criteria and learning through adaptation – before looping back into iteration or scaling.

Rather than aiming for full-scale automation from the outset, organizations are encouraged to begin with a tightly scoped, manageable pilot. Each phase feeds into the next, with learning and adaptation being central to long-term success. The circular layout reinforces the idea that AI implementation is a continuous improvement loop, where each cycle strengthens the organization's capabilities, data foundations and confidence in scaling responsibly.

From Pilot to Scale: Criteria for Advancement

Not all pilots should scale. Before moving forward, one should ask:

- Are the business KPIs showing clear improvement?
- Has the model performed reliably under realistic conditions?

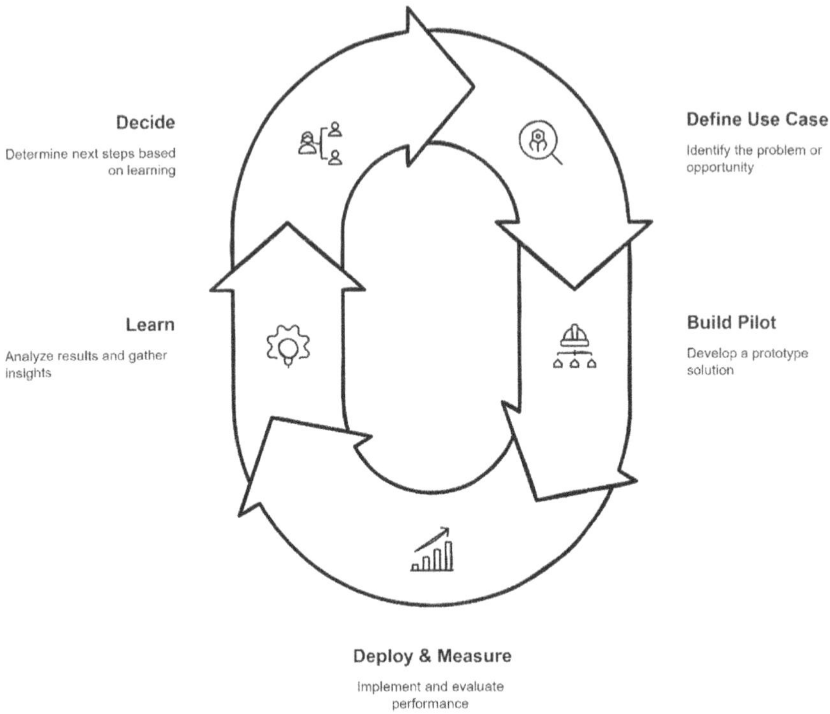

Fig. 7.7. Iterative Cycle of AI Pilot Deployment.

- Are users (internal or external) engaging positively?
- Is the infrastructure ready for expansion?

Only when these conditions are met should the project move beyond pilot. Otherwise, iterate or shelve it without hesitation.

Chapter Summary

This chapter demystifies the implementation of AI by providing a structured, phased roadmap that guides organizations from ideation to practical deployment. Rather than treating AI as a standalone technology project, it emphasizes AI as a strategic capability – one that aligns closely with business goals, customer experience and organizational maturity. Key themes covered include:

- Strategic alignment of AI with business priorities.
- Identifying high-value use cases across functions.
- Evaluating build vs. buy decisions.

- Establishing robust data and tech infrastructure.
- Running pilot projects for learning and proof-of-value.

Illustrated with real-world cases like Commonwealth Bank of Australia, Axis Bank, Coca-Cola and Starbucks, this chapter offers actionable insights for leaders, managers and technologists alike. It encourages a mindset shift – from 'Where can we use AI?' to 'What can we now achieve with AI that we couldn't before?'

Future Outlook

As businesses accelerate their digital transformation, AI implementation must evolve from a checklist initiative to a cultural and operational paradigm. The next challenge is not just adopting AI, but embedding it – into workflows, governance systems and talent strategies. Future-focused organizations will:

- Scale pilots into enterprise-wide capabilities.
- Embed ethics and transparency into AI systems from day one.
- Develop internal AI literacy across roles – not just in data science teams.
- Establish adaptive governance to ensure responsible innovation.

AI maturity is a journey – marked not by tools deployed, but by value delivered. The next chapter will explore how to scale AI responsibly, govern its use and ensure that it becomes a lasting competitive advantage rather than a transient experiment.

Discussion Questions

(1) How can your organization ensure that its AI initiatives are tied to core business outcomes rather than technical hype?
(2) Which functions in your business show the greatest pain-point urgency and data readiness? Can you identify a candidate for a pilot?
(3) What factors – cost, speed, control, explainability – would influence your decision to build an AI tool versus buying one?
(4) Is your current tech stack capable of supporting AI at scale? What changes might be required?
(5) Does your leadership team possess the awareness and capability to guide an AI transformation responsibly?
(6) What metrics will you use to evaluate whether an AI project is worth scaling?

References

Commonwealth Bank of Australia. (2025, June). *CommBank accelerates AI integration with major data migration to cloud.* https://www.commbank.com.au/articles/newsroom/2025/06/cba-ai-migration-cloud.html

Lakhani, K. R., Grushka-Cockayne, Y., Paik, J. H., & Randazzo, S. (2021). *Customer-centric design with artificial intelligence: Commonwealth bank [Case study]*. https://www.hbs.edu/faculty/Pages/item.aspx?num=61392

The Australian. (2025). *How Matt Comyn is rebuilding Australia's biggest bank with AI – and what it means for you*. https://www.theaustralian.com.au/business/technology/how-matt-comyn-is-rebuilding-australias-biggest-bank-with-ai-and-what-it-means-for-you/news-story/ac7ec17c389c2c93357d8431315458d3

Worrall, S. (2024). CommBank demonstrates the real-world benefits of AI. *Microsoft Australia News Centre*. https://news.microsoft.com/en-au/features/commbank-demonstrates-the-real-world-benefits-of-ai/

Further Readings

Deloitte. (2025). *State of generative AI in the enterprise 2024*. https://www.deloitte.com/us/en/what-we-do/capabilities/applied-artificial-intelligence/content/state-of-generative-ai-in-enterprise.html

Eastwood, B. (2025, April 1). Practical AI implementation: Success stories from MIT Sloan management review. *MIT Sloan Management Review*. https://mitsloan.mit.edu/ideas-made-to-matter/practical-ai-implementation-success-stories-mit-sloan-management-review

Gartner. (2024, October 21). *What is AI-Ready data? And how to get yours there*. https://www.gartner.com/en/articles/ai-ready-data

Gibson, K. (2024, October 9). *Building an AI business strategy: A beginner's guide*. Harvard Business Publishing. https://online.hbs.edu/blog/post/ai-business-strategy

Kervazo, F., Forsgren, M., & Narayanan, S. (2025, March 13). *From pilot to profit: Scaling gen AI in aftermarket and field services*. McKinsey & Company. https://www.mckinsey.com/capabilities/operations/our-insights/from-pilot-to-profit-scaling-gen-ai-in-aftermarket-and-field-services

Kim, W. C., Mauborgne, R., & Ji, M. (2025, September 5). Make sure your AI strategy actually creates value. *Harvard Business Review*. https://hbr.org/2025/09/make-sure-your-ai-strategy-actually-creates-value

McKinsey and Company. (2025, March 12). *The state of AI: Global survey*. https://www.mckinsey.com/capabilities/quantumblack/our-insights/the-state-of-ai

Ramos, L., Mullen, A., & Hamer, P. (2025, January 10). *The CIO's guide to building an AI roadmap that drives value*. Gartner. https://www.gartner.com/en/articles/ai-roadmap

Webster, M., & Westerman, G. (2025, January 22). Generate value from genAI with 'small t' transformations. *MIT Sloan Management Review*. https://sloanreview.mit.edu/article/generate-value-from-gen-ai-with-small-t-transformations/

Chapter 8

Scaling, Governing and Sustaining AI in Enterprises

Ideas spark, data flows,

Pilots test what business knows.

Learn, refine, then let it grow –

That's the AI way to go.

Case Study: United Parcel Service (UPS) ORION – Scaling AI on the Road

UPS, which is one of the world's largest logistics company, is a good example of the responsible scalability of Artificial Intelligence (AI) due to its measurable impact across thousands of operational touchpoints. The company's proprietary system, On-Road Integrated Optimization and Navigation (ORION), showcases the advantage of AI integrated with human input and how it can achieve enterprise-wide efficiency and transformation.

The Challenge

UPS has more than 60,000 drivers doing millions of daily deliveries for them. They encountered the traditional high-volume and high-complexity challenge, like how to optimize delivery routes, reduce servicing costs, improve fuel consumption and enhance customer service, all without disrupting the drivers' workflow or customer commitments.

Static and manual routes were the norm for delivery operations. UPS needed an intelligent system that could process real-time data, e.g., traffic,

(*Continued*)

AI and Business, 137–171

Published under exclusive licence by Emerald Publishing Limited
doi:10.1108/978-1-83708-888-120261008

(*Continued*)

package scans, customer locations, driver habits, etc. It would also be beneficial if they had the option of delivering optimized, 'drivable' routes at scale.

The Solution: ORION

The solution was found in a large-scale AI-based route optimization platform called ORION. ORION was developed over a decade ago, and it draws on the advanced algorithms available, telematics data and real-time operational updates. The attributes enabled it to create dynamic and efficient delivery routes. Additionally, it blends mathematical heuristics with practical business rules like minimizing left turns and factoring in customer specific delivery windows. The system integrates inputs from:

- GPS and on-vehicle telematics;
- historical and live traffic data;
- package volume and location;
- delivery time constraints and driver experience.

Drivers receive real-time route suggestions via their handheld Delivery Information Acquisition Device (DIAD), updated continuously as conditions change.

Implementation Strategy

UPS did not rush ORION into action. It followed a phased, iterative rollout:

- 2003–2009: Conceptual development and small-scale tests.
- 2010–2012: Controlled pilots across select regions.
- 2012–2016: Full US deployment across ~55,000 delivery routes.
- Post-2017: Dynamic optimization upgrades, real-time re-routing and deeper integration with data infrastructure.

The ORION team collaborated with data scientists, engineers and frontline drivers to ensure the system was not only intelligent but also trusted and useable.

Business Impact

- 100 million fewer miles driven annually.
- 10 million gallons of fuel saved per year.
- Approximately $300–$400 million in annual savings.
- Reduced CO_2 emissions by over 100,000 metric tons.
- 2–4 additional miles saved per driver daily with dynamic re-routing.

These gains were achieved without requiring major operational overhauls, thanks to ORION's seamless fit into existing workflows.

Lessons in Scaling AI

UPS's ORION project highlights several best practices for scaling AI:

- Human-Centred Design: Early driver resistance was addressed through redesign and engagement initiatives, ensuring AI-assisted rather than dictated.
- Infrastructure Readiness: Success was underpinned by investments in telematics, cloud infrastructure and scalable analytics systems.
- Governance and Feedback Loops: Pilot learnings were baked into model tuning, with feedback cycles involving both managers and drivers.
- Ethical and Operational Balance: ORION avoided 'over-automation' – drivers retained autonomy while benefiting from algorithmic guidance.

Questions to Think About

1. What made ORION a scalable and sustainable AI success rather than just a one-time innovation?
2. How did UPS balance algorithmic optimization with human decision-making?
3. What infrastructure and cultural elements were essential for ORION's deployment?
4. If your organization wanted to implement something like ORION, where would you start?
5 What lessons from ORION could apply to non-logistics industries or customer-facing services?

Source Note: Based on publicly available data from UPS Sustainability Reports, Business Insider and Harvard case documentation.

1. https://www.bsr.org/en/case-studies/center-for-technology-and-sustainability-orion-technology-ups#:~:text=Developed%20by%20UPS%2C%20ORION%E2%80%94or%20On%2DRoad%20Integrated%20Optimization,the%20most%20efficient%20daily%20route%20for%20drivers.&text=Next%2C%20UPS%20wanted%20to%20demonstrate%20consistent%20results.
2. Yoo, A (2017). UPS: Driving Performance by Optimizing Driver Behaviour. https://d3.harvard.edu/platform-digit/submission/ups-driving-performance-by-optimizing-driver-behavior/
3. UPS (2023). UPS's releases 21st sustainability report. https://about.ups.com/us/en/our-impact/sustainability/sustainable-services/2022-ups-sustainability-report-.html
4. Brown, D (2018). New UPS navigation tool aims to save time and money with each turn. https://www.businessinsider.com/r-new-ups-navigation-tool-aims-to-save-time-and-money-with-each-turn-2018-12
5. UPS (2018). UPS Deploys Purpose-Built Navigation for UPS Service Personnel. https://about.ups.com/us/en/newsroom/press-releases/innovation-driven/ups-deploys-purpose-built-navigation-for-ups-service-personnel.html

AI implementation rarely ends with a successful pilot. In fact, this is where the more complex, strategic phase begins. Organizations that have tested AI in isolated functions must now address the challenge of scaling these efforts across the enterprise, ensuring consistent value delivery, responsible governance and long-term sustainability.

A compelling example of this transition can be found in the case of UPS and its ORION system. What began as a pilot for route optimization evolved into a fleet-wide AI deployment, delivering significant cost savings, operational efficiency and carbon reductions. This transformation did not occur simply by adopting an algorithm – it was enabled by structured rollout planning, infrastructure maturity, strong cross-functional coordination and long-term governance. This chapter continues to develop the implementation framework presented earlier and is concerned with the examination of four key themes:

(1) Horizontal and vertical scaling of AI within and across business functions.
(2) Implementing governance and monitoring frameworks for AI performance and responsible use.
(3) Organizational and cultural change management involves workforce readiness and upskilling.
(4) Addressing dilemmas and ethical issues in the context of decision-making systems with AI.

The assimilation of AI in the form of proofs of concept (PoCs) necessitates structured stewardship, well-defined responsibility lines, organizational alignment and institution-specific culture. This enterprise chapter seeks to offer scaling frameworks while keeping the adaptive AI capabilities within the organization in check.

This chapter continues to develop the implementation framework presented earlier and is concerned with the examination of four key themes:

(1) Horizontal and vertical scaling of AI within and across business functions.
(2) Implementing governance and monitoring frameworks for AI performance and responsible use.
(3) Organizational and cultural change management involves workforce readiness and upskilling.
(4) Addressing dilemmas and ethical issues in the context of decision-making systems with AI.

The assimilation of AI in the form of PoCs necessitates structured stewardship, well-defined responsibility lines, organizational alignment and institution-specific culture. This enterprise chapter seeks to offer scaling frameworks while keeping the adaptive AI capabilities within the organization in check.

The AI Continuum: From Pilots to Optimization

The integration of AI technology into organizational operations has become a widespread phenomenon. However, there is a common concern: how to evaluate an organization's readiness to transition from conducting small-scale tests to a major, broad-scope strategic integration. While many companies seem to start with ambition and enthusiasm, the systematic evolution of AI capabilities at the cross-department, process and decision-making layer levels is often erratic.

To address this, we introduce the AI Continuum. This maturity model assists organizations in evaluating their position in the AI journey and what strategic actions are required to move forward. As mentioned in Chapter 1, AI Continuum served as a conceptual anchor but is now expanded into a five-stage framework outlining an organization's level of AI adoption, integration and reliance.

Unlike binary models where firms are labelled as 'AI adopters' or 'non-adopters,' this continuum captures degrees of maturity, spanning from initial awareness to AI-first enterprise mentality. Each stage is marked by more than just the introduction of tools or pilots and includes shifts in leadership mindset, culture, data infrastructure and governance systems.

> ***Strategic Insight:*** Positioning your organization anywhere on this continuum provides a common language for planning AI initiatives and achieving cross-disciplinary alignment. It enables business executives, technologists and policymakers to ground their conversations within structured evaluation instead of instinct, hype or intuition.

Stage 1: Awareness

At the Awareness Stage, AI is acknowledged as a transformative potential capability, but actions are far from concrete. Attending conferences, commissioning white papers and consulting engagements are some actions taken at the leadership level. However, no active teams or projects are present. Speculation around business-relevant solutions is commonplace during discussions. Organizations in this stage tend to:

- Explore AI through informal channels (e.g., vendor demos, media exposure).
- Lack of defined goals, budget or leadership commitment for AI adoption.
- Have a limited understanding of internal data quality or readiness.
- Operate without any AI-related roles, governance frameworks or use case repositories.

While it is a foundational phase, remaining too long in the awareness stage risks being outpaced by more agile competitors. However, with the right strategic push – such as forming an internal AI task force or conducting a readiness audit – organizations can transition quickly to experimentation. For example, a mid-sized manufacturing firm where the CIO has begun researching AI-based quality inspection tools, but no projects or internal capability building have yet been initiated.

Stage 2: Pilot

At the Pilot stage, organizations begin to move from theory to experimentation. AI is no longer just a discussion topic but becomes the basis for small-scale projects designed to demonstrate feasibility, validate use cases and build internal confidence. These initiatives are typically department-led, siloed and exploratory in nature. Characteristics of this stage include:

- PoCs and pilot projects developed in marketing, operations or IT.
- Reliance on external vendors, open-source tools or no-code platforms.
- Limited integration with core systems such as CRM, ERP or customer data platforms.
- Lack of coordinated data governance or model monitoring practices.
- Success criteria are often defined as post hoc, with limited linkage to long-term KPIs (Key Performance Indicators).

The primary risk at this stage is fragmentation. Without intentional guidance, various teams will apply AI independently, leading to redundant efforts, competing solutions or failure to leverage what works at scale. For instance, a chain store tries out a generative AI tool for social media posts and a chatbot for customer support FAQs, both operated by separate teams with no common architecture or learning framework.

Moving from pilot to integration involves creating shared evaluation frameworks, encouraging internal knowledge sharing and starting to consider AI not as a novelty but as a production-quality business capability.

Stage 3: Integration

The integration phase represents a key inflexion point in the AI maturity path. Here, AI is no longer a proving ground – it is integrated into live business processes. Models are rolled out to production, synchronized with enterprise systems and backed by maturing infrastructure and cross-functional teams. The following are key indicators of this stage:

- Deployment of AI models into customer-facing or operational workflows.
- Integration with enterprise data systems via APIs, data lakes or cloud platforms.

- Formation of internal AI or analytics teams with clearly defined roles.
- Introduction of data governance policies, access protocols and compliance tracking.
- Use of dashboards or alerts to track AI-driven performance indicators.

At this stage, AI begins to influence routine decision-making, whether it's approving a loan, recommending content, routing a sales inquiry or optimizing inventory. Significantly, the technical teams, together with business teams, have to tackle performance, explainability and stakeholder trust simultaneously. As an illustration, a machine learning model assists with the diagnostic image prioritization at a healthcare provider, which is integrated into the clinical workflow. Feedback from doctors aids in the iterative retraining and calibration of the model.

Integration, while improving visibility and controllership alignment, increases the complexity of ensuring model stability, drift management, automation bias, acceptance by the workforce and trust placement on the system as automation increases.

Stage 4: Optimization

In the optimization stage, value becomes continuous and measurable, so AI evolves past integration. Organizations now treat models as dynamic rather than static assets requiring continuous tuning, retraining and agile governance. This stage is characterized by:

- Routine use of Machine Learning Operations (MLOps) practices for version control, model monitoring and automated retraining.
- Clearly defined AI performance KPIs tied to business goals (e.g., conversion lift, cost savings, churn reduction).
- Feedback loops – both human and automated – that improve model quality over time.
- Executive dashboards and decision review processes that include AI output as a core input.
- Beginning of ethical frameworks, fairness audits and bias checks in high-impact domains.

At this level, AI becomes part of the organization's operational nervous system. Trust by business users in AI outputs is established, there is an increase in internal diagnostics capabilities, and the organizations have systematic management of technical debt. For example, a telecom firm uses real-time churn risk scores to dynamically determine customer retention offers. The model is also scrutinized for data drift and fairness across customer segments on a daily basis.

This stage requires improvements, not perfection, which needs to be embraced along with learning as a continual process, where cultural alignment and technical discipline are paramount.

Stage 5: AI-First

In the final stage, the organization applies the AI-first approach, in which case AI is not an auxiliary tool to strategy but becomes the strategy.

AI is fully integrated within product development and innovation, decision-making, customer engagement and other areas of the organization. Teams actively look for solutions to business problems that are AI-native, and the structure of the organization reflects roles with leadership focused on AI. Key markers of this stage include:

- Organization-wide AI literacy and training programs, including non-technical roles.
- Emergence of roles such as AI product managers, AI ethics officers or model stewards.
- Strong internal platforms for data sharing, model reuse and rapid deployment.
- AI systems that are self-optimizing, adapt to user behaviour and influence high-level strategic planning.
- A mature governance model with audit trails, compliance integration and stakeholder oversight.

For example, a global digital media company leverages AI not only to recommend content but to commission scripts, adjust promotion budgets and personalize thumbnails in real time – based on user engagement predictions across regions.

In the fifth stage, organizations consider AI as a primary capability rather than an auxiliary support instrument. They appreciate that the edge over competitors in the digital economy is earned through the pace and sophistication of the learning systems that are integrated into routine processes and decisions .

This diagram (Fig. 8.1) depicts five progressively evolved stages of organizational AI maturity, spanning from awareness to operations that are fully integrated and AI-first operations. Each stage reflects a change in mindset, capability and strategy. Organizations do not usually adopt AI in one go. They tend to shift from a casual interest to a more sustained integration in a stepwise manner. AI Maturity Continuum visualizes this journey by situating firms on a

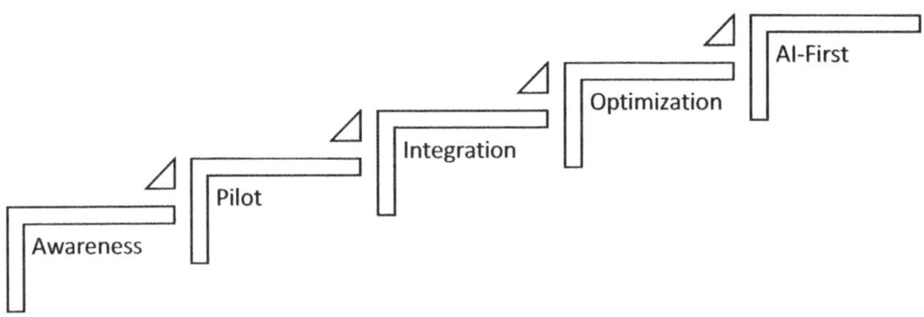

Fig. 8.1. AI Maturity Continuum.

spectrum of preparedness and sophistication. As a firm's diagnostic and planning tool, it enables decision-makers to assess their current state, set attainable targets and strategize around the cultural and operational enablers required at every stage .

The AI maturity stage markers (Table 8.1) outline the diagnostic boundaries for evaluating an organization's position in the AI journey. It helps in pinpointing expectation gaps, bridging capability gaps, aligning multi-functional silos and setting focused priorities for advancement. Aiming for coherence across the enterprise means some teams working at higher stages than others can be tolerated. During AI planning sessions, audits of digital transformation or capability reviews, this table provides clarity around where investment is most needed, who should be reskilled and how to prepare for sustainable and responsible scalable AI integration, thus enhancing decision-making.

Using the Continuum for Organizational Assessment

Familiarity with the phases of the AI Continuum offers organizations more than an academic concern – this is a pragmatic strategic tool. It is often the case that organizations do not struggle due to a lack of ambition, a lack of tools or even a lack of funding. Rather, organizations often misjudge their current state or try to pursue maturity while lacking alignment across functions. The continuum assists in avoiding this by providing a self-assessment framework to avoid the need to align all functions. This allows leaders to evaluate readiness, prioritize investments and coordinate cross-functional efforts.

Why Assessment Matters

AI maturity is uneven by nature. One business unit may be piloting advanced recommendation systems while another still struggles with fragmented spreadsheets and manual reporting. A clear-eyed assessment of the organization's maturity helps ensure that growth happens cohesively, technologically, culturally and strategically.

Moreover, AI maturity is not a fixed destination. Even organizations operating at the 'AI-First' stage must continue to monitor, recalibrate and evolve their capabilities as technologies advance and regulatory expectations shift.

How to Use the Continuum Effectively

The AI Continuum is most valuable when used not just by a single department but as a shared reference across the organization. It enables structured dialogue about where teams stand, where they differ and what it will take to progress. The following are a few things which will help you in taking care of how to use continuum effectively:

Table 8.1. AI Maturity Stage Markers.

Stage	Leadership Mindset	Data Readiness	Tooling & Infrastructure	Governance	Organizational Culture
Awareness	Exploratory, reactive	Unknown or fragmented	Vendor demos, basic dashboards	Not defined	Curious but unsure
Pilot	Experimentation-focused, siloed interest	Basic access for limited use cases	Isolated tools, PoCs	Ad hoc controls or vendor-led policies	Risk-tolerant, innovation-driven pockets
Integration	Commitment to embedding AI	Consolidated pipelines and system integration	Connected to CRM/ERP, internal teams forming	Emerging policies for compliance and access	Cross-functional collaboration begins
Optimization	Strategic review and oversight of AI performance	Automated pipelines, data quality protocols	Monitoring tools, model versioning, MLOps	Defined ethical checks, bias reviews	Learning systems embedded in teams
AI-first	AI as core to vision and strategy	Shared infrastructure, real-time data access	AI platforms, reusable models, auto-scaling	Formal boards, ethical audit logs, explainability layers	AI literacy across roles, high trust in automation

(1) Conduct a cross-functional audit: Assemble representatives from key business units – IT, marketing, finance, operations, HR – and assess each against the five continuum stages. The goal is not consensus but clarity. Differences across functions often reveal where support, infrastructure or training are needed.
(2) Assess across multiple dimensions: Use the five dimensions in Table 8.1 (leadership mindset, data readiness, tooling, governance, culture) to break down the assessment. For example, an organization might be at the Integration stage in terms of tooling but still in the Pilot stage when it comes to governance.
(3) Track progression over time: Maturity should be reviewed regularly – bi-annually or annually – as part of digital transformation or strategic planning cycles. This allows organizations to track movement along the continuum and mark gains and also identify stagnation or reversals.
(4) Establish stage-appropriate objectives: Not all organizations need to become AI-first at once. More important is establishing achievable, actionable objectives appropriate to the current stage. For instance, a Pilot-stage company might prioritize developing internal capability and creating a governance charter, instead of deploying AI-driven strategic projects.
(5) Apply it as a communication tool: The continuum is not just valuable for measurement but also for creating alignment. When technical teams, leadership and middle managers have a shared vocabulary around AI maturity, it becomes simpler to make the case for resources, control expectations and objectively measure progress.

Tip for Practice: The continuum can be inserted into organizational scorecards or digital transformation dashboards. As time passes, following the maturity track allows organizations to benchmark against peers and detect emerging capability gaps prior to becoming structural roadblocks.

With the AI Maturity Continuum, organizations can systematically assess their capabilities and chart a course for progress. This model delineates maturity into distinct stages: awareness, pilot, integration, optimization and AI-first. This division fosters strategic clarity, alignment across and within teams and improved organizational and operational decisions. Whether conducting internal assessments, planning transformations or developing briefings for executives, the continuum provides breadth as well as depth in diagnosis while illuminating directions. In the next section, we shift focus from assessing action readiness to strategizing ways to scale AI initiatives across organizational functions and enhance their impact within those functions.

AI Maturity Checklist

How to Use This Checklist

Review each statement in the checklist and place a checkmark (✔) next to those that accurately describe your organization's current practices. This is not a test – there are no right or wrong answers. The goal is to reflect on your AI journey with honesty and clarity.

Each checked item earns 1 point. After reviewing all 10 items, total your score to determine your approximate position on the AI Maturity Continuum.

✔/X	Statement
□	We have an executive sponsor or steering group focused on AI strategy.
□	At least one AI pilot or proof of concept has been completed in the past 12 months.
□	Our business units are aware of AI tools relevant to their domains.
□	We have structured, accessible data pipelines supporting analytics or AI.
□	We use AI outputs in at least one live customer-facing or operational process.
□	There is a cross-functional team responsible for AI delivery and oversight.
□	Models in production are monitored, retrained and linked to KPIs.
□	Employees beyond the IT team receive training or exposure to AI concepts.
□	Our organization has begun defining ethical, compliance or bias-related AI guidelines.
□	We consider AI capabilities when designing new products, services or workflows.

Interpreting Your Score

- 0–3: Awareness/Early Pilot: Your organization is in the early stages of exploring AI. Focus on building foundational knowledge, identifying relevant use cases and initiating pilot projects with clear objectives.

- 4–6: Integration Underway: At this stage, AI is operational in certain areas of the business, but the implementation is still disjointed. Focus on cross-silo integration and infrastructure streamlining to overcome stagnation along with governance building to strengthen holistic collaboration.
- 7–8: Optimization Phase: Companies at this phase have operationalized and are obtaining measurable results from AI systems. Continue investment in model maintenance, monitoring systems and further talent acquisition to scale in a sustainable manner.
- 9–10: AI-First Thinking: Your company now sees AI as a foundational capability. The key challenges are to maintain momentum, govern AI implementation ethically and integrate organizational learning across business functions

Note: Where gaps in scores across functions (ex: Marketing vs HR) are observed, aim to allocate attention and resources to those areas showing the most need.

It is recommended to use this checklist as a tool to evaluate progress and inform strategic planning every 6–12 months.

Scaling and Embedding AI Across the Business

Successfully piloting AI is a critical milestone, but it only marks the starting point. AI's true value is realized not from its singular applications but from its ubiquitous embedding into the enterprise's underlying structure. Scaling AI poses both a technical and organizational challenge. It requires a unified approach to funding infrastructure, operating models, talent, governance and change management. Perhaps most critically, it requires that AI be integrated as an evolving, adaptive capability, seamlessly intertwined with decision-making processes, service delivery frameworks and value generation systems rather than being treated as a self-contained project.

Scaling refers to the transition from 'AI as an Experiment' to 'AI as a System of Intelligence,' which underpins daily activities and informs tactical as well as strategic initiatives. For most firms, this means progressing in two complementary directions:

- Horizontally – by expanding AI use across business functions and departments.
- Vertically – by deepening its integration within individual functions or workflows.

Together, these scaling pathways create the foundation for AI maturity at enterprise level, allowing for cumulative learning, shared standards and reliable performance.

Horizontal Scaling: Extending AI Across Functions

Horizontal scaling refers to the deployment of AI in different and often disparate departments or business units. What used to be an isolated experiment, such as the implementation of a chatbot in customer support, can over time be replicated or adapted to other functions, including human resources, logistics, finance and supply chain. This nurtures organizational fluency in AI and establishes a shared infrastructure across the organization, increasing ROI while decreasing redundancy. The key enablers of horizontal scaling include:

(1) Frameworks and toolkits that are reusable: These can be in the form of templates, APIs or pretrained models, which are available and can foster cross-domain adoption while lowering development costs.
(2) Shared data infrastructure: A cohesive team working towards a common goal with consistent, high-quality data sources enables the use of a unified data lake or enterprise data platform.
(3) Cross-functional learning: The AI experience of one department could guide others – what worked, what did not work and the reasons behind it.

However, horizontal scaling also comes with risks. If poorly governed, it can result in:

- inconsistent standards (e.g., multiple teams using different NLP tools);
- fragmented governance;
- overlapping functionalities leading to inefficiencies.

For this reason, organizations must institute enterprise-level oversight mechanisms such as an AI Centre of Excellence (CoE), shared code repositories and federated governance models to facilitate knowledge transfer while maintaining strategic alignment.

Illustrative Example

A global healthcare provider initially used AI to triage inbound patient inquiries. Seeing strong results, the same architecture was later extended to insurance claims analysis, fraud detection, supply chain forecasting and employee performance dashboards – each leveraging similar ML infrastructure and shared data repositories.

Vertical Scaling: Deepening AI Within Functions

Vertical scaling refers to embedding AI more deeply within a single department, process or use case. Instead of replicating across teams, the focus here is to increase sophistication and coverage within an already targeted area. Vertical scaling deepens typically through these three levels:

(1) Expansion of processes: AI starts to assist with additional steps within an end-to-end workflow. A predictive maintenance model, for example, may start by detecting machine failure but later evolve to propose replacement timelines, schedule technician visits and even optimize inventory.
(2) Algorithmic refinement: Initial models might rely on basic classification systems or rules-based approaches. More sophisticated contextual models, such as reinforcement and ensemble models as well as hybrid human-in-the-loop systems, replace them over time.
(3) Interconnected AI modules: Functions begin to deploy multiple AI systems that work in tandem – for example, in a hospital setting, one model prioritizes diagnostics while another tailors treatment plans based on patient history and clinical guidelines.

Vertical scaling often requires high trust, especially where mission-critical or customer-facing decisions are involved. It demands not only reliable models but also explainability, auditability and smooth human–AI collaboration interfaces.

Illustrative Example

In radiology departments, AI may begin as a second-opinion tool for identifying anomalies. As confidence grows, it evolves into a triaging engine that prioritizes high-risk scans, generates auto-drafted reports and updates case notes in the EMR system, dramatically accelerating workflows.

Change Management and Process Redesign

Scaling AI at either level cannot occur in a vacuum. Most enterprise processes were not designed with AI in mind and therefore must be carefully examined and redesigned for AI to deliver sustained value. Here's what effective change management for AI scaling involves:

(1) End-to-end process mapping: Before integrating AI, map current-state workflows to identify pain points, decision nodes, data gaps and areas for automation. Only then can you determine where AI can augment or transform processes.

(2) Stakeholder involvement from inception: Resistance to AI often stems from fear or lack of understanding. By involving end users (e.g., clinicians, analysts, customer reps) early and letting them shape AI tools, organizations can boost adoption and surface critical contextual insights.
(3) Upskilling and AI literacy: As AI begins to affect more roles, training becomes essential – not only for developers and data scientists but also for line managers, team leads and frontline workers. AI literacy programs should include both technical orientation and ethical awareness.
(4) Redefining performance metrics: Existing KPIs may not capture AI impact adequately. For instance, success should go beyond automation rate or accuracy and include user trust, time saved, customer satisfaction and model transparency.
(5) Iterative implementation and feedback loops: Scaling should follow an agile philosophy: test, learn and refine. Small wins should be scaled thoughtfully, with built-in monitoring systems to adjust models and processes in real time.
(6) Process ownership and accountability: AI introduces distributed decision-making. To prevent confusion, clearly define ownership: who maintains the model, who interprets its outputs and who is responsible for final decisions?

Academic Insight

Scaling AI is a socio-technical transformation. It requires realignment of people, process and platform. Without attention to the behavioural and structural side of adoption, even the most sophisticated algorithms will underperform or go unused.

New Roles for Scaling AI

As AI capabilities move beyond pilots and isolated functions, traditional organizational roles and responsibilities begin to fall short. Scaling AI effectively requires the introduction of specialized roles that can bridge business and technical teams, oversee model operations and ensure that ethical and operational standards are maintained as complexity increases. Here are three emerging roles that are becoming increasingly critical in organizations scaling AI:

These roles (Table 8.2) support a more stable and accountable AI ecosystem and are essential as organizations aim to reduce technical debt, institutionalize learning and drive adoption across levels.

Table 8.2. Emerging Roles for Scaling AI in Organizations.

Role	Key Responsibilities
AI champion	Typically, a senior executive who provides strategic sponsorship for AI initiatives. Champions help secure funding, remove organizational barriers, advocate for cross-functional buy-in and ensure AI efforts align with business priorities.
AI translator	Acts as a liaison between domain experts and data science teams. Translates business problems into AI requirements and communicates model outputs in a way that is meaningful to stakeholders. Helps prevent mismatches between technical delivery and business expectations.
MLOps lead/Model steward	Focuses on operationalising AI. Oversees model deployment, performance monitoring, retraining schedules, data drift detection and compliance tracking. Maintains model health over time and ensures reliable outputs in changing environments.

Case Story: Apollo Hospitals (India)

Apollo Hospitals, one of Asia's largest healthcare groups, offers an illustrative example of how AI can be scaled strategically and responsibly within a high-stakes domain.

Initially, Apollo piloted AI systems to generate automated discharge summaries and support antibiotic prescribing. These tools saved physicians and nurses hours of daily documentation time and reduced variability in care delivery. Encouraged by these results, Apollo developed a roadmap for broader AI adoption. Key strategies included:

- Incremental scaling across specialties: Once proven in general medicine, similar models were extended to departments like cardiology and oncology, with domain-specific retraining to account for contextual variation.
- End-user engagement: Doctors were involved early in testing and validating models. Their feedback was used to refine interfaces and improve interpretability.
- Governance and review boards: All AI outputs were reviewed for clinical safety, and internal oversight committees ensured models adhered to evolving ethical and legal frameworks.
- Digital upskilling programs: Clinical and administrative personnel trained to interpret and flag AI-generated confidence scores and outputs.

As demonstrated by Apollo, responsible scaling, change readiness, process alignment and scaling are interconnected. The initiative reported saving hours of clinician time each day and is now being deployed throughout the hospital network, with AI integrated into strategic IT planning.

Source:

Reuters (2024, March 13). Apollo Hospitals bets on AI to tackle staff workload. https://www.reuters.com/business/healthcare-pharmaceuticals/indias-apollo-hospitals-bets-ai-tackle-staff-workload-2025-03-13/

Monitoring, Optimization and Governance

Implementing AI models is just the start of value realization. Once in operation, these models need to be continuously monitored, optimized in terms of performance and governed in a structured manner to keep them accurate, ethical and aligned with business goals. As AI gets integrated into critical operations, its performance and accountability need to be managed as proactively as any human-driven process or enterprise system.

Monitoring and optimization are not just technical requirements but they are strategic drivers. Poorly monitored or infrequently retrained models can cause operational inefficiencies, customer dissatisfaction, compliance risk or reputational harm. Furthermore, neglecting to oversee AI deployments end-to-end, across functions, teams and applications can lead to siloed practices and ethical blind spots.

Tracking Key Metrics: From ROI to Model Drift

Successful AI monitoring starts by specifying the correct performance metrics. These need to extend beyond such conventional measures as accuracy or precision to incorporate business, behavioural and operational aspects.

Model drift (Table 8.3) may arise because of external reasons (changes in the market, customer behaviour) or internal reasons (introduction of new product lines, updated policies). Common drift detection methods like KL divergence, Population Stability Index (PSI) or rolling window analysis can indicate when retraining or reengineering is needed.

Illustrative Example

A health insurance provider with an AI model for claims evaluation observed increasing rejection rates for one particular demographic over time. An examination disclosed data drift caused by policy eligibility and patient history format changes, needing model retraining and new data validation procedures.

Table 8.3. Common Performance Dimensions.

Metric Type	Examples
Business outcomes	Return on investment (ROI), cost savings, revenue lift, time to resolution
Model health	Prediction confidence, false positives/negatives, latency
Adoption metrics	Number of active users, user trust, override rate, engagement ratio
Drift indicators	Data distribution shifts, feature importance changes, output variance

Model Maintenance and Retraining

After being deployed, an AI model is prone to entropy. Its predictive capability diminishes over time if it is not retrained or recalibrated proactively. Maintenance, therefore, needs to be considered a lifecycle function rather than an after-deployment activity. Best practices for AI model maintenance are as follows:

(1) Scheduled retraining cycles: On a monthly or quarterly basis, based on model utilization and sensitivity.
(2) Trigger-based retraining: Driven by drift detection, regulatory changes or business rule modifications.
(3) Monitoring feedback loops: Incorporating human review data (e.g., overrides, corrections) for enhancing subsequent iterations.
(4) Model versioning and rollback: Keeping secure backups and tidy records of updates for compliance and debugging.

Models can unintentionally become biased, less accurate or unsuitable for the prevailing decision environments without regular monitoring. Keeping high-fidelity logs and retraining history is also crucial for compliance with regulations, particularly in industries such as banking, insurance and healthcare.

Building an AI Governance Structure

As AI gets widespread, organizations have to transform their governance mechanisms to capture the intensifying influence of machine-based decisions. A sound AI governance system maintains consistency between technical performance, ethical responsibility and business goals. The main elements of an AI governance framework are as follows:

(1) AI Ethics Board: A cross-disciplinary team (including legal, compliance, technical, and business stakeholders) that:
    - reviews high-risk models and their ethical implications;
    - approves guidelines on fairness, privacy and accountability;
    - oversees transparency practices (e.g., explainability standards, impact assessments).
(2) Data Quality and Audit Mechanisms: Governance begins with reliable inputs. This includes:
    - routine data audits for accuracy, completeness, timeliness;
    - policies for responsible data sourcing and access control;
    - metadata standards and documentation practices.
(3) AI Steering Committee: A strategic coordination body responsible for:
    - portfolio review of all AI initiatives;
    - cross-functional alignment and budget allocation;
    - risk management and regulatory compliance.

Illustrative Example

To comply with GDPR, a European fintech start-up integrated an AI steering committee for customer-facing models. With proprietary fairness audits, the committee mitigates regulatory risk and builds customer trust by enforcing explainability thresholds prior to model deployment.

Governance must be proportionate to risk. Low-impact AI applications (e.g., content tagging or workflow prioritization) may require lightweight review while high-stakes systems (e.g., credit scoring, medical triage, hiring recommendations) demand more rigorous oversight.

Case: Stitch Fix (Retail Fashion)

Stitch Fix (https://www.stitchfix.com/), an online fashion subscription company, uses AI to predict customer preferences and make clothing recommendations. However, their system isn't static, continuously learning from user feedback. When customers return items or leave ratings, the data feed into algorithms, which are retrained regularly to improve future curation. Their AI is monitored by human stylists, who adjust recommendations and flag model failures.

This hybrid approach – algorithmic prediction paired with human oversight and continuous optimization – is now seen as a gold standard in retail AI governance. Stitch Fix uses dashboards to track override rates, adoption levels and accuracy shifts, treating model performance as a living metric rather than a fixed output.

Sources:

https://www.tacticone.co/blog/stitch-fix-revolutionizing-retail-with-generative-ai

https://roundtable.datascience.salon/how-stitch-fix-uses-ai-to-predict-what-style-a-customer-will-love

https://www.forbes.com/sites/bernardmarr/2018/05/25/stitch-fix-the-amazing-use-case-of-using-artificial-intelligence-in-fashion-retail/

Monitoring, optimizing and governing AI systems is essential not just for performance but for trust, compliance and long-term value realization. Organizations must treat AI as a strategic asset that evolves over time, not as a one-time deployment. Metrics must be multi-dimensional. Retraining must be methodical. Governance must be structured. As AI adoption deepens, governance is not a constraint – it is an enabler. The ability to scale responsibly, ethically and adaptively will distinguish leaders from followers in the next wave of AI-driven transformation.

Ethical and Cultural Considerations in AI Deployment

Half the challenge lies in developing the relevant AI systems. The other half places equal weight on organizational culture, ethics and responsibility when deploying the systems. This chapter will explore privacy, transparency, fairness and the accompanying cultural transformations necessary to incorporate them. It will include case studies, such as bias in facial recognition technologies and how to counteract that bias.

Designing for Privacy, Transparency and Fairness

Ethical principles must be purposefully integrated to ensure responsible AI:

- Privacy by Design: Limit data capturing, anonymize the data and encrypt it and acquire informed consent at every point, including throughout the AI lifecycle.
- Transparency and Explainability: Clear model documentation, human-readable explanations (via XAI methods) and accessible user notifications about AI use build trust.
- Fairness and Bias Mitigation: Several approaches reduce disparate impacts, including diversified training datasets, algorithmic fairness techniques and consistent bias audits.

Establishing ethical frameworks – or adopting recognized ones such as IEEE or EU Trustworthy AI – assists in aligning societal norms and legal requirements with compliance on AI projects. Ensuring compliance on issues of privacy, transparency and fairness from the start guarantees that the system is as ethically sound as it is technically resilient.

Cultural Readiness: Mindset, Trust and Empowerment

Ethical deployment depends on shifting organizational mindsets, not just deploying new tools:

- Building Digital Trust: Employees and users need clarity on how AI affects them, why decisions are made and how they can intervene.

Checklist for Monitoring and Governing AI Systems

Use the following checklist to evaluate whether your organization has the necessary systems in place to monitor, maintain and govern AI responsibly. This tool is the most effective when reviewed jointly by cross-functional teams (technical, business, compliance).

✓/X	Item
□	We track AI performance using both technical metrics (e.g., accuracy, latency) and business KPIs.
□	There is a defined process for detecting and responding to data or concept drift.
□	AI models are retrained on a scheduled or trigger-based cycle.
□	We log and version all model updates and can roll back if needed.
□	Feedback loops are in place to integrate user corrections or decisions into model learning.
□	An AI governance or ethics board exists to review high impact use cases.
□	We conduct regular data quality audits and document data sources and assumptions.
□	Explainability standards are established and required before deploying customer-facing models.
□	User adoption, override frequency and trust metrics are tracked actively.
□	Our organization has mapped AI risks and defined escalation protocols for adverse outcomes.

How to Use This Checklist

Review each item and mark it only if it is currently in place and consistently applied.

- Score 8–10: Strong governance maturity. You're in a good position to scale responsibly.
- Score 5–7: Moderately prepared. Prioritize formalizing feedback loops and governance structure.

(*Continued*)

(*Continued*)

- Score <5: High risk. Start with assigning responsibility for AI governance and oversight.

As your AI impact expands, use this checklist from time to time. Remember, it's not just for compliance; it's a strategy towards sustainable, trustworthy operations.

- Empowered Workforce: Offer AI literacy programmes – covering technical principles and ethical concerns – to frontline employees, managers and support functions
- Culture of Accountability: Clarify ownership – who is responsible for AI errors, monitoring bias and adjudicating decisions. Establish escalation protocols alongside AI systems.

A top financial institution observes that when its advisory chatbot inadvertently misallocated support tickets, open communication with customer service teams – and the capacity to modify the model – assisted in enhancing trust. Ethical AI is not code; it's an ideology infused into organizational DNA.

Case Story: Bias in Facial Recognition (Disguised)

In 2023, a major US hospital facial-recognition technology was deployed to clinics for patient verification. Routine audits post-launch flagged a 15% false-negative rate – misidentification and access delays – particularly among darker-skinned patients. Factors cited included:

- Lack of standardized bias testing or demographic analysis for pre-deployment evaluation.
- Consent procedures not presented, nor were opt-out choices provided.
- Training data heavily skewed towards lighter skin tones.

Directive actions included:

(1) Bias audit and corrective regression with new image data:

- Human-in-the-loop review reinstated to resolve mismatches under bias audit and corrective regression with new image data.
- Governance added ethical board approval alongside quarterly audits and demographic performance reports.
- Patients informed via posters, consent was needed and processes for refusal were detailed; breached transparency.

Corrective measures resulted in over 60% reduction of misidentification and improved perception of fairness and safety among patients.

In the next section, we examine the managerial dilemmas and organizational challenges arising from the integration of AI as an enterprise capability instead of trusted automation.

Common Pitfalls and Managerial Dilemmas

The promise and enthusiasm that AI draws are often overshadowed by new difficulties it poses when integrated into business processes. Organizational values, readiness and expectations greatly impact the ability of a business to effectively integrate AI. Management issues regarding AI frequently arise from systematic boundaries where a decision must be made, which is what we call a managerial dilemma.

These issues lie somewhere between ethics, accountability and trust, which is why they are so difficult to resolve. Such decisions usually concern the delegation of authority to machines, communication of capabilities to stakeholders and the navigational approach to unintended consequences that would maintain progression instead of setting it back. Understanding these dilemmas is essential not only for preventing failure but also for fostering responsible leadership in AI governance. The following discussion provides a comprehensive analysis of AI governance frameworks with an industrial focus, identifying multi-layered pitfalls and decision-making points.

Operational Pitfalls

Operational pitfalls arise when considering how human elements and frameworks intersect with AI systems automation as an operational opportunity. A shift to automation, when implemented without due consideration for human variability, real-world variability or user needs, creates systems that are rigid and inflexible and therefore brittle. User disengagement, friction and diminished performance often result from model overreach, opaque logic or flow inequity – issues that stem more from organizational incoherence rather than technical shortcomings. Three practical risks stand out from AI implementation:

- Systems disengagement from nuanced human judgement occurs when over-automation is utilized. An example would be a logistics firm that employed an AI engine to reroute deliveries during peak traffic periods. Although this was a time efficiency solution, the system repeatedly missed Service Level Agreements (SLAs) because it was unaware of weather-related disruptions, leading to immense frontline frustration.
- The black-box syndrome refers to when users of a system lack the understanding of its internal workings and processes. In customer service, agents often override AI-powered recommendations because the underlying logic is hidden, so they do not trust the outputs of the system. Trust erodes through the absence of explainability.

- Employee disengagement tends to happen when automation tools that increase surveillance or decrease individual agency are introduced too rapidly. One European bank tried to optimize efficiency with an AI-driven 'productivity dashboard' that monitored employees' actions without training them or providing an opt-in. Adoption stagnated as pushback increased.

The above examples show that the dangers of AI are not solely technological; they intersect with social and systemic dimensions. Smooth sailing here calls for more than just thoughtful design. These challenges require understanding and proactive change leadership.

Managerial Dilemmas in Practice

Managerial dilemmas stem from the perplexing decisions leaders encounter when AI starts to impact critical or sensitive areas of an organization. Unlike more apparent risks, these dilemmas offer options that are in sharp juxtaposition to one another: urgency vs accountability, efficiency vs empathy and automation vs autonomy. The correct choice can be situational and hinge on the organization's culture, values, appetite for risk and level of governance maturity. What matters here is the acceptance of conflicting situations found in the framing of issues, not in the attempt to eliminate them. It is crucial to build pathways devoid of bias while providing reasoned deliberation to mitigate assumptions.

Should You Automate Performance Appraisal?

With the vast amount of data available, AI-driven systems can evaluate employee performance based on rate of completion, email sentiment analysis and other relevant metrics. A leading software company in the United States piloted an AI system designed to streamline annual reviews and minimize bias. EPC (majorly refers to Engineering, Procurement and Construction companies) flagged 'quiet' employees who received low collaboration scores despite high client satisfaction. The company has since updated the algorithm to factor in qualitative feedback, but the problem persists. In evaluating people, can human judgement truly be replaced by efficiency?

How Should AI Failures Be Communicated?

A digital lending platform in the financial services industry incorrectly denied hundreds of users due to an error in its credit risk assessment model. At first, the company claimed the problem stemmed from 'technical errors' without naming AI. This drew backlash from advocates of transparency and the impacted users themselves. As a result, the company publicly corrected its statement, developed a new FAQ section explaining the workings of its AI and instituted a manual appeals process. Trust was partially regained; however, the incident highlighted the need for AI failures to be addressed with humility and systematic responsibility.

These examples are not singular illustrations. Once AI is integrated into the more sensitive domains of healthcare, recruitment, lending or legal analysis, such dilemmas will be standard. Equally as important as improving algorithms and upgrading infrastructure is preparing leaders to tackle them with unambiguous insight and bold resolve.

This Table 8.4 aims to stimulate proactive thinking among strategists, compliance officers and AI leaders. It shifts from treating dilemmas as scarce anomalies to recurring tensions that require constant management, which agile transparency and flexible governance (dynamic adaptability) resolve. Although contexts differ across organizations, documenting approaches to these dilemmas assists in balancing innovation with responsibility. This is critical as the scale of AI adoption accelerates across regions and domains .

This Table 8.5 can help managers and designers calibrate their governance efforts. High-stakes dilemmas – those involving real people's lives, livelihoods or rights – require deliberate governance mechanisms and accountability layers. In contrast, low-stakes applications can be guided by iterative feedback and user testing. The key is to match governance intensity to potential impact, ensuring resources are focused where ethical risk is highest and trust is most vulnerable.

Reflection Prompt: Navigating AI Dilemmas With Integrity

- What criteria do you consider determining whether an AI-driven decision is 'high-stakes,' particularly one that affects people?
- Do your current procedures for reporting and reviewing failures address communication sufficiently, especially within sensitive contexts?
- What discussions are necessary to solidify internal boundaries for responsibility when an AI system inflicts damage or produces confusion?
- What organizational principles may help you reflect upon responses to AI grey-zone dilemmas?

Tip: Discuss these prompts in leadership reviews, cross-functional planning sessions or AI ethics workshops. Use them to define your 'red lines,' escalation policies and principles for responsible automation.

The Human–Machine Balance: Strategic Decisions for Managers

As AI systems grow more powerful and more embedded, managers face a recurring challenge: where should human insight end and machine logic begin? This balance is not just a technical decision but a strategic one. Knowing when to rely on human intuition, when to leverage AI's computational speed and how to integrate the two effectively is central to responsible and high-performing AI deployment.

Table 8.4. Managerial Dilemmas, Risks and Mitigation Strategies.

Managerial Dilemma	Context/Scenario	Associated Risk	Suggested Mitigation Strategy
Automating performance appraisal	AI system evaluates employee performance based on metrics like communication tone, task logs or time spent.	Strips away nuance; may penalize non-quantifiable but valuable behaviours (e.g., mentoring, creativity).	Use AI for augmentation, not automation; support with 360° feedback and manager validation.
Communicating AI failures	An AI tool makes an erroneous recommendation or classification affecting a customer, employee or policy.	If not disclosed, users may feel manipulated or deceived; loss of reputation and internal morale.	Define clear disclosure protocols; communicate failure causes, not just corrections.
Delegating final decisions to AI	AI is used to finalize loan approvals, medical diagnoses or legal outcomes with minimal human intervention.	May create legal liability if AI decision is contested; weakens transparency and auditability.	Mandate a human-in-the-loop checkpoint; ensure explainability for final decisions.
Using AI in sensitive domains (e.g., Hiring)	AI screens job applicants using NLP to score resumes or video interviews for behavioural traits.	May reproduce past hiring biases encoded in historical data; legal and ethical red flags.	Use diverse training data; conduct bias audits; allow appeals and human review layers.
Balancing AI efficiency with employee autonomy	AI monitors workflows and auto-assigns tasks, but removes control or flexibility from human workers.	Over-reliance can result in disengagement, pushback, or silent workarounds by employees.	Design adaptive AI tools with user feedback loops; empower teams to override or adjust.

Table 8.5. Comparing High-Stakes vs Low-Stakes AI Dilemmas.

Dimension	**High-Stakes Dilemmas**	**Low-Stakes Dilemmas**
Examples	Hiring, loan approvals, medical decisions	Content tagging, internal analytics, task automation
Impact scope	Affects individual rights, safety, access or legal standing	Impacts efficiency, workflow or internal processes
Risk profile	Legal liability, ethical scrutiny, reputational harm	User inconvenience, inefficiency or minor errors
Mitigation required	Human-in-the-loop, audit trails, ethics review	Lightweight monitoring, usability testing
Communication approach	Transparent disclosure, formal escalation protocol	Informal feedback loops, optional explanations
Frequency	Less frequent but highly consequential	Frequent and embedded across departments

When to Trust AI vs Human Judgement

AI excels in pattern recognition, data-heavy processing and tasks that benefit from scale, consistency and speed. In contrast, human judgement integrates contextual factors, empathy, ethics and dealing with ambiguity.

A classic case is found in medical imaging. While AI tools may outsmart radiologists in spotting subtle anomalies in volumes of scans, they still depend on physicians for diagnoses, explanations and communication with patients. Managers face the question of whether to use AI as an assistant, recommender or final decision-maker. This depends on the level of risk involved, how the information can be interpreted and the sensitivity of the contextual factors.

Strategic Trade-offs in AI-Driven Decision-Making

AI technologies could enhance operational efficiency in speed, scale and accuracy, raising many decisions managers need to make due to associated trade-offs. Strategic choices often go beyond operational efficiency; they require judgement, trust, reputation and accountability. Automation integration powered by AI into workflows requires a separate layer of user experience design. User experience automation will transcend business processes and will span core organizational values associated with openness, agility and adherence to flexibility.

Real-life examples of AI trade-offs permeate almost every domain. For instance, should we replace the customer service executive with AI even if the AI system is unable to handle the emotional or complex queries? What is the customer loyalty impact when fraud detection algorithms reject too many valid claims?

Rarely is there a silver bullet in such situations when one solution can fit all. In the following framework, we attempt to capture the most typical trade-offs, their practical outcomes and some tools towards intuitive metrics for the sought equilibrium .

Through a managerial lens, Table 8.6 serves as a framing device for considering automation. It is most useful during strategy formulation or deployment review meetings when assessing the role of AI in a workflow. Leaders should not pose the question, 'Can AI do X function?' Instead, the question must be reframed to 'Should AI do X function?' while contemplating what trade-offs are acceptable within the context. Supporting decisions along these contours invites more mindful, responsible and cohesive deployment practices.

Framing Human–AI Collaboration

Human decisions and actions, along with AI systems' inputs, have to interact with each other and within the frameworks of the decision systems. This is where the design focus goes beyond the consideration of the trade-offs to look at collaboration between AI and humans. Collaboration may range from fully autonomous systems to AI where humans direct, teach or override the model.

Table 8.6. Strategic Trade-offs in Human–AI Decision Systems.

Trade-off	AI Strengths	Human Strengths	Key Considerations
Cost vs Quality	Reduces operational costs, performs at scale	Maintains nuance, handles exceptions	Use AI for repetitive decisions; route edge cases to humans
Speed vs Transparency	Delivers instant output, handles high-volume decisions	Explains rationale clearly to stakeholders	In high-stakes contexts, speed must not override explainability
Consistency vs Flexibility	Applies the same rules to all cases	Adjusts to context, considers soft factors	Consider hybrid workflows where AI offers baseline suggestions
Scalability vs Customization	Adapts to growth without incremental cost	Personalizes based on empathy, history, intent	Use AI to narrow choices; humans finalize the tailored output
Precision vs Interpretability	Optimizes outcomes based on data	Justifies decisions to peers, clients, regulators	Balance model complexity with need for explainability

Best outcomes occur when AI and humans perform complementary roles, and these include:

- AI performing complex calculations or repetitive tasks;
- humans dealing with ambiguity, exceptions and ethics;
- design algorithms to allow humans to audit, override or instruct the systems.

Illustrative Example

Consider a consumer lending platform where AI assesses risk scoring for applications. An applicant who sits at the borderline threshold gets flagged. The credit officer then reviews contextual data like recent life events or prior history, which is not captured in structured inputs, and makes the final decision. AI is helping to enhance throughput while human discretion is retained.

These collaboration modes help organizations choose an interaction model that fits the trust level, risk level and compliance needs of their operations .

This collaboration model in Table 8.7 is especially helpful in defining participatory roles within AI workflows. It assists in determining where teams will integrate human oversight, the level of autonomy that will be granted to AI systems and what protective measures will be needed. While drafting standard operating procedures, interface designs or escalation protocol setups, this model serves as a useful reference. The right balance between human and AI collaboration practices is determined by the specific task and also by the organization's risk appetite, user profile and regulatory environment.

Chapter Summary

Building on the implementation roadmap from Chapter 4, this chapter focused on the more profound challenge of scaling and institutionalizing AI throughout the enterprise. We introduced the AI Continuum as a diagnostic and planning tool so that organizations can self-assess their maturity and readiness for expansion. This chapter comprehensively maps the diverse operational, proclaimed cultural and managerial challenges in the deployment of AI, systematically exploring the structured horizontal and vertical scaling frameworks, monitoring, governance and ethical frameworks.

We examined strategic trade-offs, collaboration patterns and challenges that managers need to deal with on a daily basis – not merely about using AI systems but about making effective decisions in AI-informed situations.

Table 8.7. Models of Human–AI Collaboration.

Model	Description	Best Suited For	Key Risks/Limitations
AI-assisted decision	AI provides recommendations; a human makes the final call	Customer support, HR screening, diagnostics	Risk of cognitive bias towards AI suggestion ('automation bias')
Human-in-the-loop	A human reviews and approves or overrides AI output	Credit approval, hiring, insurance underwriting	Can slow processes; needs clearly defined escalation rules
Human-on-the-loop	AI acts autonomously, but human can intervene if needed	Dynamic pricing, fraud detection, marketing optimization	Risk of over-reliance or missed edge cases
Full automation	AI makes decisions independently without human oversight	Low-risk, high-volume tasks like spam filtering	Lack of transparency; potential for undetected errors

From AI pilots and PoCs to scaled platforms and embedded practices, this chapter outlined what it takes to move from technical experimentation to strategic transformation. Three themes emerge as core to successful AI maturity:

- Strategy: AI must be aligned with core business goals and designed to solve high-impact problems – not simply adopted for trendiness or superficial innovation.
- Structure: Without foundational data infrastructure, feedback loops, governance boards and cross-functional roles, AI efforts remain fragmented and unsustainable.
- Stewardship: AI demands not only execution but ethical leadership. Responsible scaling requires ongoing accountability, transparent communication and cultural readiness.

These are not one-time investments. They are capacities that must evolve continuously as technologies, expectations and risks change.

Crucially, this chapter invites leaders to move beyond a project mindset towards an institutional mindset, seeing AI not as a solution to implement but as a capability to build, govern and grow.

Future Outlook

As organizations advance in their AI journey, several strategic priorities come into focus:

- Operationalizing AI maturity assessments through formal scorecards and cross-departmental alignment reviews.
- Embedding AI governance into board-level oversight, particularly for firms in regulated or high-stakes sectors.
- Investing in adaptive talent models that support continuous upskilling, human–AI collaboration and emerging roles like AI translators or model stewards.
- Preparing for generative AI and autonomous agents, which will raise new questions about trust, accountability and human relevance in decision ecosystems

Ultimately, the future of AI in business is not a story of automation vs humanity but of augmentation, alignment and adaptability. Organizations that can scale AI while preserving their values will define the next wave of industry leadership.

> *AI doesn't replace decision-makers – it challenges us to become better ones.*

Discussion Questions

(1) Based on the AI Maturity Continuum, where would you place your organization (or one you know) and why?
(2) What are the key signals that indicate an organization is ready to move from pilot to platform?
(3) What are the unique challenges of horizontal scaling vs vertical scaling of AI initiatives?
(4) How can an organization build a culture of digital trust and AI literacy across non-technical teams?
(5) How should organizations communicate AI failures without undermining trust in technology or leadership?
(6) How can managers decide when to rely on AI and when to prioritize human judgement?

Further Readings

Busse, C. (2024). *The secret to successful enterprise AI? 'Human-In-The-Loop' design.* Forbes Technology Council. https://www.forbes.com/councils/forbestechcouncil/2024/08/06/the-secret-to-successful-enterprise-ai-human-in-the-loop-design

Deloitte. (2024). *Scaling artificial intelligence: Navigating the horizons of innovation.* https://www.deloitte.com/us/en/Industries/financial-services/articles/scaling-ai-in-insurance.html

Deloitte. (2024). *Three roles CEOs need to play to scale Generative AI: Leading a Generative AI-Fueled enterprise: A CEO series.* https://www.deloitte.com/us/en/what-we-do/capabilities/applied-artificial-intelligence/articles/ceo-guide-to-scaling-generative-ai.html

Holdsworth, J., Belcic, I., & Stryker, C. (2024, July 16). *What is model drift?* https://www.ibm.com/think/topics/model-drift

Zappulla, A. (2024, November 19). Business leaders risk sleepwalking towards AI misuse. *Reuters.* https://www.reuters.com/sustainability/society-equity/comment-business-leaders-risk-sleepwalking-towards-ai-misuse-2024-11-19/

Chapter 9

Business Opportunities in Metaverse

Metaverse is no longer just a virtual playground; it is the next frontier of business innovation where brands build immersive experiences, entrepreneurs create new economies, and companies unlock value beyond physical boundaries.

Case Study: Nike's NIKELAND on Roblox – Redefining Brand Engagement in the Metaverse

By 2021, Nike faced an increasingly digital-first consumer landscape where younger audiences (particularly Gen Z and Gen Alpha) were spending more time on gaming platforms than traditional media. Nike recognized that passive digital advertising would no longer be enough to build emotional connections with these digitally native consumers. The challenge was twofold:

- Engage younger consumers where they are most active – virtual worlds and games.
- Create immersive, branded experiences that go beyond traditional e-commerce or digital campaigns.

The Solution

Nike partnered with Roblox to launch NIKELAND, a persistent branded world where users could play games, interact with Nike-themed spaces and purchase virtual Nike apparel and accessories for their avatars. Key elements of the solution included:

(*Continued*)

AI and Business, 173–201

doi:10.1108/978-1-83708-888-120261009

(*Continued*)

- A virtual sports playground inspired by Nike's real-world headquarters.
- Customizable avatar outfits featuring iconic Nike sneakers and apparel.
- Branded mini-games encouraging social competition and physical movement using mobile device accelerometers.
- Limited-edition digital collectibles and opportunities for co-creation.

Implementation Strategy

Nike's approach combined strategic platform selection, brand storytelling and community engagement:

- Platform Alignment: Roblox was chosen for its large, young user base and social gaming culture.
- Immersive Storytelling: Instead of creating a static showroom, Nike designed an open, interactive world where play was central to the experience.
- Phased Engagement: Nike rolled out seasonal events (e.g., sports competitions, product launches) to sustain interest and drive repeat visits.
- Seamless Monetization: Introduced digital wearables (e.g., exclusive sneakers) that players could buy for their avatars – creating a new revenue stream.
- Cross-Channel Promotion: Nike integrated its Roblox activities with its broader marketing campaigns, creating social media buzz and earned media.

Business Impact

- Over 7 million visitors within the first three months of launch.
- Users spent an average of 20 minutes per session, far exceeding engagement metrics of traditional digital campaigns.
- Digital sneakers and avatar apparel sold out rapidly, creating a new digital commerce stream.
- Enhanced brand visibility among Gen Z and Gen Alpha audiences.
- Positioned Nike as a trailblazer in the emerging Metaverse economy.

Lessons

- Brands must meet consumers where they are: Nike recognized Roblox as a thriving digital social space and engaged its community authentically.
- Experience matters more than exposure: Passive advertising is less effective in immersive environments – experiential branding drives deeper connections.
- Virtual goods are real business: Digital assets like avatar wearables can unlock significant revenue streams and brand loyalty.
- Continuous engagement is key: One-time events are not enough – persistent worlds with evolving content maintain interest.

Questions to Think About

1. How can your brand create meaningful, interactive experiences rather than just digital advertisements?
2. What role could virtual goods play in your future revenue models?
3. How do you measure the success of brand engagement in a virtual world versus traditional channels?
4. What skills and partners do you need to design immersive, gamified brand experiences?
5. How do you ensure your brand remains authentic and respectful within a user-generated environment like Roblox?

Sources

1. https://www.forbes.com/sites/briansolis/2022/10/11/the-business-case-for-the-metaverse-creating-value-in-the-next-version-of-the-web
2. https://medium.com/%40lunawolfe01/10-metaverse-examples-of-brands-doing-it-right-241c10c55b5f
3. https://moldstud.com/articles/p-5-successful-metaverse-monetization-case-studies
4. https://www.wired.com/story/nike-will-let-people-design-and-sell-sneakers-for-the-metaverse
5. https://www.metaverse911.in/blog/brands-success-stories-in-the-metaverse
6. https://flexe.io/blog/metaverse-marketing-examples-2025/

The concept of Metaverse is no longer confined to science fiction – it has emerged as one of the most significant frontiers for business innovation and digital transformation. As companies navigate the evolving digital economy, Metaverse offers new possibilities for immersive customer experience, virtual commerce and decentralized communities. This chapter explores Metaverse through a business lens, examining its historical roots, defining features, enabling technologies and strategic opportunities. By understanding the evolution and potential of the Metaverse, businesses can prepare to engage consumers in entirely new ways and create value beyond traditional digital platforms.

History of Metaverse

The concept of the Metaverse has evolved over several decades, emerging from a mix of science fiction, technological innovation and changing internet culture. The term **'Metaverse'** was first coined by **Neal Stephenson** in his 1992 science fiction novel *Snow Crash*. In the book, he described the Metaverse as a 3D virtual world in which people, represented as avatars, interact and do business. Later, **Ernest Cline's** *Ready Player One* (2011) further popularized the idea of fully immersive digital realities used for everything from education to entertainment. With the advances in technology like virtual reality (VR) and augmented reality (AR), the Metaverse came into the mainstream. Platforms like Minecraft and Roblox started providing a Metaverse-like experience with the user-generated content produced in the ever-evolving digital world. The final game-changer was when **Facebook** was rebranded to **Meta** in 2021, explicitly stating its goal to build the Metaverse. This move brought massive attention to the concept. Companies like **Microsoft, Apple, Nvidia** and others began developing hardware and platforms to support the Metaverse environment (e.g., Mesh, Apple Vision Pro). The Metaverse today is not one single space but a **network of digital platforms** experimenting with immersive experiences (e.g., VR meetings, virtual real estate, digital avatars).

Defining Metaverse

The Metaverse is a future-oriented, interconnected digital environment where social and economic elements mirror reality. Users embodied as avatars can simultaneously interact with the environment and with each other across a range of devices and immersive technologies, such as VR, AR and spatial computing. This is done while engaging with digital assets and properties enabled by technologies like blockchain and non-fungible tokens (NFTs). The Metaverse can be defined as *'a technology-mediated virtual environment characterized by varying degrees of environmental fidelity and sociability, wherein the access device shapes the user experience with different levels of immersion'* (Di Paolo et al., 2025, p. 2). Core to its definition are three critical features: a profound sense of immersion fostering presence, real-time interactivity enabling synchronous collaboration and significant user agency over identity, creation and participation (Ball, 2022). The Metaverse market size is valued at 74.4 billion US dollars in 2023 (Statista, 2023), with more than 600 million active users worldwide as of 2024 (Hryziuk, 2024). This architecture necessitates seamless interoperability across platforms and devices, creating a unified experiential layer. Crucially, as technologist Matthew Ball emphasizes, the Metaverse is characterized by its potential for 'massively scaled and interoperable' participation, enabling thousands – potentially millions – to interact simultaneously within shared persistent spaces. The following are the core characteristics that define and differentiate the Metaverse from the real world.

- **Immersive Environments:** The Metaverse offers fully immersive 3D environments where users can interact in real time. Through VR headsets or AR overlays, users are transported into digital worlds that simulate real-life experiences, making brand interactions more engaging and memorable.
- **Persistent and Real-Time:** Unlike traditional games or websites, Metaverse environments are persistent – they exist and evolve continuously, even when a

user logs off. This persistence allows brands to maintain an ongoing presence and build long-term communities.

- **Interoperability:** One of the aspirational goals of the Metaverse is interoperability – users can move across platforms with their digital identities, assets and experiences fully intact. This opens up the possibility for cross-platform branding and seamless user journeys.
- **Digital Avatars:** Users represent themselves through customizable avatars, enabling self-expression and identity in digital spaces. Brands are using avatars for virtual product try-ons, digital influencers and personalized interactions.
- **Social and Community-Oriented:** The Metaverse is inherently social. It supports real-time communication, collaboration and co-creation. Brands are leveraging this by hosting virtual events, concerts and interactive campaigns to foster communities around their products and values.
- **Decentralization and Blockchain Integration:** Many Metaverse platforms are built on blockchain, which supports digital ownership, decentralization and the creation of unique, tradable digital assets (NFTs). This empowers users and opens new economic models like play-to-earn and creator economies.
- **Virtual Commerce (V-Commerce):** The Metaverse introduces new avenues for commerce – users can shop for both virtual and real-world goods in 3D storefronts. From virtual real estate to branded skins and digital collectables, v-commerce is redefining consumer behaviour.
- **Gamification:** Gamified elements such as quests, rewards, leaderboards and badges are deeply integrated into the Metaverse experience. Brands use gamification to boost user engagement, encourage repeat visits and foster brand loyalty.

From an organizational perspective, interpretations vary. Brian Solis, Global Innovation Evangelist at Salesforce, views the Metaverse primarily as '*a space for building community', highlighting the essential need for fostering belonging and granting users an active stakeholder role within a shared virtual environment* (McKinsey & Company, 2022). This perspective aligns with research emphasizing the Metaverse's potential to reshape customer engagement and collaborative ecosystems. Furthermore, the World Economic Forum identifies '*The Metaverse as a driver of new economic models, predicting it will unlock new opportunities for businesses and creators' through novel digital ownership and value exchange mechanisms* (WEF, 2022), positioning it as a transformative force at the physical–digital juncture (Table 9.1).

Key Technologies Empowering the Metaverse

It is essential to understand the backbone of the Metaverse, the technologies that power the Metaverse's space. It is built on the convergence of multiple advanced technologies that deliver seamless interactions, an immersive experience and

Table 9.1. Elaborates on the Opinions of Various Organizational Stakeholders in Order to Present a Comprehensive View of the Metaverse.

Expert and Role	Key Quote	Primary Theme	Citation Source
Satya Nadella (CEO, Microsoft)	'The Metaverse enables us to embed computing into the real world and to embed the real world into computing… creating a persistent digital world connected to people, places, and things.'	Physical–Digital Convergence	Microsoft Ignite 2021 Keynote (Nadella, 2021)
Jensen Huang (CEO, NVIDIA)	'The Metaverse is the next evolution of the internet… a 3D internet you can step inside. We'll see a new economy, larger than our current economy.'	Economic Scale & Evolution	NVIDIA GTC 2021 Keynote (Huang, 2021)
Tim Sweeney (CEO, Epic Games)	'The Metaverse isn't a game. It's a social experience where users have agency and ownership… It must be interoperable, open, and governed by creators.'	User Agency & Interoperability	VentureBeat Interview (Marchesoni, 2023)
Eric Yuan (CEO, Zoom)	'The Metaverse will transform remote collaboration… Imagine walking into a virtual conference room where spatial audio creates presence. This is the future of human connection.'	Enterprise Collaboration	Zoomtopia (2022) Keynote

Stephane Kasriel (Former CEO, Upwork)	'The Metaverse will democratise access to global talent and new markets. Freelancers in Lagos can design virtual stores for brands in Paris.'	Labour Democratization	World Economic Forum Panel (2022)
Brian Solis (Global Innovation Evangelist, Salesforce)	'The Metaverse is a space for building community. Belonging is the currency – users aren't just consumers; they're stakeholders shaping the virtual environment.'	Community and Belonging	Salesforce Blog Solis (2023)

create a complex virtual space. Below are some of the key technologies that are essential to understand.

(1) *Virtual Reality and Augmented Reality*
VR and AR form the immersive backbone of the Metaverse. VR transports users into fully simulated digital environments through headsets and motion sensors, which allows deeply engaging experiences. AR, on the other hand, enhances the physical world by overlaying digital elements such as images, information or 3D objects via smartphones or smart glasses. Together, these technologies blur the lines between physical and digital realities, enabling interactive virtual meetings, education, gaming and retail experiences.

(2) *Blockchain and Cryptocurrencies*
Blockchain ensures that the Metaverse operates in a decentralized and secure manner. It facilitates transparent digital ownership through NFTs, supports peer-to-peer transactions via cryptocurrencies and enables smart contracts that automate user agreements. This technology empowers users with control over their assets, identities and data, creating a trust-driven ecosystem within virtual environments.

(3) *Artificial Intelligence (AI)*
AI enhances the Metaverse by enabling intelligent interactions and dynamic content creation. It powers virtual assistants, generates lifelike avatars, personalizes experiences and enables real-time language translation. AI-driven non-player characters (NPCs) can simulate human behaviour, making virtual worlds feel more natural and responsive. It also helps analyze user behaviour for content recommendations and community moderation.

(4) *3D Modelling and Digital Twins*
Creating immersive environments and realistic avatars in the Metaverse requires sophisticated 3D modelling. Designers use tools like Blender, Unity and Unreal Engine to craft detailed virtual spaces and characters. Digital twins, which are virtual replicas of physical objects or environments, further enrich the Metaverse. This is possible due to real-time synchronization with the real world, enabling applications in industries like manufacturing, healthcare and urban planning.

(5) *Internet of Things (IoT)*
IoT bridges the physical and digital worlds by enabling smart devices to collect and exchange real-time data. In the Metaverse, IoT allows users to interact with virtual environments using real-world data inputs, such as movement, temperature or biometric feedback. This integration adds depth to simulations and supports real-time adjustments in connected virtual experiences, such as smart homes or wearable tech feedback loops.

(6) *5G and Edge Computing*
High-speed connectivity is crucial for the Metaverse, and 5G provides the low latency and bandwidth necessary for seamless, real-time interactions. Combined with edge computing – which processes data closer to the user – this technology reduces lag and enhances performance. This ensures that

large-scale virtual events, multiplayer gaming or remote collaboration remain fluid and responsive.

(7) *Cloud Computing*
The Metaverse requires vast computing resources for storing data, rendering 3D graphics and supporting global access. Cloud computing provides scalable infrastructure to host these experiences, enabling users to access virtual worlds from anywhere without heavy local processing. It supports persistent environments where changes are saved and synchronized across devices in real time.

The Metaverse: A Transformative Juncture for Business

The world stands at a pivotal juncture in the evolution of digital commerce, on the threshold between the established physical economy and the emerging, immersive landscape of the Metaverse. This moment represents not merely an incremental technological advancement but a fundamental paradigm shift poised to redefine value creation, customer engagement, and competitive dynamics. The unique attributes of the Metaverse collectively position it as a significant game changer for the global business landscape. Some of the core attributes and disruptive potential of the Metaverse are discussed in the following section.

(1) ***Immersive and Interactive Experiences:***
The Metaverse transcends traditional screen-based interaction by offering persistent, shared and 3D virtual environments. The most interesting and interactive part of the Metaverse is that the users are embodied as customizable avatars and can interact with each other and digital objects in real-time with unprecedented **spatial presence**. This fosters deeper social connections, experiential marketing opportunities and novel forms of customer engagement that blur the lines between physical and digital presence. Businesses can create branded worlds, host virtual events with global reach and offer experiential products or services that are impossible in the physical realm.

(2) ***Emergence of New Digital Economies:***
The most radical attribute of the Metaverse is its capacity to host self-sustaining digital economies. Built upon blockchain technology and digital assets (like **cryptocurrencies, NFTs** and **virtual goods**), these economies enable verifiable ownership and seamless peer-to-peer transactions. Virtual land, digital fashion, unique artwork and even virtual services can be created, bought, sold and traded, creating new revenue streams, asset classes and labour markets (e.g., virtual architects, experience designers). This fundamentally redefines concepts of value, property and work, potentially decentralizing economic activity.

(3) ***Convergence of Enabling Technologies:***
The Metaverse's viability is propelled by rapid advancements in complementary technologies, like VR, AR and AI. In a Metaverse world, VR provides deep immersion, AR overlays digital information onto the physical world and AI powers intelligent environments, realistic avatars and personalized experiences. This technological synergy is making the Metaverse increasingly accessible and realistic.

(4) ***Cross-Industry Applicability and Innovation:***
The most common misconception about the Metaverse is that it is a short-lived bubble and a source of entertainment. The disruptive potential of the Metaverse extends far beyond entertainment. It promises to revolutionize diverse sectors. Some of them are:

- Education: Enabling immersive simulations, virtual field trips and collaborative global classrooms.
- Healthcare: Facilitating remote consultations in virtual clinics, surgical training simulations and therapeutic VR environments.
- Enterprise and Remote Work: Creating persistent virtual offices for enhanced collaboration, spatial meetings and onboarding, transcending geographical limitations and potentially boosting productivity and connection for distributed teams.
- Manufacturing and Design: Utilizing digital twins for real-time monitoring, simulation and collaborative product design in virtual spaces.
- Retail: Offering virtual showrooms, try-before-you-buy experiences for digital and physical goods and entirely new forms of social commerce.

The significance for business lies precisely in this juncture. The Metaverse does not seek to wholly replace the physical world but rather to create a parallel, interoperable layer of existence and commerce. Businesses operating at this intersection have the unprecedented opportunity to design hybrid strategies, leveraging the unique attributes of the Metaverse – immersion, user agency, persistent economies and technological convergence – to unlock new markets, enhance customer experiences, optimize operations and foster innovation. It necessitates a fundamental rethinking of value propositions, organizational structures and customer relationships. While challenges regarding **interoperability**, privacy, security and equitable access remain significant, the confluence of its core attributes underscores the Metaverse's potential to be a transformative force. This helps in reshaping the very fabric of how business is conceived and conducted in the coming decades.

Metaverse-Driven Strategic Transformation

The rapidly evolving Metaverse has impacted various industries globally by creating new opportunities for customer engagement, virtual collaboration, data-driven insights and innovative marketing strategies. Metaverse has given a new way to define business–client relationships. It has opened avenues to new revenue streams through virtual products and services and continues to foster innovation in diverse businesses. According to Mancuso et al. (2024), the Metaverse serves as an archetype for how businesses engage with customers, deliver value propositions, manage relationships and scale new heights to innovation. Scholars have been debating the implementation of the Metaverse primarily from a technical standpoint while paying less attention to how these innovations and technologies can be leveraged to transform businesses (Ritala et al., 2024). Moreover, just like traditional business models, the Metaverse also poses unique challenges that have never been tackled before, like the integration of diverse technologies and developing and managing advanced engagement platforms and strategies. Additionally, scaling into uncharted territory in an ethical way is always a challenge. Hence, the following section elaborates on the tactics that firms can integrate in their strategic decision-making to drive Metaverse-driven strategic transformation.

To support the Metaverse-driven strategic transformation, we propose a three-stage business transformation approach, based on the New Value Creation Model, Reimagined Customer Engagement and Operational Innovation.

Stage 1: New Value Creation Model

The **Metaverse** has sparked the evolution of entirely new models of value creation. Unlike the traditional internet, the Metaverse blurs the boundaries between digital and physical spaces, enabling people to live, work, socialize and transact in new ways. Below are three cutting-edge models redefining economic interaction within this ecosystem. Table 9.2 brings a snippet of the three models of economic interaction.

Tokenization of Assets in the Metaverse (NFTs and Fractional Ownership)

Tokenization within the Metaverse allows for digital ownership of unique assets, like avatars, wearables, art, experiences and even virtual land, through **NFTs**. These NFTs are backed by blockchain and can be fractionally owned, traded or monetized. Metaverse has indeed added value that empowers its users to become investors and traders in virtual goods and introduces **asset liquidity** in virtual environments.

A few examples to illustrate this can be:

- Nike offered tokenized wearables where you could customize the avatar. This can be done by choosing the limited-edition Nike sneakers on the platform, which is offered by Roblox.
- A high-value virtual land parcel in The Sandbox may be co-owned by several users who share development rights or rental income.

Table 9.2. New Value Creation Models in Metaverse.

Model	Mechanism	Metaverse Use Case	User Role	Value Created
Tokenisation	NFTs, smart contracts	Tradeable virtual goods, co-owned spaces	Investor/ Collector	Liquidity, access, resale
Virtual Real Estate and Twins	Digital plots, simulation	Branded worlds, city twins, 3D campuses	Developer/ Tenant	Revenue, planning, immersion
Creator Economy	Monetization tools, platforms	Custom content, services, experiences	Creator/ Entrepreneur	Ownership, income, recognition

- Gaming industry has offered rare swords, skins or pets in games like Axie Infinity that can be bought, sold or rented as NFTs.

Virtual Real Estate and Digital Twins

The Metaverse offers real estate opportunities just like the real world. You can own land or start a virtual store, the same as you can in the real world. Another popular opportunity that the Metaverse provides is a digital twin, which is a virtual representation of a physical object, system or process that is continuously updated in real time. Digital twins enable real-world objects or systems to be mirrored in the Metaverse for simulation, management or immersive experience. Brands can generate alternative revenue streams from virtual commerce, advertising and events in the Metaverse. Also, digital twins offer cost-effective prototyping and testing in simulated environments.

Some of the brands that have leveraged virtual real estate and the phenomenon of digital twins.

- Brands like Gucci, Samsung and Adidas have purchased land and built stores in platforms like Decentraland and The Sandbox to showcase digital fashion and launch new products.
- Snoop Dogg owns 'Snoopverse' in The Sandbox, where fans attend concerts and parties.
- Cities like Seoul and Singapore are building digital twins in the Metaverse to simulate traffic, pollution and infrastructure planning.

User-Generated Content Monetization: Creator Economy

The Metaverse empowers its users to become **active economic agents by** designing, creating and monetizing their digital content. These creator economies are decentralizing wealth and giving rise to micro-entrepreneurs. **In this ecosystem, creators are directly rewarded by users, eliminating the intermediaries, thus building a community-led economy** around user identity, ownership and engagement. Some of the examples are:

- Platforms like DressX promote digital fashion designers by creating and selling virtual fashion clothing through NFTs for digital avatars.
- **Artists and performers can** host virtual galleries or concerts where entry is ticketed via NFTs or social tokens.
- In Roblox, users earn real-world income by creating games or skins with high engagement.

Stage 2: Reimagined Customer Engagement

The Metaverse is quickly transitioning from science fiction to a real-time digital universe. As a result, progressive brands are rising to the occasion by rethinking how they can connect with customers. Brands are forming deeper emotional connections with consumers through immersive and interactive experiences and multi-layered branding strategies, such as virtual showrooms, branded worlds, NFT-based loyalty programs and gamified experiences. Such an approach is transcending the traditional digital environment.

By converging entertainment, commerce and community in ways never before, brands are creating fun spaces for consumers. Fashion houses such as Gucci and Nike have created collections digitally through platforms like Roblox and Decentraland, where individuals can try and buy digital apparel for their avatars, transforming them into customer experiences. Brands can also gather real-time feedback, create together with users and share socially with users in these spaces, increasing the importance of personalization and sense of belonging. As the Metaverse solidifies and melds with AR/VR technologies and blockchain capabilities, it is becoming increasingly complex as a digital frontier in terms of how brands connect with audiences in a meaningful way. The below section discusses some of the strategies that brands use in the Metaverse:

Experiential Marketing Through Immersive Interactions

Experiential marketing in the Metaverse goes far beyond traditional digital ads. Brands offer interactive, immersive experiences that let users engage with products in a virtual space, feeling, customizing or trying them before making purchase decisions. Some of the strategies used by the brands are:

a. **Virtual product trials:**
   - **L'Oréal** offers users the ability to virtually try on makeup within a branded Metaverse environment using their avatars.
   - **BMW** allows potential customers to configure and test drive cars in a virtual showroom.

b. **Virtual Brand Games**
   - **Chipotle's virtual burrito builder** in Roblox gamifies the customer experience with free rewards.

c. **Event-based engagement:**
   - **Balenciaga in Fortnite** ran an exclusive virtual fashion drop and style competition.

Persistent Brand World

Brands are building **persistent virtual environments** – not just ad campaigns but entire digital worlds that exist independently of specific events. These are immersive spaces where users can explore, interact and return repeatedly. Some of the examples are discussed below:

- **Nike's SWOOSH Platform:** Nike has launched a Metaverse-native platform for users to collect, trade and use virtual sneakers, as well as co-create future product ideas. Users can wear NFTs in games or sell limited editions.
- **Gucci Garden in Roblox:** A virtual space reflecting Gucci's aesthetic and history, complete with hidden experiences and collectable digital fashion items.
- **Adidas' Into the Metaverse:** Offers community membership and tokenised access to exclusive experiences and drops, connected to a broader virtual ecosystem.

Community Co-Creation

The Metaverse allows brands to move beyond viewing customers as mere consumers to seeing them as stakeholders – engaged community members who co-create value, content and experiences. Inspired by Brian Solis' vision, the brand–customer relationship becomes collaborative and mutually reinforcing. Some notable customer brand co-creation examples are Adidas ALTS, BAYC, etc.

a. **Co-design of products: Nike's Swoosh** and **Adidas' ALTS** invite community members to co-create digital designs or choose the direction of upcoming collections.
b. **Community-driven storytelling: Bored Ape Yacht Club (BAYC)** built a brand entirely from user participation – members use their NFTs to create music, games and merchandise.
c. **DAO-led product development:** Web3-native brands like **RTFKT Studios** involve their NFT holders in product and creative decisions through decentralized voting mechanisms.

Stage 3: Operational Innovation in the Metaverse

The Metaverse is changing consumer experiences and how organizations are transforming internally and globally. Organizations can implement workforce development, supply chain optimization and other business operations in immersive real-time collaborative systems to maximize agility, minimize risk and foster innovation. The following are three specific operational innovations that are occurring in the Metaverse.

Virtual Supply Chain Simulations

By utilizing the Metaverse, organizations can establish a virtual model of supply chain networks in which logistics, inventory and production can be managed and tested in real time. They can simulate logistics and inventory flow in the system while testing 'what-if' scenarios to identify bottlenecks, test disruptions and improve decision-making, all without affecting any currently operating supply chain. Virtual supply chain simulation reduces the risk involved as decisions can be made against prototype formats of the supply chain. By learning and experimenting virtually, organizations can enhance resilience and agility while also preparing for procurement and distribution. Some of the collaborations that have set the foundations for the virtual supply chains.

a. **Siemens + NVIDIA Omniverse:** Siemens is creating industrial Metaverse environments where engineers and supply chain managers simulate factory workflows, inventory flow and logistics under various scenarios.
b. **Walmart:** Uses VR to train employees in inventory management and test new logistics procedures in a risk-free, virtual space.
c. **Maersk:** Developing virtual control towers to simulate port operations and optimize global container movement using real-time IoT data.

Global Collaboration Spaces

Inspired by Eric Yuan (Zoom CEO), the Metaverse introduces a new paradigm for **global, persistent collaboration**, where teams work together in **shared, immersive virtual offices**, breaking free from the limitations of flat screens and Zoom fatigue. These collaborative spaces look like:

- **Digital headquarters:** Employees from different locations log into persistent 3D environments where they can brainstorm, meet clients and interact informally.
- **Spatial audio and avatar expressions:** Platforms like **Meta Workrooms**, **Microsoft Mesh** and **Virbela** provide near-physical social cues that enrich remote collaboration.
- **Real-time co-creation:** Teams work together on digital whiteboards, 3D models or documents in fully immersive environments.

Some of the brands have already started experimenting and entering into virtual workplaces.

- **Zoom's Metaverse Strategy:** Yuan envisions Zoom evolving into an immersive workspace where meetings feel like being physically present, integrating AR/VR with spatial awareness and expressive avatars.
- **PricewaterhouseCoopers (PwC):** Created a virtual meeting environment for international clients and employees to collaborate on audits and consulting projects.
- **Microsoft Mesh for Teams:** Allows virtual meetings where participants interact as avatars and manipulate shared 3D content in real time.

Risks, Ethics and Regulatory Considerations in Metaverse

Data Privacy and Surveillance in Immersive Environments

The Metaverse is far more immersive and data-rich than traditional web platforms. In virtual and augmented environments, **users generate vast amounts of personal and behavioural data**, often without realizing it. The primary data collected include biometric information, such as eye movement, facial expressions, gestures, voice recordings, gait and emotional states. Also, a large amount of **location and spatial data** are used in the Metaverse since real-world location, movement within virtual spaces and surroundings via AR devices are monitored. Moreover, continuous interaction data is produced that account for who the users interact with, what they look at and for how long. Since purchases are made via cryptocurrencies, digital wallets or NFTs, transactional data are also saved in the Metaverse. Thus, creating a need to not just manage the data but also align the correct privacy measures to secure the data.

To better understand this concern, we must explore the key privacy and surveillance concerns in the Metaverse. VR/AR headsets and Metaverse platforms can continuously monitor users, collecting data even when they are idle. Data may be used for behavioural profiling or targeted advertising without clear consent. Moreover, third-party developers may integrate tracking tools or extract data via decentralized apps (dApps). The biggest challenge is that users are unaware of the data rules. They often don't understand the scope of data being collected, not just in the Metaverse but in any immersive experience. The standard policies designed for the Metaverse are generic and do not touch upon the nuances of immersive data.

Another challenge in data privacy lies in the ownership and control of the data. Who owns the data generated in virtual worlds – users, platform providers or developers? Without strong legal frameworks, users may have limited recourse over misuse or unauthorized sharing of data. Thus, the need to design strong and exclusive legal frameworks for the virtual immersive world is a necessity. Also, to add the centralization of immersive data makes platforms lucrative targets for hackers, increasing the risk of data theft. Leaks of biometric or identity-related information could lead to irreversible harm, including deepfakes, identity theft and blackmail.

The challenges faced by businesses in managing data privacy in the Metaverse:

The Intensity of Personal Data Collection

In contrast to conventional digital settings, where experience is measurable by clicks and text, the Metaverse allows for the capture of experiences at a much deeper and more intimate level. In the Metaverse, every gesture, blink, tone of voice and interaction can be recorded. Users often need to present biometric data (e.g., eye movement, mannerisms, gait, etc.) to be fully immersed in VR or AR space. In this space, the Metaverse can afford users opportunities to signal more detailed information, such as:

- spatial location within virtual worlds;
- emotional reactions, as indicated by haptic feedback or neural signals;
- ambient sounds in users' environments.

The sensitivity of the layers of data we collect is significant; when they are all aggregated, platforms and third parties can create rich psychographic information on the tale. This personalized and specific landscape of data doesn't just create privacy issues – it alters the nature of privacy issues.

The Mirage of Informed Consent

Informed consent, a foundational principle in data protection law, becomes problematic in immersive digital spaces like the Metaverse. Most users engage with the Metaverse through headsets and controllers, immersed in virtual narratives. This reduces both their likelihood and capacity to read and comprehend lengthy privacy notices or permissions. Additionally, interfaces in the Metaverse are often gamified or designed for flow not friction. This makes critical privacy decisions feel peripheral or obtrusive. As a result, users grant sweeping permissions without fully understanding the extent of data being accessed or shared.

Surveillance and Behavioural Profiling at Scale

With the Metaverse, platforms can follow the users in two ways: (1) what users do and (2) how they do it. This analysis includes sources of behavioural knowledge of facial micro-expressions, pupil dilation, posture and virtual body language. When analyzed by AI, the aggregated data streams represent behavioural profiles that can predict, influence or manipulate user behaviours in real time. Such visibility, privacy and surveillance can have legitimate usages (e.g., personalized experiences or prevention of abuse), but they can also lead to surveillance capitalism, political targeting, and emotional exploitation.

Interoperability and Cross-Platform Vulnerabilities

Interoperability is one of the fundamental promises of the Metaverse. It is the ability to transfer assets, identities and experiences across platforms fluidly. Such fluidity allows for the continuous and swift use of social capital and increases user experiences qualitatively. While interoperability is beneficial, it engenders the loss of significant amounts of privacy. Personal data from a given platform is at risk of exposure or misuse on another platform if adequate interoperability standards are not implemented. Avatars may own personal metadata (e.g., transaction history, preferences and social networks) that include personal identifiers that, in the absence of adequate privacy measures, are trackable and accessible across all environments. The increasing amount of data that is exchanged between platforms increases the risk for major breaches of privacy and risk of identity leaks alongwith constant fatigue.

Ambiguities Around Data Ownership and User Control

In many Metaverse environments, users are prolific creators of avatars, environments, art and social interactions. However, the ownership of these digital artefacts and the data they generate remain murky. While some blockchain-based platforms promise decentralized data ownership, most commercial Metaverse platforms retain control over user data through opaque Terms of Service (ToS). Users are rarely given meaningful control to access, modify, transfer or delete their data, undermining the data sovereignty principle.

Identity Theft and Digital Impersonation

Identity in the Metaverse can be expressed through avatars, voices and behaviours, which makes impersonation a much more sophisticated and real threat than in traditional digital economies. Impersonation using deepfakes, synthetic avatars and cloned voices lets people impersonate other people in ways like their voice or behaviour. This is leading to fraud, reputational damage and manipulation. Unfortunately, as many identity layers are being created through the immersive biometric world of the Metaverse, most identity checks are still based on traditional forms of identity, such as email authentication and passwords, which are easy to use and result in a devalued but commonplace identity verification in a rich and immersive context.

Fragmented and Outdated Legal Frameworks

While nations and regions have made progress with data protection legislation, like the European Union's General Data Protection Regulation (GDPR) and India's Digital Personal Data Protection Act, there is no international legal framework specifically designed for the Metaverse. This absence leads to inconsistent privacy standards across platforms and jurisdictions, limited regulatory oversight of cross-border data flows and significant enforcement challenges. This is stronger when platforms operate in decentralized or extraterritorial environments. The transnational nature of the Metaverse demands coordinated, adaptive regulatory responses, yet these remain in early stages of development.

A Privacy Paradox: Decentraland and Blockchain's Double-Edged Sword

Decentraland is a blockchain-based Metaverse platform where users purchase, trade and build on virtual land using cryptocurrency. All transactions and ownership records are stored on the Ethereum blockchain, making the platform decentralized and theoretically user-controlled. While Decentraland promotes decentralization and self-sovereignty, its use of **public blockchains** creates unique privacy concerns:

a. Every transaction, asset trade or land purchase is **permanently recorded on-chain.**
b. These records are **publicly accessible and immutable**, meaning user behaviour is visible to anyone, forever.

In 2022, privacy advocates noted that while Decentraland offered more autonomy, it also exposed users to irreversible data visibility, including location, transaction habits and asset values. Thus, we agree that blockchain-based Metaverse platforms pose a privacy paradox: they empower users with ownership but sacrifice anonymity and data erasure.

Challenges in the Metaverse: Societal and Ethical Dimensions

Even as the Metaverse proffers unprecedented opportunities for creativity, collaboration and connection, it is ridden with difficult sociopolitical and ethical challenges concerning trust, governance, and social acceptance. Each of these new virtual realms inevitably raises questions about privacy, security, safety, health and economic implications, much like any other digital technology. To best leverage the Metaverse as an impactful driver for innovation and profit, organizations must develop a clear understanding of its complexities and implications. Ultimately, the Metaverse will only succeed if it does so by the principles of equity, openness, inclusivity and data security. As builders, regulators and users, we now have the opportunity to influence the future direction of the Metaverse in alignment with our collective aims and values.

There are broader **social implications**, such as digital inequality and exclusion. The Metaverse demands certain prerequisites like high-end devices and stable internet, which are not accessible to all. This digital divide could deepen existing socio-economic disparities, marginalizing those without the means to participate in these virtual worlds. Moreover, social norms are still evolving in the Metaverse, often influenced by dominant cultures and corporations. There's a risk of replicating real-world hierarchies, biases and stereotypes unless proactive efforts are made to build diverse and inclusive virtual communities.

Legal Threats in Metaverse

As the Metaverse takes shape as a multifaceted digital environment that merges aspects of VR, AR, blockchain and AI technologies, it also creates a medley of legal hurdles. The Metaverse is a legal and regulatory grey area due to its being borderless, immersive and decentralized. While the legal implications of the Metaverse are still in their initial stages, the legal issues raised are already diverse and pressing. The evolving habitat for the users in the Metaverse may create new challenges for legal systems worldwide, for example, intellectual property and user privacy, fraud, harassment and property disputes unique to the Metaverse environment. A blend of upfront regulation, platform governance, user education and international legal collaboration will be paramount in ensuring a level of safety, equity and accountability in this dynamic digital space. The following illustrates the principal groups of legal risks in the Metaverse, with supporting examples and cases showcasing what should be seen as an urgent need for clear, enforceable regulatory frameworks.

Intellectual Property (IP) Infringement

One of the biggest legal issues in the Metaverse is the protection and enforcement of IP rights. The sheer volume of user-generated content in the Metaverse includes avatars, virtual clothes, branded virtual real estate and digital art; all of it may infringe copyright, trademarks and patents that have been established.

Case: Hermès vs Rothschild (2022)

In a landmark Metaverse case, luxury brand Hermès sued digital artist Mason Rothschild for selling 'MetaBirkins' NFTs (images of faux-fur Birkin Bags) for $42,000 each. Hermès's claim was based on trademark rights, and the court ruled in favour of Hermès, confirming that avatars and NFTs are also covered by traditional IP laws. The ruling established a legal precedent where the law stated that virtual representations of registered physical trademarks will be subjected to the same protection rules as their real-world counterparts. The more significant consequence of this case is that other companies with registered trademarks should monitor Metaverse platforms for unlicensed uses of their brand elements. Similarly, digital creators, such as artists and designers, need to ensure that they are properly licenced if they are using real-world assets or trademarks for their virtual design, fashion and art.

Source

https://itsartlaw.org/2024/05/07/case-review-hermes-v-rothschild/

Harassment, Abuse and Safety Violations

In such an embodied environment, online harassment's emotional and psychological effects become heightened, due to the nature of a Metaverse experience compared to social media, which operates through text or video. Victims feel violations, such as unwanted nearness, being verbally abused or sexually harassed, more acutely within Metaverse experiences as they take place in real time, spatially and are experiential.

An Example Is Sexual Harassment in Horizon Worlds: A Virtual Game.

Multiple women have reported experiencing being 'groped' or verbally harassed while playing in Meta's Horizon Worlds. One user reported her avatar was groped in the first 60 seconds inside the space. Meta had added a 'personal boundary' feature to protect you from unwanted proximity, but it was opt-in by default for a long time, drawing criticism for not having safety features in place. A 2024 article released from the Guardian stated that British police launched an investigation into the described virtual 'gang rape' of a girl under 16 in a Meta powered Metaverse game. This describes the kind of emotional and psychological trauma users can face in immersive virtual spaces similar to that of a real-world assault. Meta's protective features, 'personal boundary' and 'Safe Zone', which auto-enforce a perimeter around users, have been criticized for being insufficiently protective in those instances.

Source

https://www.theguardian.com/commentisfree/2024/jan/05/Metaverse-sexual-assault-vr-game-online-safety-meta)

The challenge lies in the absence of robust reporting mechanisms, legal definitions of harassment in virtual spaces and jurisdiction over avatar-to-avatar interactions. Existing criminal laws on assault or abuse may not yet encompass acts in VR, leading to legal voids that protect offenders. This has led to countries increasing the scope of their laws, especially in the virtual space.

Contractual Ambiguities and Digital Asset Ownership

Most Metaverse platforms operate under user agreements that provide them broad control over content, user behaviour and digital goods. These ToS are often unilaterally amendable and grant the platform the right to delete content or revoke access. This calls into question the enforceability and legitimacy of digital ownership within these ecosystems.

Property Rights in Second Life

Members of the online, virtual world of Second Life buy and sell land or items using real money. Individuals have even sued Linden Lab (the creator of Second Life) for shutting down accounts and seizing digital property, claiming ownership rights were violated. While users who spent real money on those assets (ownership) argue they are entitled to these items, the courts have generally supported the platform's ability to manage and revoke virtual goods, using their ToS as the basis. The legal status of 'virtual property' remains unresolved. Blockchain-based Metaverses using NFTs as a digital representation of value aspire to create a more substantial claim of ownership to digital assets. However, NFTs themselves are still administered by smart contracts and platform policies that are often non-transparent or ever-changing.

Source

https://secondlife.com/land

Identity Theft and Avatar Impersonation

In the Metaverse, users typically interact through avatars, which can be customized to resemble real people. This opens the door to identity theft, avatar impersonation and fraud. There have been increasing reports of individuals creating avatars mimicking celebrities, influencers or acquaintances and using them to deceive or scam other users. With advancements in voice cloning and facial rendering, the risk of **'deepfake avatars'** is growing exponentially. Victims may find their likeness or persona misused without consent, leading to reputational harm or exploitation. Currently, laws concerning impersonation and defamation do not always extend to virtual environments, especially when the avatar is a 'close resemblance' but not an exact copy. Legal remedies for such impersonation remain limited and platform dependent.

Jurisdictional and Cross-Border Legal Challenges

One of the basic legal difficulties of the Metaverse involves jurisdiction, which is determining which laws apply and where legal claims should be filed and adjudicated. Since servers, users, companies and transactions are often in different countries, determining jurisdiction is a serious legal puzzle. As an example, consider the following scenario. A user is harassed in a virtual environment hosted on servers in the United States, and the virtual environment is operated by a company that is headquartered in Singapore, while the user is located in Germany. In this example, which country's laws apply? Can the victim report the harassment to law enforcement in Germany, or do they need to pursue the reported harassment according to the company's jurisdiction?

This type of scenario will occur in real life, as courts are now dealing with cases where national laws are applied to virtual conduct. In addition, most, if not all, of the commons claimed to be public platforms on which the harassment occurred have jurisdiction clauses embedded in their ToS so that the harm victim's legal recourse is now limited to the company's specified courts or arbitration. Combining these jurisdiction limitations, whether virtual conduct, regardless of country, will be comparable to in-person jurisdictional laws, remains to be seen.

Data Privacy and Surveillance

Because of this intensive nature, all data generated from VR and AR platforms will be very extensive. VR and AR devices collect more than just basic user data (e.g., names, locations, browsing behaviour); they now also include biometric data (i.e., eye tracking, facial expressions and possibly even neural data). This granular level of information creates new privacy risks.

VR and AR Devices and Uses Linked to Meta (or Facebook): The Oculus

Facebook's VR platform Oculus faced serious backlash for requiring users to use Facebook accounts to log in to their devices. By linking technologies with sensitive usage data, the obvious violation of a user's consent rights and the creation of a monopoly were vastly critiqued. Meta may have changed their tune regarding their terms of use, but what they did emphasize is that user consent, when used in an immersive environment, is a far more complicated process when compared to plain old digital platforms, which already face scrutiny regarding consent practices.

Regulations such as the GDPR and California Consumer Privacy Act (CCPA) are still not specific enough where the Metaverse is concerned. Also, the concerns around what other profiling, manipulation and surveillance companies or actors will do with biometric information are raising new ethical and privacy considerations when the biometric data are collected from a user. These challenges span from identity and behavioural norms to safety, regulation and inclusivity.

Chapter Summary

This chapter examined the evolution of the Metaverse from its early conceptualizations in science fiction to its current status as a dynamic, immersive digital ecosystem. We discussed the defining features of the Metaverse – immersion, interactivity, persistence and interoperability – and explored its core enabling technologies, including virtual and augmented reality, blockchain, AI and 3D modelling. Through real-world examples and case studies, we demonstrated how businesses across sectors – from fashion and retail to education and enterprise collaboration – are leveraging the Metaverse to create new economic opportunities, enhance customer engagement and redefine business models. Importantly, the chapter highlighted the need for ethical considerations, such as privacy, equity and digital well-being, as firms navigate this emerging space.

To make the discussion more engaging we have developed an A–Z dictionary of the Metaverse world (Appendix).

Future Outlook

As the Metaverse evolves from fragmented platforms into integrated digital economies, several strategic imperatives will guide business innovation:

- Building immersive brand ecosystems that extend beyond marketing into commerce, customer service and community-building.
- Developing interoperable virtual assets and experiences that can seamlessly transition across metaverse platforms and devices.
- Creating new business models in virtual real estate, digital collectibles and avatar customization, driving both consumer engagement and monetization.
- Establishing governance frameworks to address data privacy, content moderation and user well-being in immersive environments.
- Investing in metaverse-ready talent models, including 3D experience designers, virtual community managers and metaverse marketing strategists.
- Preparing for convergence with emerging technologies, such as AI-driven avatars, blockchain-enabled economies and spatial computing interfaces.

Ultimately, the future of the Metaverse in business is not merely a technological evolution but a reimagining of how value is created, shared and experienced across digital and physical worlds. Businesses that combine creativity with responsibility will shape this next chapter of digital commerce and community. To explore the A to Z of Metaverse, refer Appendix.

> The Metaverse will not replace physical experiences – but it will challenge businesses to create more meaningful digital ones.

Discussion Questions

(1) What business value do we want to unlock in the Metaverse?
(2) What core objectives should drive your Metaverse strategy?
(3) Which technologies and infrastructure are required for effective Metaverse engagement?
(4) How can businesses monetize in the Metaverse?
(5) What legal, privacy and IP protections are essential in virtual spaces?
(6) In what ways can immersive Metaverse experiences enhance customer engagement?
(7) How might the Metaverse transform internal operations like training and remote collaboration?
(8) Which risks and unintended consequences of Metaverse implementation should you anticipate?

References

Ball, M. (2022). *The metaverse: And how it will revolutionize everything*. Liveright Publishing.

CRN. (2021, November). Microsoft Ignite 2021: Satya Nadella's 5 'Key Attributes' to drive cloud. *CRN*. https://www.crn.com/slide-shows/cloud/microsoft-ignite-2021-satya-nadella-s-5-key-attributes-to-drive-cloud. Accessed on October 2024.

Di Paolo, F., Mancuso, I., Bettiga, D., Lamberti, L., Messeni Petruzzelli, A., & Panniello, U. (2025). Metaverse business transformation: Four companies' virtual experiences. *Management Decision*, *63*(13), 349–371.

Hryziuk, C. (2024). Exploring the future: 20 metaverse stats for 2024. *EMBRYO*. https://embryo.com/blog/metaverse-stats-2024

Mancuso, I., Petruzzelli, A. M., Urbinati, A., & Matzler, K. (2024). Leadership in the metaverse: Building and integrating digital capabilities. *Business Horizons*, *67*(4), 331–343.

Marchesoni, E. (2023, February 4). *The current state of metaverse interoperability: Where design framework must go from here*. VentureBeat. https://venturebeat.com/virtual/the-current-state-of-metaverse-interoperability-where-design-framework-must-go-from-here

McKinsey & Company. (2022, August 23). *Building the next big experiences*. https://www.mckinsey.com/capabilities/growth-marketing-and-sales/our-insights/building-the-next-big-experiences. Accessed on September 10, 2025.

NVIDIA. (2021). *AI and the future of industries* [Conference session]. NVIDIA GTC Fall 2021. https://www.nvidia.com/en-us/on-demand/session/gtcfall21-a31660/?playlistId=playList-c53b029c-8ebf-49b8-9bca-ddddb90a82a6. Accessed on December 2024.

Ritala, P., Aaltonen, P., Ruokonen, M., & Nemeh, A. (2024). Developing industrial AI capabilities: An organisational learning perspective. *Technovation*, *138*, 103120.

Solis, B. (2023, January 30). *McKinsey: A CEO's guide to the metaverse*. BrianSolis.com. https://briansolis.com/2023/01/mckinsey-a-ceos-guide-to-the-metaverse/. Accessed on December 2024.

Statista. (2023). *Metaverse - Worldwide*. https://www.statista.com/outlook/amo/metaverse/worldwide. Accessed on September 22, 2024.

World Economic Forum. (2022). *Davos Annual Meeting 2022 – Global Economic Outlook* [Video]. World Economic Forum. https://www.weforum.org/videos/davos-annual-meeting-2022-global-economic-outlook-original/. Accessed on October 2024.

Zoom. (2022, November 10). *Thank you for 'exploring new dimensions' at Zoomtopia 2022!* [Blog post]. Zoom. https://www.zoom.com/en/blog/zoomtopia-2022-recap/

Further Readings

Bruni, R., Colamatteo, A., & Mladenović, D. (2024). How the metaverse influences marketing and competitive advantage of retailers: Predictions and key marketing research priorities. *Electronic Commerce Research*, *24*(2), 965–982.

Mazzù, M. F., Pozharliev, R., & Sala, I. D. (2025, May). Luxury in the metaverse: A digital renaissance or a fading mirage? *California Management Review*. https://cmr.berkeley.edu/2025/05/luxury-in-the-metaverse-a-digital-renaissance-or-a-fading-mirage/

Sung, E., Kwon, O., & Sohn, K. (2023). NFT luxury brand marketing in the metaverse: Leveraging blockchain-certified NFTs to drive consumer behavior. *Psychology and Marketing*, *40*(11), 2306–2325.

Wongkitrungrueng, A., & Suprawan, L. (2024). Metaverse meets branding: Examining consumer responses to immersive brand experiences. *International Journal of Human–Computer Interaction*, *40*(11), 2905–2924.

Appendix: The A–Z of the Metaverse

Letter	Term	Description
A	Avatar	A digital representation of a user within a virtual world or game.
B	Blockchain	A decentralized digital ledger used to verify ownership of digital assets.
C	Creator Economy	An ecosystem where individuals monetize their content, goods and services.
D	DAO (Decentralised Autonomous Organization)	A community-led organization with rules encoded in smart contracts.
E	Extended Reality (XR)	An umbrella term for VR, AR, and MR technologies creating immersive experiences.
F	Fungible Token	A digital asset where each unit is interchangeable with others of the same type.

(Continued)

(Continued)

Letter	Term	Description
G	Gamification	The application of game-design elements to engage users in non-game contexts.
H	Haptics	Technology that simulates touch and motion feedback in virtual environments.
I	Interoperability	The ability of digital assets and experiences to work across multiple platforms.
J	Journey Mapping (CX)	The process of designing and analyzing the customer experience in virtual environments.
K	Keyframe Animation	A technique used to animate 3D objects and avatars in virtual worlds.
L	Land Parcel (Virtual)	A plot of digital space in a Metaverse platform that can be owned or leased.
M	Mixed Reality	A blend of physical and digital environments where users interact with both virtual and real-world elements simultaneously.
N	NFT (Non-Fungible Token)	A unique digital asset representing ownership of a virtual item or collectible.
O	Open Metaverse	A vision for decentralized, interoperable virtual spaces not controlled by a single company.
P	Play-to-Earn	A gaming model where players earn cryptocurrency or digital assets through gameplay.
Q	Quest	A task or mission assigned to players in a gamified virtual world.
R	Real-Time Rendering	The process of generating graphics instantly as users interact with the environment.
S	Smart Contract	Self-executing code on a blockchain that governs transactions automatically.

(Continued)

Letter	Term	Description
T	Telepresence	Technology enabling people to feel virtually present in remote environments; critical in Metaverse meetings and collaboration.
U	User-Generated Content (UGC)	Content created by users rather than the platform's developers.
V	Virtual Reality (VR)	A fully immersive digital environment accessed through head-mounted displays.
W	Wearables (Digital)	Virtual clothing and accessories worn by avatars.
X	XR Platform	A technology environment supporting VR, AR and MR content and experiences.
Y	Yield Farming	Earning passive income through staking digital assets in DeFi platforms connected to Metaverse economies.
Z	Zero-Knowledge Proofs	Cryptographic methods for verifying data without revealing the underlying information, useful in secure virtual transactions.

Chapter 10

Navigating the AI Landscape: Ethics, Governance and Responsible AI

> The true test of intelligence is not what a machine can do – but whether we dare to ask if it should.

Case Study: Housing and Policing – Life-Altering Decisions

In 2022, SafeRent Solutions, a tenant-screening company, used an Artificial Intelligence (AI)-powered risk-scoring algorithm to evaluate rental applicants in Massachusetts. A lawsuit filed by civil rights groups revealed the system disproportionately gave lower scores to Black and Hispanic voucher holders, effectively denying them housing opportunities.

At the same time, facial recognition systems used by U.S. law enforcement agencies resulted in multiple wrongful arrests of Black individuals – including Nijeer Parks, arrested in 2019[1] – raising concerns about racial profiling, insufficient oversight and the erosion of due process (CNN, 2021).

The Challenge

- Bias in Algorithmic Design: Models trained on historical or unbalanced data perpetuate racial and socioeconomic bias.
- Opacity and Lack of Accountability: Affected individuals have no clear mechanism to contest algorithmic decisions.
- Legal and Ethical Risks: Violations of the Fair Housing Act and constitutional rights (e.g., wrongful arrest without probable cause).

(*Continued*)

[1]https://edition.cnn.com/2021/04/29/tech/nijeer-parks-facial-recognition-police-arrest

AI and Business, 203–225

Published under exclusive licence by Emerald Publishing Limited
doi:10.1108/978-1-83708-888-120261010

(*Continued*)

Solution

- Litigation and Public Advocacy: Civil rights organizations sued SafeRent; the firm agreed to a $2.3 million settlement and suspended its use of the algorithm.
- Policy Recommendations: Advocates pushed for mandatory algorithmic audits, explainability and tenant redress mechanisms.
- Facial Recognition Moratoria: Cities, such as San Francisco and Boston, suspended the use of facial recognition by police departments.

Implementation Strategy

- Regulatory engagement to establish standards for transparency and bias mitigation.
- Collaboration between civil society, technologists and legal experts to assess ethical risks.
- Adoption of AI ethics checklists, impact assessments and independent audits before deployment.

Business Impact

- Reputational Risk: Tenant-screening firms and law enforcement agencies faced national criticism.
- Legal Consequences: Settlements, lawsuits and stricter regulatory scrutiny.
- Operational Changes: Increased demand for ethical AI frameworks and explainable models in the housing and policing sectors.

Lessons Learnt

- Biased training data leads to discriminatory outcomes, even in 'objective' systems.
- Algorithms must be transparent, contestable and regularly audited.
- Fairness must be context-specific – not just technically defined but socially understood.
- Human oversight remains critical in high-stakes applications like housing and law enforcement.

Questions to Think About

- Should automated systems be allowed in domains that directly affect human rights and freedoms?
- Who should be held accountable when an algorithm causes harm?

- What safeguards are necessary before deploying AI in the public interest?
- How can marginalized communities be included in algorithm design and testing?

Sources

https://www.theguardian.com/technology/2024/dec/14/saferent-ai-tenant-screening-lawsuit
https://www.teenvogue.com/story/artificial-intelligence-policing-encode-justice

The Ethical Imperative in the Age of AI

AI is a profoundly disruptive technology that demonstrates a sustained and meaningful impact on society globally, as well as on how people interact. The potential of AI is vast; it can drive unprecedented levels of productivity, promote the democratization and expansion of access to critical services, lead to significant advances in product innovation across all sectors, and contribute to economic development by enabling new methods of innovation and research and helping to promote potential solutions to our greatest challenges.

However, with the rapid and ubiquitous incorporation of AI into various sectors and for all elements of everyday life, several ethical and societal issues must be thoughtfully considered. Of important ethical and societal issues that must be thoughtfully considered. These issues are complex, related to specific notions of fairness, transparency, accountability, privacy and the potential misuse of AI. That is, while the power of AI to offer meaningful solutions to important problems is allowing for direct and potentially substantial benefits, it also creates the potential for direct harm if meaningful caution is not established. Societal impact must be a design specification, meaning those involved in AI and in society must shift from implementing practices that are characterized as reactive to practices characterized as proactive.

To suitably mitigate the AI's potent influence, we need to first comprehend and define the nuanced interrelationships between AI ethics, AI governance, algorithmic bias, and finally, responsible AI. AI ethics will effectively operate as the motivations informing the principles to define the principles around the right and wrong use of, and development of, AI. AI governance will translate ethical principles into practical policies, frameworks and practices of governance, providing a check mechanism that supports risk minimization and accountability. Algorithmic bias should be viewed as a critical failure point within AI, as it represents the occasions when AI output is unfair, discriminatory and unequal. Finally, responsible AI is seen as the overall holistic practice that includes ethics and governance and seeks to act to develop and deploy ethical, rightful and transparent AI that engages through mitigating bias through the entire AI lifecycle. Since trust in AI systems remains a barrier for the advocates of AI as a technology, responsible AI should be seen as consistent with meaningful engagement. The amount of work needed to move from aspirational ethics to acting on ethics in practice for real-world AI systems cannot be underestimated. This means that AI ethics and AI governance cannot simply engage in thinking and theorizing; they must join forces. Rather, this is the beginning of interdisciplinary work and technical practices so that there are useful, practical and effective technical tools, specific use-case policy guidelines and so on.

AI Ethics: Foundational Principles and Dilemmas

AI ethics is a multidisciplinary area of inquiry that aims to understand and address the moral consequences of AI. The overall aim is to leverage AI's potential societal goods while minimizing its intrinsic hazards and possible negative implications. Essential to the ethos of AI ethics is a set of normative standards that define ethical principles and guidelines for AI. It is essential to have normative standards to support ethical decision-making around the whole AI lifecycle and to provide a basis for distinguishing between right and wrong. The ultimate aim of AI ethics is for AI technologies to be designed and applied in alignment with key human social values, human social rights and human social goods, which promote equity, safety and human and societal well-being.

Key Ethical Frameworks

AI ethics essential principles are described in numerous frameworks but usually consist of accountability, fairness, privacy, safety, transparency, sustainability, the intention of AI for societal good and user-centred AI design. The essential principles identified above are salient examples of ethics in AI, though there are many other essential principles that researchers emphasize. Some of the key principles are data responsibility (keeping data safe and ensuring it is fair and reliable), explainability (making decisions by AI comprehensible), robustness (designing systems resilient against errors and attacks), inclusion (giving everyone equal access to the benefits of AI), moral agency (establishing who is responsible for AI), value alignment (ensuring AI incorporates common human values), trust and actively preventing technology misuse. The European Commission developed the world's first ethics guidelines for trustworthy AI, consisting of four ethical principles based on fundamental rights. These included respect for human autonomy, prevention of harm, fairness and explicability.

There are frameworks for ethical AI across the globe, from different international standards bodies and different corporations, but each has contributed understandings and frameworks to the map of responsible AI.

EU AI Act's Ethical Principles

The European Union's strategic approach to AI is firmly rooted in fostering both excellence and trust, with a strong emphasis on ensuring that AI remains human-centric and trustworthy. The EU's ethics guidelines for trustworthy AI advocate for systems that are not only lawful but also ethical and robust throughout their entire operational lifecycle. Key principles guiding this framework include:

- *Respect for Human Autonomy*: AI systems must be designed to augment, complement and empower cognitive, social and cultural skills, allowing for genuine choices and control within work processes. AI systems must not unduly subordinate, coerce, deceive, manipulate or herd humans. This principle reinforces the necessary view of AI as tools to enhance human capabilities, not replace or degrade them. Hence, careful decisions must be made about their design to prevent usurpation of the power of individual agency.
- *Prevention of Harm*: AI systems will be safe, secure and technically robust to minimize unintended harm and prevent unacceptable harm and not be open to pernicious use. There are special obligations to care for vulnerable people and groups, for the natural environment as a whole, and for all beings with life. This makes each ethical aspect of AI not only about its direct human impacts but also about the health and well-being of the environment and society as a whole. This fits the ethics of AI, across the board, into the larger framework of doing holistic risk assessments.
- *Fairness:* This principle has both substantive and procedural aspects. Substantively, fairness demands equitable and just distribution of benefits and harms, freedom from unfair bias, discrimination and stigmatization, and more. Fairness as a substantive principle may include any important aspect of fairness, such as fostering equal opportunity. Procedurally, fairness ensures that individuals can contest and seek effective redress for decisions AI systems have made. The principles used may require clear accountability and an appropriate degree of accountability.
- *Explicability:* This principle is crucial for building trust with users because it requires some introspection and transparent practices, clear communication around the AI system's potential for capacity and ultimate purpose, and explainable decisions to those affected by those decisions. With 'black box' algorithms, in addition to these options of traceability, auditability and transparent communications, an examination is necessary in order to assess the rights-protecting implications of the system's use. Finally, the circumstances and extent to which a faulty output may affect the situation should inform the level of explicability, while realizing that there are technical limitations to being fully explicable with AI models. While the ethical basis for explicability indicates we should at least understand a machine's rationale, there are limits in clarity with many AI model designs and executions, especially with AI operating in high-stakes contexts.

OECD AI Principles

These principles, adopted in 2019 and amended in 2024, seek to foster the development and application of innovative AI systems. They help promote trust as well as respect for human rights and democratic values. They are organized around five core value-based principles.

- Inclusive Growth, Sustainable Development and Well-being: This principle leverages AI's unique potential to address global challenges with a focus on enabling equitable social progress across communities. The focus is to achieve mutual benefits for people and the planet, which may include human capacity, fostering creativity, including underrepresented groups, mitigating inequality (economic, social and gender) and protecting the natural environment. Hence, this supports inclusive growth, well-being and sustainable development alongside environmental sustainability.
- Respect for the Rule of Law, Human Rights and Democratic Values: AI actors are required to uphold the rule of law, human rights and democratic as well as human-centric values at all stages of the AI system's lifecycle. This encompasses non-discrimination and equality, freedom, dignity, individual autonomy, privacy and data protection, diversity, fairness, social justice and the internationally recognized rights to labour. It also includes recognition and actions to address the misuse of information and disinformation due to AI technologies while upholding other rights, including the right to freedom of expression as protected by relevant international law. This principle sets an actionable legal and moral boundary for the advancement of AI technology while understanding its impact on the exercise of basic freedoms.
- Transparency and Explainability: AI actors are required to commit to transparency in relation to AI systems and responsible disclosure. Meaning AI actors provide relevant and commensurate information to the context and contemporary practices to ensure a collective comprehension of AI systems (both capabilities and limitations), advocate for knowledge by the stakeholders on a broader scope concerning their engagement with AI systems (also at the workplace), and, if helpful and practicable, provide step-by-step reasoning for how data sources, factors, processes or reasoning lead to certain outputs, enabling the affected parties to contend AI decisions. This principle will help to foster trust and enable stakeholder engagement to scrutinize AI systems.
- Robustness, Security and Safety: AI systems must display robustness, security and safety throughout their life cycle. This will ensure proper performance of AI systems (a) during normal use, (b) during foreseeable use or misuse and (c) during less predictable adverse conditions (external factors). AI systems must not introduce an unreasonable safety and/or security risk. There must be provisions for the AI systems that pose a risk of unreasonably harming, misbehaving, overriding, repairing and safely decommissioning. This principle emphasizes the need to build safe, robust and secure AI systems that are safeguarded against both unintentional errors and intentional hostile actions.

- Accountability: AI actors can demonstrate accountability for all AI systems and for implementing all of the above, depending on role, context and consistency with the contemporary state of the art. This accountability includes ensuring traceability (datasets, methods, decisions), adhering to a systematic risk management approach over the AI lifecycle, and assuming responsible business conduct regarding risks associated with AI. Accountability is an essential step to realize responsibility and ensure that ethical failings or harms can be attributed and remedied.

UNESCO Recommendation on the Ethics of AI

Adopted in November 2021 by 193 member states, this recommendation offers a global framework for ethical AI use, emphasizing human rights, environmental sustainability and inclusivity. Its 10 principles include:

- *Proportionality and Safety*: AI development and use should be proportionate to the intended use and should do no more than the minimum necessary to achieve the intended use, and should not include excessive potential for harm. AI should not be designed and/or used in a way that is harmful to people and/ or the environment, including for discriminatory purposes, mass surveillance and/or psychological manipulation. The replicated method of AI should be appropriate, proportional, balanced and follow established, reliable scientific principles. The principle of proportionality and safety clarifies a vital boundary in practice, namely that AI applications must occur within permissible and non-harmful limits.
- *Safety and Security:* Involves an emphasis on eliminating and/or minimizing unintended harms, security risks and vulnerabilities of the AI system throughout its life cycle to ensure the safety of people, environmental systems and ecosystems. This includes implementing prevention and sustainable models of access to data that minimize risk for privacy while allowing access to high-quality data to fit the intended use of the models (training and/or validation). It reflects the notion that without strong technical safeguards in place to mitigate both accidental and malicious harms, the path forward for AI is unsuitable.
- *Equity and Non-Discrimination:* Requires AI entities to protect principles of equity, social justice and non-discrimination. In practical terms, this means equity in availability of AI technology and equitable access to the benefits of AI technology for everybody, with an understanding of diverse needs based on characteristics such as age, culture, language, ability, gender and socio-economic status. It seeks to encourage open access/entry into AI systems that connect users with content that is locally relevant to the user's experience while ensuring that linguistic rights and recognition of cultural diversity are respected.
- *Sustainability*: Emphasizes advancing environmental, social, cultural and economic dimensions for sustainable societies. AI systems must be designed

for energy efficiency, focusing on minimizing consumption and carbon footprint. Lifecycle ramifications (from production to disposal) must also be accounted for. Interoperability with other existing systems has been encouraged, and duplication will be avoided. This can point out the extent of AI's fallibility on an environmental footprint and reminds us to be better stewards of the environments in which we live and develop.

- Right to Privacy and Data Protection: Privacy is a foundational human right. The collection, use, sharing, archiving and deletion of data must follow the applicable legal frameworks, including the data subject's reasons for consent and informed consent. A multilateral approach to global data protection standards is recommended. This principle reiterates the role of strong data governance for protecting individual rights while navigating an increasingly data-centric AI domain.
- Human Supervision and Human Decision: This principle deals with the question of responsibility for decisions being made by AI systems, including the ease with which those decisions can be automated. While it does acknowledge the role of human responsibility in decisions affecting human life or health, AI cannot erase the responsibility of the operator. The principle maintains human control and moral agency at the top of AI systems, especially for decisions that are consequential.
- Transparency and Explainability: Core to human rights, defining a way of being able to look at the decisions taken by AI and reinforce their legal grounds. The amount of transparency and clarity will depend on the context and the consequences of their meaning. The public must be made aware when AI algorithms are making a decision that affects either their security or their human rights, and be allowed to ask questions, seek clarity and challenge. This gives individuals choices to understand and challenge AI decisions that affect them.
- Responsibility and Accountability: All AI actors must always take responsibility and an ethical duty for all decisions and actions based on AI systems and be in full compliance with national and international legislation. Appropriate oversight, impact evaluation (e.g., audits) and accountability are needed by all actors in the lawful AI ecosystem to fortify the legal and ethical responsibility to arrive from all actors.
- Awareness and Education: There is a need for collaboration between public authorities, civil society, the media, academia and the private sector to promote media literacy, civic involvement and digital skills training that takes into consideration cultural and linguistic diversity. There must be a culture of ethical AI across all sectors. This requires public awareness, preparedness and informed discussion about AI.
- Adaptive Governance and Collaboration: Large multinational companies should always be compliant as set out by their national sovereignty and laws of the international stage. In order for the benefits of AI to be distributed equitably, a strong, complex international collaboration will be needed on all fronts – legal, technical and ethical – starting with the largest and hiring within and developing AI products, processes and services to last.

Ethical Dilemmas in Practice

The theoretical principles of AI ethics often confront complex dilemmas when applied in real-world scenarios, highlighting the nuanced challenges of AI deployment.

Case 1: Autonomous Vehicles (AVs)

The ethical implications of AVs are frequently explored through variations of the classic 'Trolley Problem,' which poses a dilemma: should an AV be programmed to sacrifice its passenger to save a greater number of pedestrians, or vice versa? The fundamental ethical conflict in AVs lies between prioritizing the interests of the passenger (e.g., arriving safely, quickly and cheaply) and those of the broader community (ensuring road safety for all users).

From a utilitarian perspective, the only option is to try to reduce total fatalities, even at the cost of the AV's passenger. Studies indicate that most people consider this morally superior to other options, contributing to the tension. On an individual level, people prefer to buy AVs designed to prioritize their passengers. Here we have a tough social problem: individual interests can conflict with the collective good, which creates tension and hinders public acceptance of utilitarian AV programming. The deontological position would assert that compromising prices is not the right thing to do, and it would advise never swerving from an AV if the alternative is to intentionally hurt others, even if it saves more lives. Keeping the AV on track, even with more fatalities, might be thought of as 'merely foreseen harm' and thus more permissible from a theory of ethics perspective. This situation highlights the comparative moral weight of intentional action versus inaction. There is also an offshoot of this called a 'Rawlsian algorithm,' after contractarian philosopher John Rawls, which proposes that an AV's software could estimate the approximate chance of survival for each person who would be in a crash and calculate their current course of action based on what they would agree to if they didn't know who they would be in this crash. This approach attempts to introduce a form of impartial decision-making, but its practical implementation is complex, requiring the AV to identify and categorize individuals based on social factors, which is currently beyond sensor technology capabilities.

Source:

https://analyticsindiamag.com/ai-features/the-moral-dilemma-of-embedding-ethics-into-autonomous-vehicles/

Case 2: Lethal Autonomous Weapons Systems (LAWS)

LAWS are reliant on the use of sensors and algorithms for decision-making, and in some instances, remove the requirement for real-time human involvement to set objectives, select targets and launch an attack. While only a handful of autonomous systems are in operation at present, the notion of fully autonomous systems raises serious ethical issues as they develop rapidly.

One conception as to why LAWS may be unacceptable is that they cannot comply with even the existing principles of military ethics. Critics have argued that no matter how advanced, computers do not have the ongoing and creative thinking processes to visualize and interpret the nuanced complexity of war in real-time; LAWS would remain completely hamstrung in their ability to distinguish a combatant from a non-combatant, with the safety and well-being of non-combatant persons remaining a high risk of destruction. More fundamentally, the questions are, should robots be allowed to make autonomous decisions in relation to killing human beings, or should humans always be required to maintain the ultimate decision-making authority? Autonomous weapon systems will further legitimize this objectification of human targets by increasing our limitations on tolerable collateral damage, including death. Hence, robots will lessen human involvement in decision-making; thus, the moral agency of an operator making ethical decisions is also diminished by either their reliance on technological mediation or automation bias.

Additionally, the combined notion of LAWS can potentially greatly lower risks to human soldiers; it may unintentionally encourage the next wars, as deaths can be politically deterrent. Moreover, robot armies could become weapons of mass destruction that can be intercepted by hackers seizing control and using them against their makers, or AI itself might be used militarily to also cause mass deaths and mass destruction. There are no general international laws around military robots, and the potential for control and limitations to AI use is also a barrier moving forward. This ethical dilemma stresses the absolute need for the international community to come together and develop regulatory and governance regimes before the general use of such systems is emplaced.

Source:

https://www.asil.org/insights/volume/29/issue/1

Case 3: AI Surveillance Technologies

The use of AI technology in surveillance systems has raised serious concerns about ethical issues such as privacy, bias and accountability. The proliferation of surveillance cameras and sensors, especially those equipped with AI, can foster an all-encompassing feeling of being surveilled even in public places, thereby violating individual privacy rights and diminishing the ability to remain anonymous. An important ethical issue is the risk of bias and discrimination in the AI surveillance system. For example, biases in AI facial recognition systems exist – some AI facial recognition systems exposed higher errors for people of colour and women. This should create serious concerns about fairness and equal treatment under the law if AI facial recognition systems were used to make significant decisions. Such racial bias may lead to misidentifications or wrongful arrests and serve to worsen disparities in already marginalized communities. That said, AI surveillance systems may unfairly surveil vulnerable groups and perpetuate ecological over-policing, as communities are not always surveyed but are targeted with surveillance analysis, fostering increasing feelings of oppression.

The complexity of AI systems may lead to confusion and impede transparency and accountability. We can understand that AI systems can be induced to understand specific facets of their decision-making journey by the data produced by operating models. Once AI systems identify an understanding, it becomes impossible to ascertain how the AI systems arrived at specific decisions or answers. This is concerning as both an entity and an individual, because it becomes even more challenging to hold any given person (or organization) accountable for the decisions made by the AI-driven policy. The complexity also creates potential for risk where unintended consequences impacting the individual could either not be addressed or resolved.

There is also a risk of a chilling effect on individual agency derived from the responsibility of controlling the surveillance. AI surveillance can create oppressive policy structures that affect how individuals choose to engage with others or allow themselves to behave. People may self-censor their interactions or emotional expressions, fearing negative feedback from AI monitoring systems and pervasive surveillance by governments or corporations. While some states and municipalities have enacted regulations requiring consent for biometric data collection, federal laws specifically regulating facial recognition technology are currently lacking in some jurisdictions, leaving significant gaps in protection.

Source:

https://ovic.vic.gov.au/privacy/resources-for-organisations/artificial-intelligence-and-privacy-issues-and-challenges/

AI Governance: Frameworks and Implementation

AI governance encompasses the processes, policies and standards guiding the responsible, ethical and secure use of AI technologies. AI governance addresses the possible risks related to AI's capability of producing biased outputs, non-compliance and security and privacy breaches by establishing policies and frameworks that contain necessary controls. It encompasses the processes of designing, developing, deploying, implementing and operating AI systems while defining best practices and processes for accountability, transparency and bias-free operations of datasets and AI systems.

AI governance responsively rests on several foundational principles, which include:

- Fairness and Bias Mitigation: creating AI systems that apply fairness as a guiding principle in the eradication of bias.
- Transparency and Explainability: AI systems must be understandable, accessible and accountable. AI technologies need to be demystified.
- Privacy and Data Protection: ensures that AI systems and the environment operate legally and ethically by protecting identifiable personal information.
- Accountability and Governance: AI systems and their outputs can be traced to legal entities through roles, documentation and oversight systems that govern them.
- Safety and Security: ensuring resilient access to and reliable operation of AI while preventing unauthorized use and access, and also maintaining confidentiality and integrity.

Societal Impact: Assesses and manages the positive and negative influences with respect to the economy, culture and social dynamics owing to the technologies.

National and International Governance Frameworks

Governments and international organizations are actively developing regulatory frameworks to manage AI's impact and ensure its responsible development. The following section discusses the developments in Europe, China, the United States and the United Kingdom.

EU AI Act

The Artificial Intelligence Act of the European Union (EU AI Act) is regarded as the first in the world to provide a comprehensive regulatory framework for AI. The regulation takes a risk-based approach to compliance, assigning different rules to AI depending on the risk it poses. The act classifies AI systems into four levels of risk: unacceptable, high, limited, minimal or no risk.

- Unacceptable Risk: Risks that undermine the safety, livelihood and rights of individuals will lead to a total ban. The harms include any AI-driven social manipulation/exploitation of vulnerabilities, social crediting, risk evaluation for one-off criminal acts on an aggregate basis, non-targeted web facial recognition/face database scraping, non-targeted CCTV face recognition/face database extraction, emotion recognition for educative and occupational contexts, biometric profiling to deduce safeguarded common attributes and unconsented real-time remote biometric identification in public bounding spaces for law enforcement.
- High Risk: These systems include those with identifiable use cases that pose serious health, safety or human rights risks. Examples of high-risk AI systems encompass their application in essential services, remote biometric identification, law enforcement activities that could infringe upon core human rights, critical infrastructure, education (such as credential evaluation or grading), safety evaluations for products and services, policing, managing a workforce, migration and border control, as well as the functioning of justice and democratic institutions. Such systems need to satisfy stringent pre-market conditions like risk evaluation and discrimination-free data collection, reliable human oversight, documented engineering processes, sufficient and clear deployer guidance, mechanized checks for human oversight and consistently trustworthy operations.
- Limited Risk: This category requires transparency regarding AI use. The Act mandates specific disclosure obligations, such as informing users when they are interacting with an AI system (e.g., chatbots) and requiring machine-readable formats to mark AI-generated content (e.g., deepfakes).
- Minimal or No Risk: The majority of AI systems fall into this category (e.g., AI-enabled video games, spam filters) and are not subject to specific rules under the Act.

The EU AI Act is expected to become a global standard, much like General Data Protection Regulation (GDPR) influenced personal data privacy regulations worldwide, spurring the development of AI governance and ethics standards internationally.

US AI Policy Framework

The U.S. response to AI governance involves a patchwork of executive orders, existing laws and negotiations. The U.S. Executive Order on AI of October 2023 lays the groundwork for federal agency use of AI and emphasizes safety, equity and national security in its approach. The major mandates of the U.S. Executive Order on AI and existing civil rights laws are as follows: (1) require safety testing of AI; (2) require watermarking of any AI-generated content; (3) exercise federal oversight for AI utilization in healthcare, defence, or other national security class sectors; (4) promote the establishment of an AI workforce; and (5) encourage global AI cooperation. Existing civil rights laws apply to (1) preventing prohibited conduct, regardless of the AI model used to achieve those ends – in education, healthcare, hiring, housing, financial services and purchasing goods and services – under existing civil rights laws; (2) there are legal requirements that exist, such as SR-11–7 for model governance in banking – banks must identify model risk and exercise effective model risk management, including transparency and understanding of any AI models used; and (3) the U.S. also has the Algorithmic Accountability Act (US) that applies to AI fairness.

China's AI Governance Strategy

China is an emerging power in AI with an articulated governance framework and an ambition to be a global leader in AI by 2030. China's approach to AI governance is to promote innovation while injecting prudential safeguards to try to prevent additional social or economic harms from emerging from this type of technology. This type of model is especially attractive to developing countries where there are opportunities for learning, skill development and economic growth while also striving for societal cohesion.

The centralized AI governance framework articulated in the AIGC Content Moderation will examine precursory elements regarding the traceability and authenticity of content that is developed through any type of AI model to ensure information does not flow that could be found to contradict local regulations. Each service provider is required to identify AI-generated content (i.e., visual, auditory or textual) with unique watermarks, in addition to identifying content material that could confuse the public. Service providers that are categorized as higher risk and that help generate 'public opinion attributes or social mobilization capacities' face more rigorous regulatory requirements, ranging from file requirements for algorithms used for recommendations to security assessments.

Data protection: There were minimal changes to the overall regulatory elements that apply to AI governance roles that can refer back to obligations already articulated in the 2021 Personal Information Protection Law (PIPL). PIPL outlines a range of duties that AI service providers need to consider (under PIPL); they include whether there are lawful bases for processing and whether consent will be required for personal data processing i.e., collection (inputs), training (processing), and use (outputs) with obligations of accountability imposed and numerous rights already put in place for data subjects. The objective is to ensure that any processing of personal data is not harmful to users or undermines social public order, which would prioritize a priori behaviour model sort of consideration if a machine learning model, also under certain considerations, that liability could arise when public order is being regulated.

Algorithmic Governance: This pillar distinguishes algorithmic management as a regulatory feature that has its provisions regarding security, ethicality and clarity of algorithms. Security is key for services with 'public opinion attributes or social mobilization capabilities,' with the requisite information needing submission to the CAC on algorithms. Ethicality requires algorithms to have an ethical basis, meaning, for instance, the use of AI to create discriminatory content based on protected characteristics is prohibited. This principle also applies to vulnerable groups, who are protected classes. Nevertheless, these protected classes will be 'particularly encouraged and protected.' Clarity requests companies provide information and disclosures as it pertains to the services they provide, including the advertisements and recommendations, and disclose AI-generated products that simulate humans.

UK AI Regulation Approach

The UK government has opted for a 'pro-innovation and business-friendly approach' to AI regulation and does not have specific AI legislation yet. While an AI bill is being created, publication of it has been delayed until it can align with the approaches taken by the US. In the meantime, organizations and regulators are endorsing the government's Policy Paper (UK Government, 2023), containing cross-sectoral principles that regulators may interpret and apply to AI in their sectors while maintaining five value-based principles:

- Safety, security and robustness: AI systems must ensure continuous risk identification and management during operation.
- Adequate explainability and transparency: AI systems should build trust and eliminate potential harms while being appropriately transparent and explainable.
- Equity: AI systems must not breach legal rights, arbitrarily discriminate against individuals or generate discriminatory market outcomes.
- Accountability and governance: There should be a possibility for oversight to be applied to AI systems with defined accountability by regulators.
- Contestability and redress: Users must be provided with appropriate means to contest AI-enabled decisions or actions deemed harmful.

The UK government will not be establishing another AI regulator, but existing regulatory bodies (ICO, CMA, FCA, Ofcom) will assist a range of context-dependent approaches to underpin AI development with a central government function for coherence and willingness to share information with one another. The UK government also launched the AI Opportunities Action Plan to accelerate the uptake of AI, with new initiatives.

UN AI Governance Initiatives

The United Nations embraces AI governance through an eagerness to build AI to advance the Sustainable Development Goals (SDGs) while sharing its benefits with the world. The UN establishes an Independent Scientific Panel on AI to facilitate international governance of AI through a multidisciplinary approach and initiated a Global Dialogue on AI Governance, which is meant to embrace all stakeholders.

UN agencies have over 40 sister agencies, and they are involved in AI projects all over the world, from predicting food crises to measuring water productivity to mapping schools, all the way to the optimization of communications. The most important consideration is the protection of human rights throughout the AI lifecycle, with a particular focus on freedom of expression, equality and non-discrimination, as well as the significant impact of AI on exacerbating existing inequalities. The UN Office for Digital and Emerging Technologies (ODET) was created to support AI governance.

Council of Europe Framework Convention on AI

The Council of Europe AI framework was adopted on 17 May 2024, and it started collecting signatures on 5 September 2024. This is the first treaty of its kind – international and legally binding – dealing with AI, human rights, democracy and the rule of law. The Convention aims to both aid the progress of technology and ensure that all activities concerning the lifecycle of AI systems are aligned with these vital values.

The Convention establishes a risk-based approach to the implementation measures, which are scaled based on the impact on human rights, democracy and the rule of law. Foundational principles include respect for individuals and their freedom, non-discrimination, privacy, personal data protection, transparency, oversight, accountability, reliability and promotion of safe innovations. The Convention will extend to AI used by public authorities or private entities acting under the authority of public officials, which allows some latitude in the use of provisions regarding the private sector. The convention obliges parties to carry out risk and impact assessments and provide rights to individuals to challenge AI-driven decisions.

Global Partnership on AI (GPAI)

GPAI was created in June 2020 as a voluntary, multi-stakeholder initiative of 44 member states that seeks to advance responsible AI development and use on the basis of human rights, inclusion, diversity, innovation and economic growth while striving towards the 2030 Sustainable Development Goals. GPAI is creating a multidisciplinary group of experts in industry, government, civil society and academia to conduct world-class research and pilot projects in core areas of AI activities.

The work Oxford has established is based on the OECD AI Principles. GPAI organizes work through working groups on data governance (plus metrics), responsible AI (including for pandemic response), the future of work and commercialization and innovation. The OECD hosts the GPAI Secretariat and is collaborating with GPAI's Centres of Expertise (in Paris, Montreal and Tokyo) as they use the OECD's national and international frameworks to assist with testing, piloting and scaling. GPAI seeks to promote human-centred and trustworthy AI, to bolster the global AI safety framework, and to help develop international collaboration.

Corporate Governance Initiatives

In addition to national and multilateral frameworks, leading companies are building their internal governance and best practices to support responsible AI development and deployment.

IBM: IBM's guidance for Responsible AI is organized around its 'Pillars of Trust': explainability, fairness, robustness, transparency and privacy. IBM approaches responsible AI with an end-to-end, holistic view, which begins with defining principles aligned to organizational values, educating employees, embedding ethics throughout the AI development life cycle (from data gathering to monitoring), safeguarding users' privacy and promoting human oversight. This would also include establishing a cross-functional AI ethics team and creating ethics review boards.

Google: A responsible AI approach at Google includes its set of AI principles, focused on bold innovation and responsibly developing and deploying that innovation in collaboration with others. The Responsible Innovation team at Google is responsible for guiding the implementation of responsible AI, evaluating every product with a detailed ethical review and impact assessment. Google also provides a range of tools to increase transparency, such as Explainable AI, Model Cards and an open-source toolkit (TensorFlow). For generative AI specifically, the responsible AI toolkit offers a set of guidelines related to application design, safety alignment, model-ready evaluation and safeguards, including watermarking tools (SynthID Text) and content safety classifiers (ShieldGemma).

Microsoft: Microsoft's strategy around responsible AI is guided by its Office of Responsible AI (ORA), and supported by a company-wide Responsible AI Council. The ORA is responsible for the Responsible AI Standard that provides guidance about what responsible AI means and addresses six key principles – fairness, privacy and security, reliability and safety, inclusiveness, transparency and accountability – in terms of action items for all AI projects. Microsoft Digital, the internal IT organization, has been developing workflow tools to support these standards to enable logging of projects, assist developers with determining impact assessments and simplify the review process. With this development, they have put responsible AI principles into the software development lifecycle. Examples of internal AI projects include facilities agents, campus event agents and dining agents with practical applications of these principles.

Atlassian: The values that drive Atlassian's approach to responsible AI are open conversations, trust and safety, accountability and learning and empowerment. Their use of AI begins with transparency, which they outline through the things they openly communicate about their products in terms of capabilities, data access and data use, while striving to provide complete, accurate and helpful information. Trust is earned from using secure, private and reliable products and consistently improving them with customer collaboration. While being accountable for responsible AI use is mostly a collaborative process, it involves feedback loops and constant learning. Empowerment drives the unexpected results of a project that builds inclusive and fair products by making diversity, equity and accessibility priorities in the products that they build.

Algorithmic Bias: Identification, Impact and Mitigation

Algorithmic bias occurs when machine learning algorithms produce systematic (unfair) and discriminatory results. Often intentional or unintentional (often based on the datasets used for training or biases in society), bias in algorithmic decision-making creates unfair and discriminatory insights and outputs. Bias has damaging effects in AI and decision-making, as it can cause harm through erroneous decision-making, reinforce discrimination and inequalities, and produce distrust in AI and institutions. Bias has a damaging economic and legal impact on companies; they may face severe consequences for failing to comply with laws and regulations, such as significant fines or penalties from the EU AI Act.

Sources of Bias

Bias can occur in algorithms at many different levels of the algorithm lifecycle:

(1) **Biases in Training Data:** Flawed data (as in non-representative, incomplete, historical and 'bad' data) is a source of bias and the most significant maintainer of algorithmic bias. If AI systems are based on biased output data that is used in the decision-making, this becomes a feedback loop that may compound or build bias into growing biased (and therefore skewed) outcomes over time – as opposed to analyzing the answer for more bias or biasness. Bias can also occur from the way that data has been categorized, algorithmic learning from correlation and learning (and not using) other crucial factors. This can be problematic in image datasets where datasets tend to include datasets that represent disproportionately more respondents with lighter skin and disproportionately fewer respondents with darker skin.

(2) **Biases in Algorithmic Design:** Programming mistakes or developer choices can unintentionally embed human biases into the system. This could happen if an AI designer weights the elements of the decision process in a biased way or if they build in subjective rules based on their own conscious or unconsciously biased perceptions. For example, if a hiring tool uses gender as one of the attributes equally important as others based on the training data, discrimination may occur.

(3) **Biases in Proxies:** AI often uses proxies such as race or gender with other attributes. These proxies may inadvertently cause bias for sensitive attributes. For instance, proxies such as postal codes represent economic status.

These proxies can adversely impact certain postal codes with specific racial demographics.

(4) **Biases in Evaluation:** Evaluations that are influenced by biases from the evaluators add bias to the algorithm results. Such biases are not neutral, and data-based algorithms are neutral. An individual's or corporation's decision to act on an algorithm's output may be based on their biases, leading to unfavourable outcomes. Additionally, the AI tools can create 'hallucinations,' which result in irrelevant selection as the basis of non-existent factors.

Responsible AI: Holistic Implementation for a Trustworthy Future

Responsible AI describes the ethical, transparent and accountable approaches and frameworks in the development, implementation and use of AI systems. It seeks to align AI technologies with human ethics and values, uphold and protect essential rights, and provide equity and security. It further aims to foster the welfare of the individual or society as a whole. Responsible AI considers the social, regulatory, governance and oversight implications as well as the ethical frameworks and long-term consequences of AI.

Responsible AI is fundamentally built upon three core pillars:

- **Regulation of AI**: Establishing legal frameworks and policies to govern AI development and use.
- **Standardization of AI**: Developing technical standards and best practices to ensure quality, reliability and interoperability.
- **Ethical AI**: Integrating moral principles and values into the design and application of AI systems.

This tripartite foundation ensures that AI benefits society as a whole by minimizing risks and maximizing positive impacts.

Implementation Best Practices for Businesses

To implement responsible AI practices, organizations need to establish formalized principles and then put them into action through effective AI governance, training and technical processes.

- **Developing Principles:** Recognizing and addressing the ethical boundaries involving human agency and oversight, privacy and data governance, technical robustness and safety, transparency, diversity, non-discrimination and fairness, social and environmental stewardship, and accountability is paramount for an organization's principled values. Responsible AI should be developed through a group of practitioners in AI ethics who are composed of ethicists, technicians from different fields of study, legal practitioners and

organizations, and organization leaders and business operators. Due to the diversity of backgrounds and perspectives, the practitioners help create the values and the ongoing changes of those values.
- **Integrating Ethics across the Entire AI Development Cycle:** Responsible AI development, as AI ethics and framework, can be integrated into the entire pipeline of AI development. Including processes to pre-emptively identify and mitigate all identified and potential biases, frameworks for bimodal assessments of AI for fairness, and processes that continuously support transparency, including explainability of AI systems made clear, and documentation to explore support transparency principles.
- **Protecting Private Data:** Safeguards must exist in strong data governance practices and AI governance practices with rigorous governance that can protect the privacy and sensitive data of the end user and trustworthy AI practices. This includes ways to communicate our data usage and policies, explicit permission with informed consent, and using ethical principles in data protection laws such as GDPR.
- **Specific Practices for Implementation**:
  - **Assess content readiness**: Before integrating AI, evaluate the content being worked with. Much business data is unstructured, requiring additional processing for AI to understand and extract value.
  - **Support content with metadata**: Metadata management helps AI models understand and contextualize content, acting as a roadmap for accurate interpretation and reducing skewed or outdated outputs.
  - **Look for secure, responsible AI tools**: Select AI tools that adhere to their principles, comply with data privacy regulations, do not train models using customer content, and have built-in safeguards against misuse.
  - **Test AI's effectiveness**: Regular testing is crucial to ensure the AI model delivers desired results in terms of accuracy, efficiency and data processing without distortion.

Ubiquitous AI across all sectors demands a comprehensive, proactive approach to its ethical implications, governance, algorithmic bias and responsible deployment. This analysis has shown that AI's transformative potential is directly correlated with its ability to cause unintended harm and highlights that ethical concerns cannot simply be additive; they must be foundational in the design and implementation of AI. The challenge remains the incorporation of abstract ethical principles into concrete, enforceable practices and mechanisms.

The global landscape aimed at addressing these ethical and social issues, evidenced by similar frameworks from the EU, OECD and UNESCO, as well as industry frontrunners, indicates shared values around ethical principles, such as fairness, transparency, accountability, privacy and human oversight. These frameworks are established in the understanding that whether legally binding or voluntary, these frameworks would provide ample guardrails; they have a responsible approach with people's values and communities' well-being at the forefront. As shown in numerous field-tested studies in areas such as criminal justice, hiring, health and money, algorithmic bias from flawed training data or design reproduces and exaggerates existing social inequalities, which produces harmful discriminatory outcomes and erodes trust. The rise of generative AI technologies posed new challenges in the areas of truthfulness, copyright and the massive misuse potential.

Managing these risks requires a multi-pronged approach. On a technical level, this will rely on robust data-centric practices (variety of data, pre-processing), bias-aware algorithm design, and the adoption of effective Explainable AI (XAI) tools and fairness measures to help make 'black box' models visible and disparities known. On an organizational level, this will entail a solid governance structure around AI (i.e., about planning, process and people), monitoring and auditing, and a culture that emphasizes ethical considerations across the entire AI lifecycle. Most importantly, human oversight and diversity of stakeholders, from inception to deployment, remain critical to ensuring AI systems substantiate human values and the collective interest. Ultimately, engaging responsibly with the complex and evolving AI landscape is more than a compliance exercise; it is a strategic requirement for the trustworthiness of systems to achieve equitable access and augment human potential not only in the broader terms of social responsibility but by championing not just social order but a just and fair society. The impact of evolving AI technology continues to be significant; it is through adequate governance and an adaptability to learn that progress can be linked as productive or in the best interest of humanity.

Chapter Summary

This chapter has examined the ethical, legal and governance dimensions of AI in business and society. It highlighted that while AI offers immense potential for innovation, efficiency and inclusion, it simultaneously raises critical challenges related to bias, transparency, accountability and human rights. The discussion traced the evolution of AI ethics from normative principles – such as fairness, explicability and accountability – to their operationalization in global frameworks including the EU AI Act, OECD AI Principles, UNESCO Recommendations and emerging national policies. Through real-world cases – from tenant screening and facial recognition to autonomous vehicles and lethal autonomous weapon systems – the chapter demonstrated that ethical failures in AI are not merely technical flaws but social and governance breakdowns. The closing section on Responsible AI underscored the need for multidisciplinary collaboration and proactive design to ensure that AI systems remain lawful, ethical and trustworthy throughout their lifecycle.

Future Outlook

Looking ahead, the governance of AI will increasingly depend on harmonizing international standards while retaining sensitivity to local contexts. The next decade will witness the mainstreaming of algorithmic audits, explainable models and ethical certifications as part of business compliance. The convergence of AI with technologies such as quantum computing and synthetic data will further complicate ethical oversight, demanding adaptive governance capable of responding to dynamic risks. Importantly, ethical AI will shift from being a compliance exercise to a strategic differentiator – companies that embed fairness, privacy and transparency into their business models will enjoy greater stakeholder trust and resilience. Collaboration between regulators, technologists and civil society will remain essential for transforming aspirational ethics into enforceable practice.

Discussion Questions

(1) How can organizations operationalize ethical AI principles such as fairness and transparency in day-to-day decision-making?
(2) In what ways might algorithmic governance mechanisms both empower and constrain human agency?
(3) Should high-risk AI systems – such as those used in policing or housing – be regulated differently from commercial applications like marketing or logistics?
(4) What role should international collaboration play in establishing global AI governance frameworks?
(5) To what extent can Responsible AI become a source of competitive advantage rather than regulatory obligation?

Websites

https://digital-strategy.ec.europa.eu/en/policies/european-approach-artificial-intelligence

https://www.sap.com/resources/what-is-responsible-ai

https://www.informatica.com/resources/articles/ai-governance-explained.html

https://www.accuray.com/blog/overcoming-ai-bias-understanding-identifying-and-mitigating-algorithmic-bias-in-healthcare/

https://publicsafety.ieee.org/topics/ethical-considerations-in-the-use-of-facial-recognition-for-public-safety/

https://www.numberanalytics.com/blog/ethics-of-ai-surveillance

https://aiforgood.itu.int/about-us/un-ai-actions/

https://artificialintelligenceact.eu/

https://www.microsoft.com/insidetrack/blog/responsible-ai-why-it-matters-and-how-were-infusing-it-into-our-internal-ai-projects-at-microsoft/

https://analyticsindiamag.com/ai-features/the-moral-dilemma-of-embedding-ethics-into-autonomous-vehicles/

References

CNN. (2021, April 29). *He was innocent. But a facial recognition 'match' got this Black man arrested.* CNN. https://www.cnn.com/2021/04/29/tech/nijeer-parks-facial-recognition-police-arrest

UK Government. (2023). *Policy paper: A pro-innovation approach to AI regulation.* https://www.gov.uk/government/publications/ai-regulation-a-pro-innovation-approach/white-paper. Accessd on August 30, 2025.

Further Readings

Hagendorff, T. (2020). The ethics of AI ethics: An evaluation of guidelines. *Minds and Machines*, *30*(1), 99–120.

Bostrom, N., & Yudkowsky, E. (2018). The ethics of artificial intelligence. In *Artificial intelligence safety and security* (pp. 57–69). Chapman and Hall/CRC.

Ortega-Bolaños, R., Bernal-Salcedo, J., Germán Ortiz, M., Galeano Sarmiento, J., Ruz, G. A., & Tabares-Soto, R. (2024). Applying the ethics of AI: A systematic review of tools for developing and assessing AI-based systems. *Artificial Intelligence Review*, *57*(5), 110.

Minkkinen, M., Niukkanen, A., & Mäntymäki, M. (2024). What about investors? ESG analyses as tools for ethics-based AI auditing. *AI & Society*, *39*(1), 329–343.

Chapter 11

The Future of AI in Business

AI is not a matter of tomorrow – it is unfolding today. The future belongs to those who are actively learning, experimenting, and building with AI now. AI is no longer optional; **it is essential**.

And so, the question is simple yet profound: **Will you be a bystander – or a builder of the future?**

Case Study: Tesla's Full Self-Driving: Driving Towards an Autonomous Future

Tesla Inc., founded in 2003, is widely recognized as a leader in the electric vehicle (EV) market. However, Tesla's ambition extends far beyond manufacturing electric cars; it envisions a future where transportation is autonomous, intelligent and service-based. Operating within the automotive industry, Tesla has become a disruptor, not only in the EV segment but also in autonomous driving, Artificial Intelligence (AI)-powered software, energy solutions and digital mobility services.

The global automotive industry is undergoing a seismic shift driven by electric mobility, connectivity and automation. With competitors like Waymo, Cruise and traditional automakers developing autonomous vehicles, the race is on to create a fully self-driving car that can navigate complex urban environments without human assistance. Tesla stands apart in this race by relying entirely on computer vision and AI, without using Lidar – a choice that has sparked intense debate within the industry.

The Challenge: Turning Vision Into Safe Autonomy

Tesla's goal of achieving Level 5 autonomy – full self-driving under any conditions – faces several intertwined challenges:

(*Continued*)

AI and Business, 227–253

Published under exclusive licence by Emerald Publishing Limited
doi:10.1108/978-1-83708-888-120261011

(*Continued*)

- Complex Driving Environments: Real-world roads are unpredictable, featuring erratic drivers, poor weather, temporary construction and ambiguous signage.
- Massive AI Training Requirements: Training an AI to handle billions of driving scenarios requires volumes of data, computing power and advanced neural networks.
- Regulatory and Public Trust Issues: Regulators worldwide have raised concerns about safety, transparency and accountability. Tesla has faced criticism over the marketing of 'Full Self-Driving,' given that the system remains in beta.
- Technological Roadblocks: Many competitors use Lidar for precise mapping, but Tesla chose a vision-first approach, arguing that humans drive by vision, not radar or Lidar. This creates a more difficult technical challenge but promises lower costs and easier scalability if successful.

The Solution

Tesla's approach to solving autonomous driving centres on an end-to-end AI-powered vision system:

- Tesla's Full Self-Driving (FSD) software is powered by neural networks trained on billions of miles of real-world driving data, covering diverse road conditions globally.
- Tesla developed Dojo, a custom AI supercomputer designed to train its neural networks faster and more efficiently, processing visual data from its entire vehicle fleet.
- Every Tesla on the road contributes data – capturing road edge cases, mistakes and successful manoeuvres – fuelling a flywheel of continuous AI improvement.
- Tesla's ultimate vision is a robotaxi service where car owners can rent out their autonomous Teslas, transforming the company from a car manufacturer into a mobility platform.

Implementation Strategy

Tesla's implementation strategy departs from the traditional product launch mindset:

- Tesla uses its own customers as beta testers. Its 'FSD Beta' programme grants early access to enthusiasts who drive in real-world conditions, feeding data back to Tesla's servers.
- Unlike most automakers, Tesla controls its entire ecosystem, like, hardware, software, AI models and even semiconductor design, enabling faster, more coordinated AI deployment.
- Tesla's AI doesn't learn from a single region but from drivers across North America, Europe and Asia, allowing it to adapt to global road diversity.

- By focusing exclusively on camera-based data, Tesla simplifies its hardware stack and aims for a scalable, cost-effective global rollout.

Business Impact: Creating a New Mobility Ecosystem

- Tesla anticipates revenue from not just car sales but also from autonomous ride-sharing services and subscriptions to the FSD package, potentially unlocking multi-billion-dollar service revenues.
- By shipping hundreds of thousands of partially autonomous vehicles, Tesla has established itself as a leader in on-road AI.
- Tesla's autonomy narrative is a major driver of its market valuation, positioning the company as a technology platform rather than just a car manufacturer.
- Traditional automakers and tech companies are accelerating their autonomy programs in response to Tesla's progress, shifting industry R&D priorities.
- Tesla has also sparked critical discussions about the safety of releasing beta software for real-world driving, pushing regulators to re-examine AI oversight.

Lessons

- Leverage Data Scale: Tesla's competitive edge lies in its unmatched dataset of real-world driving, proving that data quantity and diversity are essential for scaling AI.
- Vertical Integration Fuels Speed: By owning both hardware and software, Tesla eliminates coordination bottlenecks that slow down AI iteration in traditional companies.
- AI is Iterative, Not Perfect at Launch: Tesla's bold decision to launch imperfect but improving systems highlights that waiting for perfection delays innovation.
- Public–Private Tensions: AI-driven disruption inevitably attracts regulatory scrutiny; proactive engagement is critical but challenging.
- Vision-Led AI is Scalable (But Risky): Eschewing Lidar and relying solely on cameras shows that simplicity can drive scalability but comes with significant technical risks.

Questions to Think About

1. Can Tesla's AI-first approach in a safety-critical industry be applied to other sectors, such as healthcare or finance?
2. What ethical considerations arise when deploying AI that affects human safety, even in beta form?
3. How important is vertical integration for successfully scaling AI initiatives?

(*Continued*)

(*Continued*)

4. What industries beyond transportation might be disrupted by autonomous systems and AI-as-a-Service models?
5. How should regulators balance the need for safety with the need for rapid AI-driven innovation?
6. Will customers accept machines making life-critical decisions in uncertain, real-world scenarios?

Source Note: Based on Publicly Available Data.

1. https://www.youtube.com/watch?v=ODSJsviD_SU
2. https://www.youtube.com/watch?v=j0z4FweCy4M
3. https://www.youtube.com/watch?v=Ucp0TTmvqOE
4. Tesla Annual Report: https://ir.tesla.com/#quarterly-disclosure
5. https://electrek.co/guides/tesla-autopilot/
6. https://www.cnbc.com/video/2024/10/10/tesla-robotaxis-will-be-a-game-changer-says-wedbushs-dan-ives.html?

As AI becomes a core driver of business strategy, organizations must look beyond today's applications and prepare for tomorrow's possibilities. This chapter explores how AI is shaping the future of business – from the rise of AI-driven innovation and autonomous systems to the evolving regulatory landscape and the global race for AI leadership. It challenges readers to shift from thinking of AI as a tool for efficiency to viewing it as a catalyst for entirely new business models, competitive strategies and industries. In doing so, the chapter offers a roadmap for how forward-thinking companies can anticipate change, harness emerging AI trends and build sustainable, responsible and innovative AI-powered businesses.

Anticipating the Next AI Frontier

The opening case of Tesla's pursuit of Full Self-Driving systems illustrates a profound truth: the future of AI in business is not something distant and hypothetical – it is unfolding in real time, through the ambitions, innovations and experiments of today's organizations. Tesla's efforts to create autonomous vehicles are not only reshaping transportation but also redefining how we think about AI's role in core business models.

The journey of A in business began decades ago with **rules-based automation** and predictive analytics. Initially confined to data processing and statistical modelling, AI evolved through advancements in machine learning, natural language processing and computer vision. Early adopters focused on automating repetitive tasks, such as fraud detection in banking or personalization in e-commerce. These applications delivered efficiency gains, but AI's role was largely supportive – enhancing existing processes rather than transforming business models.

Today, however, AI is entering a new era where it is no longer a back-end optimization tool. It is becoming a front-line decision-maker, innovator and market creator. Businesses are no longer asking how AI can improve what they already do; they are asking what entirely new possibilities AI can unlock. As AI shifts from task automation to autonomous decision-making and creative problem-solving, it is reshaping industries ranging from healthcare and retail to logistics and energy.

Why Anticipating Future AI Trends Matters

For business leaders, anticipating future AI trends is not optional – it is a matter of competitive survival. Companies that merely react to today's AI capabilities will find themselves permanently behind the innovation curve, much like firms that underestimated the transformative power of the internet, cloud computing or mobile technologies. Anticipating AI's next frontier allows companies to:

(1) Prepare for business model disruption: Whether it's autonomous transportation, AI-generated product design or predictive maintenance services, AI is changing what customers expect and how value is created.
(2) Build strategic agility: Fast followers often struggle to retrofit AI into rigid processes, while innovators integrate AI into their core strategy and culture from the outset.
(3) Create future-ready workforces: The rise of AI changes the roles, skills and leadership competencies required in organizations.

Ultimately, companies that timely anticipate AI's trajectory will lead the market, and those that wait for certainty may never catch up.

Emerging Drivers of the Future AI Landscape

Though multiple forces are accelerating the next wave of AI transformation, here are several prime forces which are profoundly affecting the adoption of AI:

- Technological Maturity: Advances in large language models (LLMs), computer vision, reinforcement learning and edge AI are making once-futuristic applications commercially viable. Custom-built AI infrastructure – such as Tesla's Dojo supercomputer or Google's TPU– is further lowering the barriers to AI scalability.
- Evolving User Expectations: Consumers and businesses alike now expect hyper-personalized, instantaneous and intelligent experiences. In industries from fashion retail to healthcare diagnostics, customers no longer distinguish between 'digital' and 'AI-driven' – they clusters simply expect smarter, more predictive services.

- Economic and Competitive Imperatives: The economic potential of AI is vast. IDC projects trillions of dollars in incremental business value through AI-driven products and services. Simultaneously, the rise of AI-first competitors and platform ecosystems is pressuring incumbents to innovate or risk irrelevance.

The question before businesses is no longer 'when will AI impact us?' but rather 'how will we shape its impact today, for the business of tomorrow?'

Fig. 11.1 illustrates three foundational drivers that fuel AI's rapid advancement in business. Technological maturity creates the infrastructure for commercially viable AI solutions. User expectations shape the demand for personalized, seamless and intelligent services. Economic imperatives drive organizations to innovate continually to stay competitive. Together, these forces act as the 'fuel cells' powering AI's evolving role from a support function to a strategic growth enabler.

AI-Driven Innovation and/or AI-as-a-Service (AIaaS)

The future of AI in business will not be defined just by smarter algorithms or faster computing power. It will be shaped by how companies rethink their business models, creating values, revenue streams and customer relationships. AI is no longer a behind-the-scenes operational tool; it is now a front-line driver of product design, service delivery and customer experience innovation. A powerful example of this transformation is the rise of AIaaS platforms, which enable

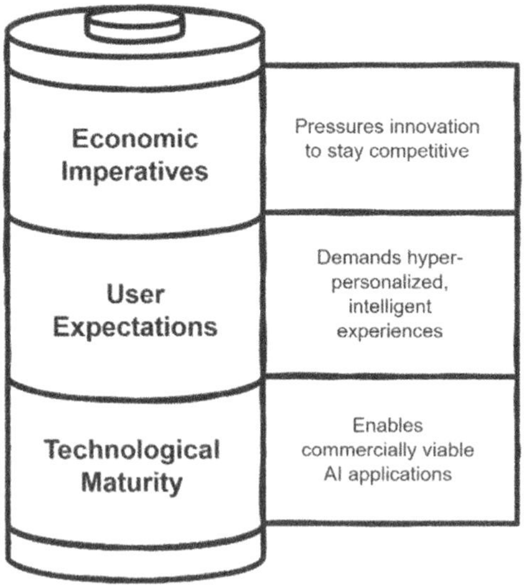

Fig. 11.1. The Core Drivers Powering the Future of AI in Business.

businesses of all sizes to access advanced AI capabilities without developing them in-house. What cloud computing did for IT infrastructure, AIaaS is now doing for intelligence – lowering entry barriers, democratizing innovation and accelerating adoption across industries.

But beyond enabling access, AI is transforming the very architecture of business models. Companies are moving from selling products to delivering intelligent services and creating adaptive, data-driven customer experiences. This shift can be understood across three key archetypes of AI-driven business models.

The Rise of AI-Driven Business Models

The integration of AI is inspiring a profound shift in how companies create, deliver and capture value. Instead of simply applying AI to automate back-end processes, forward-thinking firms are embedding intelligence directly into their products, services and customer experiences. This has led to the emergence of new business models where AI is not an add-on feature, but the core enabler of the offering itself.

These models broadly fall into categories such as smart products-as-a-service, data-as-a-service and process-as-a-service, each demonstrating how AI transforms traditional value chains into continuously evolving, intelligent ecosystems.

Smart Products-as-a-Service

Traditional products are being infused with AI to become dynamic, self-improving services. Consider Siemens, whose industrial machinery now integrates predictive maintenance algorithms, enabling equipment to monitor its own health and schedule servicing before a breakdown occurs. Customers no longer buy machines; they subscribe to uptime and operational continuity.

In the mobility space, Uber leverages AI for adaptive pricing, adjusting fares in real-time based on demand, traffic and competitor activity. This AI-driven dynamic pricing transforms ride-hailing from a transactional service into a constantly optimized marketplace.

Streaming giant Netflix offers another example. Its content recommendation algorithms use AI to deliver hyper-personalized viewing experiences, keeping users engaged and reducing churn. The product is no longer just the content itself but the personalization layer that curates it.

Data-as-a-Service

AI-driven businesses are increasingly treating proprietary data as a monetizable asset. Companies like Thomson Reuters and Experian aggregate, refine and license industry-specific data sets that power other organizations' analytics, credit decisions or compliance efforts. In this model, the business becomes a data refinery – processing raw information into actionable intelligence sold to partners and competitors alike.

As AI models require continuous learning from diverse data sources, companies that control niche, high-quality data will command new forms of strategic advantage.

Process-as-a-Service

Beyond products and data, AI is now enabling the servitization of business processes. Hyperautomation platforms such as UiPath and Automation Anywhere provide enterprises with robotic process automation (RPA) bots and AI modules that automate repetitive workflows – from invoice processing to compliance checks.

Instead of hiring staff to perform these tasks or build custom software, companies can subscribe to intelligent processes delivered via the cloud. This radically lowers the cost of automation, allowing even mid-sized firms to streamline operations with AI-powered agility.

These examples represent just the first wave of AI-driven business models. As AI capabilities continue to evolve, we will see businesses invent entirely new 'as-a-service' categories, where the boundaries between products, platforms and services blur. In such a world, the true product is not the software or hardware itself, but the continuous stream of intelligence and outcomes it delivers.

AIaaS: Democratizing Access to AI

For decades, artificial intelligence was the exclusive domain of large technology companies and specialized research teams. Developing advanced AI systems required rare technical talent, costly infrastructure and years of experimentation. But with the rise of AIaaS platforms, this paradigm has changed dramatically.

Today, businesses across industries – whether a healthcare startup, a logistics company or a retail brand – can access cutting-edge AI tools through cloud platforms, Application Programming Interface (APIs) and plug-and-play modules. Microsoft Azure AI, Google Cloud AI and Amazon Web Services (AWS) lead this democratization, offering scalable machine learning models, vision recognition services and conversational AI engines on a subscription basis. What once required an army of data scientists is now available on demand-often through just a few lines of code.

Beyond general-purpose platforms, AIaaS is evolving into industry-specific solutions. In financial services, for instance, startups use prebuilt fraud detection models to secure digital payments without developing algorithms from scratch. In customer service, AIaaS chatbots handle millions of support tickets, allowing companies to deploy conversational interfaces without building their natural language processing (NLP) models. Even more transformative is the API-first economy, where companies integrate AI capabilities into their products in hours rather than months. Whether it's face recognition in security apps, sentiment analysis in marketing platforms or route optimization in delivery apps, these

AIaaS offerings act as modular intelligence layers, ready to be embedded wherever needed.

This democratization is levelling the playing field. Previously, only tech giants could afford to run complex AI workloads on custom-built hardware. Today, a small startup in Bangalore or Berlin can build AI-powered solutions by renting compute power, pre-trained models and developer tools from cloud providers. The barriers to entry for AI innovation have been dramatically reduced.

However, AIaaS is not just a technical convenience – it is becoming a business model enabler. Companies are rethinking their value propositions by offering intelligence as part of their service portfolio, creating new revenue streams through subscription-based AI features. Looking ahead, AIaaS will continue to evolve beyond individual tools towards end-to-end solutions. Future AIaaS platforms will offer business-ready modules for entire processes – such as dynamic pricing optimization, customer churn prediction or supply chain forecasting – making it easier for businesses to adopt AI without deep technical expertise.

In this way, AIaaS is not only democratizing access to AI technologies but also reshaping the global competitive landscape, allowing businesses of all sizes to compete with intelligence-driven agility.

Table 11.1 illustrates how AIaaS models enable diverse industries to embed intelligence into their core operations. Rather than building AI from scratch, companies are adopting ready-to-integrate AI services, unlocking new revenue streams, operational efficiencies and customer experiences across sectors.

Innovative Case Snapshots: Tales of AI in Action

The future of AI in business is not a distant vision – it is already being written in boardrooms, factories and customer journeys around the world. The following cases illustrate how leading companies are crafting the next chapter of AI-driven business innovation, each with its own unique ambition and execution.

1. A New Kind of Teammate: Industrial Copilots by Siemens and Microsoft

Picture a factory floor buzzing with the hum of machines and the click of keyboards. In this space, human engineers and AI copilots work side by side. Siemens and Microsoft are reimagining industrial productivity through Industrial Copilots – AI-powered assistants embedded within manufacturing operations.

These copilots analyze equipment data in real time, predict when machines will need maintenance and even recommend optimization strategies for production lines. Instead of passively monitoring dashboards, workers now engage in a dynamic conversation with AI, asking questions like: 'How can we improve throughput by 10% today?' The answers arrive in seconds,

(*Continued*)

(*Continued*)

backed by machine learning models and industrial data lakes. In this story, AI is no longer the operator in the shadows – it is the co-pilot in the cockpit.

Sources:

https://www.siemens.com/global/en/products/automation/topic-areas/industrial-ai/industrial-copilot.html
https://news.microsoft.com/source/2024/10/24/siemens-and-microsoft-scale-industrial-ai/
https://news.microsoft.com/source/2023/10/31/siemens-and-microsoft-partner-to-drive-cross-industry-ai-adoption/
https://newsroom.sw.siemens.com/en-US/siemens-microsoft-ai/

2. AI in the Doctor's Office: Healthcare Bots for Diagnostics

Imagine walking into a healthcare clinic, but instead of waiting for hours to see a doctor, you start your visit with a smart diagnostic assistant. Across hospitals and digital health platforms, AI-powered chatbots and virtual assistants are reshaping patient journeys. These bots collect symptoms, analyze medical histories and cross-reference vast clinical databases to suggest possible diagnoses – long before the physician enters the room.

In countries facing physician shortages, these bots act as frontline caregivers, conducting triage, booking appointments and even recommending lifestyle interventions. This is not science fiction – it is the present reality in digital health ecosystems, where AI bridges the gap between growing healthcare demands and limited human resources.

3. Personalizing Retail, One Consumer at a Time: Victoria's Secret and Swarovski

The age-old art of retail has found a new muse: AI. Brands like Victoria's Secret and Swarovski are using AI-powered personalization engines to create shopping experiences that feel handcrafted for each customer.

Behind the scenes, AI analyzes browsing behaviour, purchase patterns and style preferences to recommend the right products, at the right moment, through the right channel. What once required personal stylists and boutique-level service is now being delivered at global scale – whether online, in-app or in-store. For these brands, the future of retail is not about inventory; it is about intimacy at scale, powered by algorithms.

Sources:

https://www.victoriassecretandco.com/news-releases/news-release-details/victorias-secret-co-create-new-ai-powered-shopping-experiences

https://www.centricsoftware.com/blog/how-ai-is-driving-hyper-personalized-shopping-experiences/
https://cloud.google.com/transform/victorias-secret-gen-ai-digital-retail-customer-experience
https://blog.google/products/google-cloud/victorias-secret-google-cloud-ai/

4. The AI Concierge of the Workplace: Moveworks in IT and HR

In the fast-paced world of digital workplaces, where employees juggle dozens of tools and platforms, Moveworks has introduced an AI-driven concierge. Instead of filing IT tickets or emailing HR for policy questions, employees now chat with an AI assistant embedded in Microsoft Teams or Slack.

The bot resets passwords, unlocks accounts, answers HR queries and routes complex issues to the right teams – all autonomously. What was once a source of frustration for employees is now a seamless, conversational experience. Moveworks demonstrates how enterprise AI is moving from the server room to employee's daily workflow, quietly improving productivity one request at a time.

Sources:

https://www.moveworks.com/us/en/resources/blog/how-ai-has-changed-hr-for-the-better
https://www.moveworks.com/us/en/solutions/ai-for-hr

The Bigger Picture

These are not isolated success stories. They are glimpses of an AI-powered business world where machines don't just automate tasks – they empower people, personalize experiences and reinvent industries. Each case reflects a broader truth: the future belongs to businesses bold enough to reimagine what they offer, how they deliver it and whom they serve – with AI as their creative partner.

AI as a Strategic Decision Partner

For decades, AI was seen as a tool for operational efficiency – automating routine tasks and crunching large datasets faster than humans could. But the next frontier of AI is much more ambitious: becoming a strategic partner in decision-making, helping leaders solve complex business problems, explore new markets and prepare for uncertain futures.

No longer confined to back-office analytics, AI is now supporting frontline strategy discussions, offering scenario models, simulations and real-time insights that help executives make better, faster and smarter choices.

Table 11.1. AI-as-a-Service Business Models Across Key Industries and Use Cases.

Industry Sector	AIaaS Application Areas	Example Use Cases	Leading Platforms/Players
Manufacturing	Predictive maintenance, process optimization, quality inspection	AI models that predict equipment failure, optimize energy use or detect defects	Siemens MindSphere, IBM Maximo, Azure IoT
Retail and E-commerce	Personalization engines, dynamic pricing, recommendation systems	Real-time product recommendations, automated promotions, pricing adjustments	Salesforce Einstein, AWS personalize, Google retail AI
Healthcare	Diagnostic AI, patient engagement, workflow automation	AI-driven radiology insights, patient triage bots, automated appointment booking	IBM Watson health, Google health AI, Microsoft cloud for healthcare
Financial services	Fraud detection, credit scoring, robo-advisory	Real-time transaction monitoring, automated loan approvals, AI investment advisors	FICO, Zest AI, Amazon fraud detector
Logistics and supply chain	Demand forecasting, route optimization, warehouse robotics	AI-powered shipment routing, inventory management, real-time logistics insights	Blue Yonder, Manhattan associates, Google cloud supply chain
Human resources and IT	Chatbots, ticket resolution, talent analytics	Automated HR query handling, IT support ticket closure, AI-driven hiring recommendations	Moveworks, ServiceNow, Oracle HCM AI
Energy and Utilities	Smart grid optimization, predictive asset management	AI predicting energy consumption patterns, optimizing energy storage	GE digital, Schneider electric EcoStruxure, Azure energy AI

Shifting From Human-Centric to AI-Augmented Strategy

Traditionally, strategic decisions were driven by human experience, intuition and fragmented data points compiled into reports. But in a world of continuous disruption, this approach is no longer sufficient. AI enables businesses to simulate countless 'what-if' scenarios in real-time, weighing trade-offs that would overwhelm human cognition.

In financial services, for example, AI-powered portfolio management tools forecast market shifts and optimize investment allocations in response to changing global conditions. In retail, AI anticipates shifts in consumer sentiment and inventory dynamics, helping leaders plan product launches and pricing strategies with greater confidence.

But this shift is not about replacing human decision-makers. Instead, it is about augmenting human judgement with machine precision. McKinsey refers to this as the emergence of the 'superagency' – organizations where human creativity and AI work together to drive breakthrough performance.

Superagency: Empowering Humans With AI

The concept of superagency redefines the roles of leadership teams. In this model, AI is not a silent engine in the background; it is an active participant in strategic conversations. Whether it's assessing the risks of entering a new market or modelling the impact of supply chain disruptions, AI brings data-driven clarity to boardroom decisions.

Consider how companies are using large language models (LLMs) like GPT and Claude to analyze thousands of market research reports, social media conversations and economic forecasts, synthesizing them into concise, actionable briefs for executives. What once took weeks of analyst work now happens in minutes. This human–AI partnership enables businesses to:

- Make more confident decisions in fast-moving markets.
- Challenge assumptions with evidence-based insights.
- Free leadership time from routine analysis to focus on creative, long-term thinking.

Of course, the effectiveness of AI as a strategic partner depends on data quality, model transparency and human oversight. AI can surface patterns and possibilities, but the ultimate responsibility for decision-making – and its ethical implications – still rests with human leaders.

In the future, the most successful companies will be those that cultivate leaders who are not just technologically literate but strategically fluent in working with AI. These organizations will use AI not only to optimize the present but to invent the future.

Preparing for Future AI Trends: Responsible and Sustainable Growth

Preparing for the future of AI in business requires more than technological upgrades. It demands a strategic mindset shift towards responsible innovation, sustainable growth and ethical governance. As highlighted in recent studies from McKinsey (2025), IDC (2024) and PwC (2025), organizations that proactively engage with AI's emerging trends – while embedding trust and transparency – are better positioned to lead the next wave of business transformation.

Future Trends Shaping AI in Business

According to McKinsey's State of AI Report (2025) and IDC's AI Opportunity Study (2024), several key trends are redefining how businesses will adopt and expand AI in the coming years:

- **Generative and Agentic AI:** Beyond chatbots and content creation, generative AI is now powering product design, legal analysis and autonomous workflows. Companies like Salesforce (with Agentforce) and OpenAI (with GPT agents) are embedding AI into the core of work processes.
- **Edge AI and Next-Gen Infrastructure:** As per McKinsey, the demand for AI-optimized data centres is growing at 30–33% annually, driven by the need for edge computing, latency reduction and cost optimization.
- **Quantum-AI Convergence:** McKinsey and Morgan Stanley forecast that quantum computing, when combined with AI, will unlock breakthroughs in complex optimization and drug discovery, offering multibillion-dollar market potential.
- **Sustainability in Focus:** AI's rising energy demands are prompting businesses to invest in green data centres powered by renewables. South Australia, for example, is planning 'hyperscale' renewable-powered AI hubs to meet this demand sustainably.

Responsible AI and Governance

Trust is the foundation of sustainable AI growth. As PwC's AI Predictions (2025) report highlights, organizations that lead in AI governance outperform their peers in adoption rates, innovation velocity and stakeholder trust. Leading practices in Responsible AI include:

- **Governance Structures:** Establishing Chief AI Ethics Officers and dedicated AI oversight committees.
- **Transparency Reporting:** Publishing explainability, bias and privacy metrics, as seen in Microsoft's and Google's AI transparency reports.
- **Risk Mitigation:** Deploying robust model validation and monitoring to detect drift, bias and unintended consequences.

Despite these best practices, Deloitte's recent surveys reveal that fewer than 10% of global organizations have mature AI risk frameworks in place – an alarming gap that must be addressed.

Building Future-Ready Workforces

Technology alone is insufficient. Businesses must cultivate AI fluency across leadership, operations and frontline teams. According to IDC (2024), over 60% of companies cite talent shortages as the biggest barrier to AI scaling. In response, nations and businesses are launching large-scale upskilling programmes in AI, quantum and robotics.

Equally critical is cultural transformation. Future-ready firms foster a learning mindset, cross-functional collaboration and openness to AI-human partnership – hallmarks of McKinsey's 'superagency' model.

Aligning AI With ESG Priorities

Sustainability is becoming a core lens through which AI strategies are evaluated. The environmental footprint of training large models is non-trivial; by some estimates, deep learning could consume nearly 0.5% of global electricity by 2027. Forward-looking companies are now:

- Investing in energy-efficient AI infrastructure and renewable-powered data centres.
- Integrating AI's carbon impact into ESG reporting.
- Using AI to optimize energy consumption, waste reduction and circular economy models.

ESG-AI alignment is not only a compliance issue, it is an opportunity to differentiate through purpose-driven innovation.

Is Your Business Ready for the Future of AI?

As AI continues to shape the future of industries, organizations must evaluate not only their technological investments but also their readiness in terms of governance, culture, sustainability and strategic foresight. This quick check is designed to help you reflect on your organization's AI preparedness across key dimensions highlighted in industry research (McKinsey, IDC, Deloitte, 2025).

It is not an exhaustive audit but a rapid pulse check to identify areas where you are strong and where you may need to strengthen your focus.

(*Continued*)

(*Continued*)

How to Use This Quick Check

For each statement below, assign your organization a score:

✔ Fully Achieved (2 points)
~ In Progress/Partial (1 point)
× Not Yet Started (0 points)
After completing all items, add your total score and refer to the interpretation section below.

AI Readiness Checklist

Score	Area	Readiness Question
	1. AI Governance and ethics	Do we have an AI governance framework with clear accountability, transparency standards and ethical risk policies in place?
	2. Responsible AI deployment	Are we implementing explainability tools, bias monitoring and compliance reporting in our AI systems?
	3. AI skills and Workforce readiness	Are we reskilling our workforce for AI, data literacy and automation competencies across all levels of the organization?
	4. Sustainability and ESG Alignment	Do we measure and mitigate the environmental and social impacts of our AI infrastructure and processes?
	5. Scalable and sustainable technology infrastructure	Have we invested in energy-efficient, future-ready AI platforms and data infrastructure (including cloud and edge solutions)?
	6. Future trends awareness	Are we actively tracking and preparing for emerging trends like generative AI, agentic AI, edge computing and quantum-AI convergence?

(Continued)

Score	Area	Readiness Question
	7. Regulatory and Geopolitical readiness	Do we have processes in place to track global AI regulations and anticipate geopolitical risks impacting AI trade and operations?

Interpreting Your Results

Score Range	AI Readiness Level	What It Means for Your Business
11–14	Future-ready leader	You have a proactive, strategic approach to AI. Your organization is positioned to lead in AI-powered innovation and sustainability. Focus on continuous improvement and sharing best practices.
7–10	Emerging practitioner	You are making progress but still have key gaps to address. Prioritize areas where AI governance, sustainability or technology readiness are incomplete. Accelerate leadership engagement and strategic alignment.
0–6	At risk of falling behind	Your AI readiness is limited and likely reactive. Immediate focus is needed on building governance frameworks, upskilling your workforce and investing in sustainable AI platforms. Consider partnerships or advisory support.

Suggested Next Steps

- Conduct a deeper AI maturity assessment.
- Develop an action roadmap aligned with your business strategy.
- Engage leadership teams to close gaps across governance, skills and infrastructure.
- Monitor AI trends quarterly and adjust your strategy proactively.

Preparing for the future of AI is not just a technical endeavour. It is a leadership challenge – one that demands vision, agility and responsibility. As the next sections will show, these principles must be embedded in the strategic roadmap of every business seeking to thrive in the AI-powered future.

Strategic Roadmap for Future-Ready Businesses

Preparing for the future of AI is not about one-time investments or isolated pilot projects. It requires an ongoing, strategic commitment to embedding AI into the core of business models, leadership mindsets and organizational capabilities.

Leaders who take a structured, future-focused approach to AI will not only adapt to the next wave of technological change but will shape the industries they operate in. The roadmap ahead calls for clarity of vision, disciplined experimentation and a sustained focus on ethics and responsibility.

Strategic Imperatives for Business Leaders

Before leaders can set their organizations on a future-ready AI journey, they must first align their strategic intent with the evolving realities of AI. It is no longer enough to treat AI as an isolated technology project. Instead, it should be viewed as a transformational force that will shape how companies create value, compete in their industries and define their customer relationships. With this broader perspective, leaders must craft a vision that integrates AI into the heart of business strategy, not as an add-on but as a core driver of future growth and resilience.

Crafting a Future-Ready AI Vision

The first imperative is to develop a clear, actionable AI vision that aligns with your broader business strategy. This vision should articulate how AI will contribute to revenue growth, operational resilience, customer experience and competitive positioning. Without this alignment, AI risks becoming fragmented across functions, disconnected from enterprise value creation.

Balancing Experimentation and Scalability

Future-ready businesses must strike a balance between agile experimentation and scalable deployment. Experimentation allows teams to test new AI use cases, learn fast and pivot as needed. But without a pathway to scale – whether through cloud platforms, internal AI centres of excellence or robust governance – AI will remain trapped in isolated pilots that never deliver meaningful impact.

Investing in Ethical, Responsible and Sustainable AI

Finally, leaders must embed ethical and environmental considerations into their AI strategy from the start. This means investing in bias mitigation, privacy-preserving technologies, transparent algorithms and green compute solutions. Responsible AI is not a regulatory box-ticking exercise – it is a driver of long-term trust and brand reputation.

Practical Steps Forward

Turning strategic intent into tangible results requires clear, practical actions. Future-ready businesses move beyond vision statements to build the internal capabilities, partnerships and learning cultures needed to operationalize AI across the organization. This next section outlines actionable steps to help leaders translate strategy into sustained AI-driven impact.

Build Internal AI Capabilities and Ecosystems

Future-ready companies don't outsource their AI strategy. They build internal teams, platforms and data ecosystems that enable continuous AI development. This includes cultivating AI product managers, Machine Learning Operations (MLOps) engineers and data governance specialists who can translate AI strategy into scalable solutions.

At the same time, businesses must break down silos between technical and business teams, creating cross-functional AI squads that align technology with business value.

Partner With AI Innovators and Academia

No company can master AI alone. Strategic partnerships with AI startups, technology providers and academic researchers accelerate innovation and close capability gaps. Many industry leaders co-create new AI solutions with startups or fund applied AI research in areas like explainability, healthcare AI or sustainable computing.

These collaborations allow companies to stay at the cutting edge of AI developments without shouldering the entire burden of R&D themselves.

Embrace Continuous Learning and Regulatory Monitoring

The AI landscape is evolving faster than most regulatory frameworks. Future-ready businesses invest in continuous learning programmes that keep leadership and frontline teams up to date on AI trends, tools and risks.

They also develop proactive regulatory monitoring capabilities, ensuring that AI deployments comply with emerging global standards such as the EU AI Act, U.S. state-level regulations and sector-specific compliance requirements.

A strategic AI roadmap is not a static plan; it is a dynamic capability. The companies that thrive in the AI-powered future will be those that can learn faster, adapt smarter and act with ethical purpose. AI maturity will no longer be measured solely by technology adoption but by how well organizations integrate AI into their vision, culture and systems of accountability.

Industry Leaders on AI's Future in Business: Shaping the Narrative

Understanding the future of AI in business requires listening to those who are leading its development and deployment. Before exploring their insights, it is important to reflect on why these industry perspectives matter – and how they help shape our understanding of what lies ahead.

Why Industry Perspectives Matter

The future of AI in business is not being shaped in isolation – it is being actively envisioned, debated and executed by industry leaders across sectors. These are the voices of those building the AI platforms, deploying them at scale and steering their industries through unprecedented change. Their insights are vital because they move beyond technical possibilities to focus on practical strategies, human impacts and ethical considerations.

From my perspective, understanding what these leaders foresee is essential for students, managers and business strategists alike. It helps ground the discussion of AI's future in real-world strategic thinking, not speculative fiction. Importantly, it reminds us that AI is neither utopian nor dystopian by nature; its trajectory depends on how thoughtfully we lead its adoption.

This section highlights recent viewpoints from tech giants, financial leaders and global strategists, drawn from TEDx talks, interviews, podcasts and industry reports between 2023 and 2025. These are summarized insights, designed to inspire critical thinking about where AI is headed next (Table 11.2).

Table 11.2. Key Industry Perspectives: A Cross-Sector Snapshot.

Leader	Company	Industry Segment	Viewpoint on AI's Future in Business
Sam Altman[a]	OpenAI	AI research	Predicts a future where AI agents autonomously perform cognitive work, increasing productivity and reshaping business operations.
Marc Benioff[b]	Salesforce	Enterprise software	Argues that AI is transforming teams, with many operational tasks already handled by AI, enabling human workers to focus on creativity and strategy.

Table 11.2. *(Continued)*

Leader	Company	Industry Segment	Viewpoint on AI's Future in Business
Jamie Dimon[c]	JPMorgan chase	Finance and banking	Believes AI will augment nearly every financial role and foresees a future where AI-driven workflows dominate banking operations.
Jensen Huang[d]	Nvidia	Semiconductors and AI	Envisions a future where every worker has an AI co-pilot, enhancing creativity, efficiency and complex problem-solving.
Andy Jassy[e]	Amazon	Cloud and retail	Sees AI as the most transformative technology of our lifetime, urging companies to adopt AI aggressively to stay competitive.
Arvind Krishna[f]	IBM	IT services and AI	States that AI is moving from hype to business value, with CEOs focusing on scaling AI agents and data architectures for sustainable growth.
Satya Nadella[g]	Microsoft	Software and cloud	Predicts AI agents will fundamentally change how enterprises interact with data, shifting from apps to autonomous agent-driven experiences.
Sundar Pichai[h]	Google	Internet and platforms	Believes AI will create net positive outcomes in work, increasing human productivity and driving new waves of innovation and job creation.

[a]https://www.inc.com/ben-sherry/sam-altman-says-ai-agents-will-transform-the-workforce-in-2025/91103146

[b]https://www.inc.com/kit-eaton/salesforces-ceo-just-said-ai-now-does-half-of-all-company-tasks/91208114

[c]https://www.jpmorganchase.com/ir/annual-report/2023/ar-ceo-letters

[d]https://www.crn.com/news/ai/2024/6-bold-statements-by-nvidia-ceo-jensen-huang-on-ai-s-future

[e]https://www.itpro.com/business/business-strategy/amazon-ceo-andy-jassy-ai-job-cuts

[f]https://www.cio.inc/ibm-ceo-says-ai-now-about-unlocking-business-value-a-28380

[g]https://opusresearch.net/2025/01/07/2025-the-end-of-enterprise-saas-as-we-know-it/

[h]https://opusresearch.net/2025/01/07/2025-the-end-of-enterprise-saas-as-we-know-it/

What These Views Tell Us About the Future

Across industries, some clear themes emerge from these leaders' perspectives:

(1) **AI is Already in Action:** These are not future plans but present realities. AI agents, copilots and predictive models are already transforming workflows in tech, finance, retail and logistics.
(2) **A Shift Towards Autonomy:** The future of business is moving from simple automation to autonomous, decision-making systems that work alongside or independently of humans.
(3) **Strategic Urgency:** Leaders consistently warn that AI is a now-or-never moment – businesses that wait risk falling permanently behind.
(4) **Human + AI Partnership:** Despite automation, these leaders emphasize human creativity, ethics and strategy as critical differentiators in an AI-powered world.

This quadrant chart visually maps the dominant themes identified by global industry leaders in their discussions about the future of AI in business. The vertical axis represents the emphasis placed by industry leaders, ranging from low to high, while the horizontal axis reflects key industry themes, spanning from human–AI partnership to full autonomy. The four quadrants (Fig. 11.2) capture the major narratives shaping AI's evolution in business:

Together, these themes highlight how industry leaders are simultaneously focused on driving technological autonomy and fostering meaningful human–AI collaboration, while maintaining a sense of urgency about preparing for the future.

This discussion highlights that the future of AI in business is already being built – and debated – by today's leaders. While their industries differ, their message is clear: AI is not an optional upgrade but a strategic imperative. For

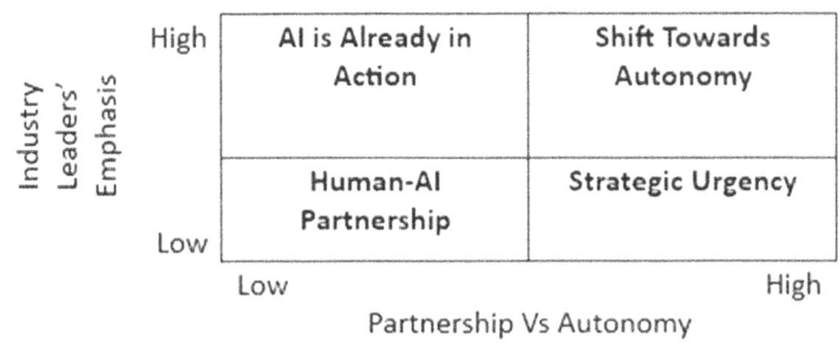

Fig. 11.2. Industry Perspectives on AI's Future – Key Themes and Emphases.

business professionals, the takeaway is not to copy what these giants do but to understand how they think:

- Adopt AI with a clear vision, not blind enthusiasm.
- Balance efficiency gains with responsible leadership.
- Prepare your teams, culture and strategies for continuous AI evolution.

The future will belong to businesses that are not just using AI tools but building AI-ready mindsets.

Chapter Summary

This chapter explored how AI is transforming the future of business, not as a distant possibility but as an active, unfolding reality. Beginning with Tesla's pursuit of full autonomy, we examined how AI-driven innovation is creating new business models, shifting from product sales to intelligent services and empowering autonomous systems across industries.

The chapter highlighted how AI is democratizing intelligence through AIaaS, allowing businesses of all sizes to access powerful AI tools. Crucially, AI is no longer confined to back-office automation; it is becoming a strategic decision partner, shaping market simulations, scenario planning and executive-level decision-making. Future-ready companies are embedding AI into their leadership mindsets, organizational culture and business ecosystems. The chapter concludes with a cross-sector perspective from global industry leaders, showing that AI is already transforming workflows, creating autonomous systems and shifting the competitive landscape. Also to figure out the industry specific futuristic AI trend map, refer Appendix A and a template is added to the strategic AI adoption path in Appendix B.

Future Outlook

Looking ahead, the future of AI in business will be defined by those who take action now. The convergence of generative AI, autonomous systems, quantum-AI integration and ethical governance will create new opportunities – and risks – that businesses must navigate. Key priorities for the future include:

- Scaling responsibly: Building AI systems that are ethical, transparent and aligned with ESG goals.
- Driving autonomy: Moving from simple automation to intelligent, self-improving systems that transform industries.
- Shaping global leadership: Anticipating and influencing AI governance frameworks and geopolitical shifts.
- Empowering people: Cultivating superagency workplaces where human creativity and AI intelligence drive shared success.

The ultimate question remains: Will your business passively experience the future of AI – or actively shape it? To conclude, this chapter closes with the reminder:

> The future of AI in business is not written by algorithms but by those bold enough to harness them with purpose, responsibility, and vision.

Discussion Questions

(1) How can business leaders move beyond incremental automation to craft a truly future-ready AI strategy?
(2) What leadership qualities and organizational mindsets are most important for navigating AI-driven business transformation?
(3) In what ways are AIaaS and data-driven business models democratizing innovation across industries?
(4) How can businesses proactively close gaps in AI governance, risk management and compliance readiness?
(5) What are the limits of AI in strategic decision-making, and how should human oversight be maintained?
(6) How might the convergence of quantum computing and AI change current AI strategies?

Further Readings

IDC Corporate. (2024, October 24). *IDC Unveils 2025 FutureScapes: Worldwide IT industry predictions*. https://my.idc.com/getdoc.jsp?containerId=prUS52691924

Kaurav, R. P. S. (2025, March). *AI is making roads safer: Here's how it's preventing accidents before they happen" future mobility media*. https://heyzine.com/flip-book/e1e9143017.html#page/38

Microsoft. (2025, April 22). *How real-world businesses are transforming with AI — with 261 new stories*. https://blogs.microsoft.com/blog/2025/04/22/https-blogs-microsoft-com-blog-2024-11-12-how-real-world-businesses-are-transforming-with-ai/

Mollick, E. (2024). *Co-intelligence: Living and working with AI*. Penguin Publishing Group.

Roetzer, P., & Kaput, M. (2022). *Marketing artificial intelligence: AI, marketing, and the future of business*. Matt Holt.

Wurth, E. (2025, May 13). *Leaders must move fast to close the AI trust gap*. https://www.theaustralian.com.au/business/tech-journal/leaders-must-move-fast-to-close-the-ai-trust-gap/news-story/6959fb8a47fda51acb30093fd18d5fec

Appendix A: Industry-Specific AI Trend Map (2025–2030)

Industry	Key Emerging AI Trends (2025–2030)	Expected Impact	Adoption Outlook
Automotive & Mobility	Autonomous vehicles, AI for traffic optimization, predictive fleet management	Disruption of mobility services; shift to robotaxis	High
Healthcare	AI-assisted diagnostics, personalized treatment plans, AI for clinical trials	Improved patient outcomes; new service models	Very high
Retail & E-commerce	Generative AI for hyper-personalization, demand forecasting, intelligent search	Personalized shopping at scale	High
Manufacturing	AI-driven predictive maintenance, digital twins, autonomous production planning	Reduced downtime, enhanced quality	High
Financial Services	AI for fraud detection, autonomous trading, AI in risk management	Faster, smarter financial operations	Very high
Logistics & Supply Chain	Autonomous warehouses, AI route optimization, demand sensing	Fully automated supply chain orchestration	High
Energy & Utilities	Smart grid optimization, AI for energy trading, predictive asset maintenance	Energy efficiency, reduced outages	Moderate to high
Education	Personalized learning platforms, automated grading, AI tutors	Enhanced learning experiences	Moderate
Public Sector & Governance	AI for citizen services, predictive policing, smart cities planning	Improved service delivery, social risks	Moderate

Appendix B: Strategic AI Adoption Roadmap Template

This template provides a structured roadmap for organizations aiming to adopt AI strategically. It guides leaders through vision-setting, capability building, and sustainable scaling – aligned with the future-focused imperatives discussed in this chapter.

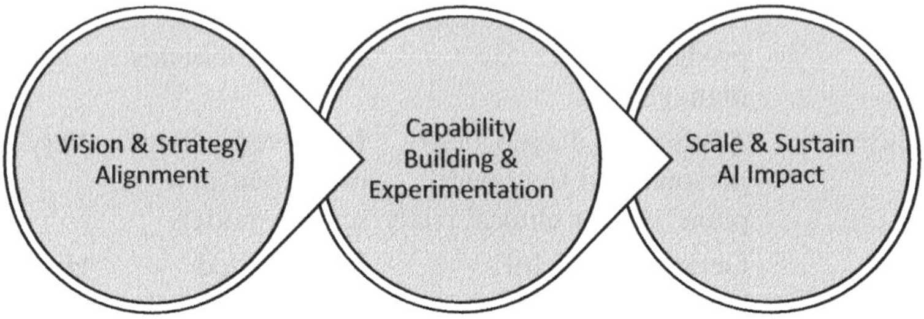

Phase 1: Vision & Strategy Alignment

Action Areas	Key Questions	Outputs
Define AI vision & objectives	What business outcomes will AI enable?	AI vision statement, strategic goals
Align with business strategy	How does AI align with growth, efficiency, or innovation?	Business-AI strategy map
Identify priority areas	Which functions (e.g., marketing, operations) will lead?	Priority use cases shortlist
Secure leadership commitment	Who will sponsor and govern AI initiatives?	Executive sponsors, AI steering group

Phase 2: Capability Building & Experimentation

Action Areas	Key Questions	Outputs
Build internal AI teams & skills	Do we have the right talent and partners?	AI teams, talent roadmap
Develop data & tech infrastructure	Are data and cloud platforms AI-ready?	AI-ready data platform, tools stack

(Continued)

Action Areas	Key Questions	Outputs
Launch pilot projects	What small-scale experiments will we run?	Proof of concept pilots
Establish AI Governance	How will we manage ethical risks & compliance?	Governance framework, RACI chart

Phase 3: Scale & Sustain AI Impact

Action Areas	Key Questions	Outputs
Scale successful use cases	How will we move from pilot to platform?	Enterprise AI platform roadmap
Measure business impact	What KPIs will track AI-driven outcomes?	AI impact dashboards
Drive continuous learning	How will we upskill teams over time?	Learning paths, AI capability maturity map
Monitor regulations & risks	How will we stay compliant globally?	Regulatory compliance tracker

Chapter 12

From Strategy to Reality: AI Case Studies Across Business Sectors

While theory informs, it is practice that transforms.

Artificial Intelligence (AI) is transforming the ways in which businesses operate, compete and grow, as it is no longer reserved for theoretical models or pilot programme initiatives. However, the journey to real-world AI adoption is complicated and often requires a process of trial and error. This is where case studies become invaluable learning aids, as they help to illustrate the ground-level implementation of AI and the strategic decisions, operational hurdles and tangible results that lie beyond the theoretical frameworks.

This chapter presents a comprehensive collection of business case studies that highlight the multifaceted roles of AI within organizational functions. To provide the readers with both authenticity and depth, we adhere to a dual approach:

- ***Primary case studies*** derive from interviews with industry executives and decision-makers. These stories capture first-hand insights on the reasons, processes and organizational learnings associated with AI initiatives.
- ***Secondary case*** studies rely on documented narratives from credible public domain sources. These include primary international corporations known for their AI strategies, which serve as scalable lessons and documented cross-domain.

The lived experience and public evidence presented in this chapter demonstrate the various ways in which AI can be practically applied and what others can learn from those leading the way.

Methodology

A dual-sourcing approach is utilized to ensure that the case studies have relevance and rigour. Firstly, primary data is gathered from industry leaders for first-hand insights, and secondary data is sourced from credible public sources.

AI and Business, 255–273

doi:10.1108/978-1-83708-888-120261012

Each data stream was analyzed separately to derive actionable information for AI implementation across diverse sectors.

Primary Case Study Selection and Data Collection

An open call was shared with public relations experts and professional groups, inviting organizations that would like to participate in this research project. From the 22 responses received, we focused on nine organizations based on the following two major factors:

(1) Proactive participation in the development, deployment or provision of AI-related infrastructure, and
(2) Academic willingness to share implementation details with utmost transparency.

Tailored, context-specific, structured questionnaires were sent to respondents via email. We received completed interviews from four senior-level professionals from the offices of founders, CTOs and directors. There were no ethical challenges in the research because all participants endorsed a Non-Disclosure and Participation Consent Contract guaranteeing confidentiality, the option to withdraw and research integrity. The following Table 12.1 summarizes the organizations interviewed and their focus areas in AI:

These cases capture a wide spectrum of AI applications – from sales and marketing to wellness and open-source innovation – anchored in distinct organizational contexts.

Secondary Case Study Selection and Sources

Secondary cases were selected based on the visibility and maturity of AI strategies within globally recognized firms. The aim was to highlight well-documented examples of AI deployment that are widely cited for their impact and innovation. Sources included company reports, academic journals, industry white papers, press releases, news features, blogs, YouTube interviews and company websites, with validation checks conducted to ensure credibility and currency.

Data Analysis Approach

Primary and secondary case data were analyzed independently. For primary interviews, thematic coding and keyword clustering were used to extract common patterns. In some cases, word clouds were generated to illustrate dominant themes. Secondary cases were narratively synthesized to examine strategies, tools used, outcomes achieved and industry implications.

Table 12.1. Summary of Primary Case Study Interviews.

Company	Sector	Role Interviewed	AI Focus Area
Enlog	Energy and IoT	Co-founder and CTO	Energy optimization, predictive maintenance
Ridge advertising	Digital marketing	Director	Generative AI for graphics
Solh	Mental health and wellness	Founder	Stress detection, predictive well-being
Weam AI	Open-source AI platforms	Co-founder and CEO	AI tool management, agentic automation

Limitations

This study acknowledges several limitations. The primary cases reflect (a) a small, (b) self-selected sample with, (c) regional concentration in Asia, particularly India and (d) rely on self-reported data. (d) Disclosure constraints also limited the depth of information in some cases. The secondary cases, while globally sourced, (e) may reflect success bias, as they predominantly feature celebrated examples of AI adoption.

Part A: Primary Case Studies (Based on Interviews)

This section presents case studies developed through first-hand interviews conducted as part of this book's research. These cases offer an insider's view into how diverse organizations – ranging from AI-native start-ups to sector-specific innovators – are designing, implementing and evolving their AI strategies.

Each case draws directly from executive perspectives and on-the-ground insights, highlighting both successes and setbacks. The structure used is consistent, enabling comparison across use cases and contexts, where relevant, direct quotations from interviews are included to preserve authenticity and voice. The following cases are not anonymized and have been shared with full participation consent.

Enlog: AI for Energy Optimization

Ayush Gupta
Co-Founder & CTO, Enlog

Context and Background

Enlog is a deep-tech climate and energy start-up based in Gurugram, India, specializing in AI-powered IoT systems for smart energy management. Co-founded by Ayush Gupta (CTO), the company targets buildings and facilities struggling with energy waste and operational inefficiencies.

The AI Initiative

Enlog developed in-house AI models to monitor and optimize real-time energy use via edge computing and cloud-integrated systems. Their platform leverages:

- Machine learning for anomaly detection.
- Predictive analytics to forecast usage and schedule maintenance.
- Reinforcement learning to improve system behaviour over time.

Their first major success involved identifying energy anomalies in hotel air conditioners and PG facilities using proprietary IoT sensors and time-series analysis.

Motivation and Goals

The company aimed to solve persistent problems in energy management:

- Cut energy bills through real-time optimization.
- Enable predictive maintenance to prevent outages.
- Deliver user-friendly insights that required minimal technical knowledge.

> AI helped us build a smart, self-managing layer over energy usage – not just a dashboard, but an invisible engine for savings. —Aayush Gupta, Co-Founder & CTO

Challenges in Implementation

- Technical: Voltage fluctuations, sensor noise and unreliable internet connectivity required resilient data pipelines.
- User Adoption: Facility managers were unfamiliar with AI insights and sceptical about algorithm-driven decisions.
- Cultural: Transitioning from manual systems to autonomous control required trust-building and gradual automation.

Strategic Alignment

AI was embedded from the outset, championed by the co-founders and supported by R&D and product teams. As the CTO noted,

> We wanted AI to work quietly in the background – making energy as smart and effortless as flipping a switch.

The initiative aligned with Enlog's climate mission and helped differentiate its offerings in an increasingly sustainability-driven market.

Results and Lessons Learnt

- 15–20% energy savings across pilot deployments.
- 4,000+ tonnes of CO_2 offset.
- ROI realized within 6–8 months for most clients.
- New roles like AI Ops Engineers and Energy Analysts emerged, reflecting the operational shift towards intelligence-driven facilities.

Unexpected outcomes included improved equipment life and stronger client trust due to transparent, actionable insights.

Quotable Insight

> Solve real problems, not just build cool tech... Grounding AI in business pain points is what creates real impact.

Discussion Questions

(1) How did Enlog's early integration of AI into its business model help it overcome implementation barriers?
(2) What factors enabled Enlog to build trust with facility managers unfamiliar with AI systems?
(3) In what ways could Enlog's approach to energy optimization be applied in public infrastructure?

Ridge Advertising: Generative AI in Creative Services

Arghya Chakravarty
Director, Ridge Advertising

Context and Background

Ridge Advertising is a digital marketing agency serving clients across sectors like consumer goods, education and government. Led by Director Arghya Chakravarty, the agency specializes in brand management, social media and performance marketing. The company saw early potential in integrating generative AI to enhance speed and cost-efficiency in visual content creation.

The AI Initiative

Ridge adopted generative AI tools to replace conventional photoshoots and streamline creative production. Their design team began using multiple third-party platforms to generate:

- photorealistic AI-generated models;
- short-format videos for campaigns;
- enhanced storyboarding and visualizations.

This initiative focused on reducing turnaround time and dependence on physical resources.

Motivation and Goals

Leadership viewed AI as a means to boost efficiency and creative flexibility.

- Create cost-effective visuals and campaign assets.

- Experiment rapidly with new formats and concepts.
- Stay competitive in a fast-evolving creative tech landscape.

> Technology is always a differentiator in creative agencies – you either resist it or adapt early. —Arghya Chakravarty, Director

Challenges in Implementation

- Resistance from experienced graphic designers who had to relearn workflows.
- Post-production inconsistencies in AI-generated visuals, requiring new QC processes.
- A learning curve in integrating AI tools seamlessly into agile design workflows.

Strategic Alignment

The AI initiative was driven by the creative leadership, with strong support from the design team. Weekly knowledge-sharing and monthly training helped build internal capability.

> We share openly with clients the pros and cons of generative AI…
> It's about augmenting creativity, not replacing it.

Results and Lessons Learnt

- 80–85% cost savings on campaigns where AI replaced traditional shoots.
- Faster delivery: AI-driven videos completed in 5 days vs. 15–20 days.
- Teams became more agile, with growing expertise in multi-tool AI environments.

Unexpectedly, Ridge found that the turnaround speed and scalability of AI helped them win new accounts with tighter budgets and timelines.

Quotable Insight

> Generative AI isn't here to replace creativity – it unlocks new forms of it we couldn't afford before.

Discussion Questions

(1) What were the key enablers for successful adoption of AI in Ridge's creative workflows?
(2) How can generative AI transform visual storytelling in agencies with limited resources?

(3) What quality control risks arise when replacing traditional production with AI tools?

Solh: AI for Mental Health and Stress Detection

Kapil Gupta
Co-Founder & CEO, Solh

Context and Background

Solh is an AI-driven wellness start-up focused on building systems that detect and manage stress before it escalates. Founded by Kapil Gupta, Solh offers a full-stack emotional wellness platform that integrates AI, psychology and behavioural science to intervene early and empathetically.

The AI Initiative

Solh developed in-house AI tools for stress detection and response, including:

- Prarambh life: Addiction recovery plan for substance uses addiction and new behaviour addiction.
- Streffie – a facial scanning kiosk that tracks 68 facial points to detect stress biomarkers.
- Multilingual NLP models to interpret journal entries in 12+ Indian languages.
- Smart Dashboards with predictive analytics to flag team or organizational-level burnout.

- 3 months programme and 6 months programme depending upon the level of addiction, from low to high.

The company also deployed reinforcement learning to enable intelligent nudges like break suggestions or call rescheduling.

Motivation and Goals

Solh sought to scale empathy using AI – capturing stress signals that humans often miss or ignore:

- Detect stress early, especially in high-pressure work environments.
- Empower HR and leadership with actionable emotional insights.
- Bridge cultural and linguistic barriers in mental health support.

> We didn't adopt AI because it was trendy. We used it because it let us listen better – to what people couldn't say. —Kapil Gupta, Founder

Challenges in Implementation

- Cultural stigma around discussing mental health, especially in corporate settings.
- Data invisibility: emotional states are hard to quantify and justify on balance sheets.
- Model sensitivity: AI had to detect stress without overreacting or violating privacy.

Strategic Alignment

AI was not an add-on – it was the foundation of Solh's value proposition. The entire product strategy was built around using AI to surface invisible pain points in real time.

> We use AI as a microscope, not a magnifying glass – something that sees what's too small to notice, not something that dramatizes it.

Results and Lessons Learnt

- 27% reduction in burnout flags across pilot groups.
- 42% drop in sick leave for logistics clients using nudges.
- 9% lower attrition where managers used Solh AI dashboards.

Beyond numbers, employees reported feeling emotional validation – many for the first time. AI insights gave them language and space to discuss hidden stress.

Quotable Insight

> If your AI doesn't understand emotion or culture – it doesn't understand anything.

Discussion Questions

(1) How can AI be designed to support emotional well-being without breaching privacy?
(2) What role does cultural context play in designing mental health AI solutions?
(3) Could Solh's approach be replicated in sectors like education or manufacturing?

Weam AI: Open-Source Platforms for AI Integration

Ronik Patel
Founder and CEO, Weam.ai

Context and Background

Founded by Ronik Patel, Weam AI is an open-source platform that helps digital agencies and tech start-ups manage, deploy and customize AI tools. The company emerged from the founder's own struggle to manage multiple AI accounts, rising costs and lack of control over AI workflows. It now serves as a unified interface for accessing and managing leading AI models.

The AI Initiative

Weam AI built a collaborative AI environment where users can:

- Access multiple LLMs (e.g., OpenAI, Gemini, Claude) from a single interface.
- Create shared workspaces with documents, prompts and Pro agents.
- Fine-tune models and workflows based on internal business logic.
- Self-host or deploy on secure cloud and local environments.

The platform offers both open-source and enterprise versions for flexibility and control.

Motivation and Goals

Weam AI aimed to solve practical, everyday barriers in AI adoption:

- Simplify access to AI tools for teams without deep tech expertise.
- Avoid vendor lock-in and rising subscription costs.
- Enable real control over data, privacy and workflow customization.

> Everyone talks about AI's potential. But companies struggle because no one gives them the system to make it work. —Ronik Patel, Co-founder & CEO

Challenges in Implementation

- Fragmentation in tools and user access across teams.
- Difficulty tracking usage, cost and value from various AI tools.
- Assumptions about what users want vs. what they actually need.

The breakthrough occurred when the team pivoted from building features to solving real deployment challenges.

Strategic Alignment

The product vision was tightly aligned with the company's open-source values: transparency, adaptability and community-driven growth.

> The real problem was not technical. It was human, shared accounts, confusion and lack of control. We gave users the clarity they didn't know they needed.

Results and Lessons Learnt

- 87% faster onboarding for team AI use.
- 40% reduction in AI tooling costs due to visibility and control.

- Strong engagement from enterprise clients who needed customizable, private deployments.

By providing centralized access and control, Weam AI empowered non-technical users and made AI sustainable for growing teams.

Quotable Insight

> Listen early, build later. Real user problems shape better AI tools than any roadmap ever could.

Discussion Questions

(1) What trade-offs does open-source AI present for enterprises managing sensitive data?
(2) How can companies structure their AI usage to avoid cost overruns and user confusion?
(3) What lessons from Weam AI can be applied to public sector or educational deployments?

AI in Practice: A Cross-Case Summary of Emerging Business Priorities

The word cloud derived from the interviews reveals a clear pattern in how businesses across sectors are approaching AI – not as a futuristic gamble, but as a pragmatic enabler of speed, precision and personalization (Fig. 12.1).

Automation With a Human Focus

Terms like automation, workflow and lead scoring highlight how AI is being used to optimize repetitive tasks, freeing human talent for more strategic roles. Yet this is not about replacement; company like Solh explicitly emphasize AI as a scalpel, not a hammer, augmenting human empathy and judgement rather than substituting it.

Personalization and Engagement at Scale

Words like personalization, customer experience and multilingual support reflect a shared ambition: to make every interaction feel human, even when AI is behind it. Businesses are leveraging conversational agents, generative AI and predictive analytics to tailor communication, support and content in real time.

Ethical and Responsible AI by Design

Several companies – particularly those working in sensitive areas like mental health (Solh) or energy infrastructure (Enlog) – foreground transparency, data segregation and ethical AI as non-negotiables. There is growing maturity around

Fig. 12.1. Word Cloud: Primary Interview Case Themes.

governance, hallucination control and feedback loops to ensure models behave responsibly and are explainable.

Smart Systems for Real-Time Decisions

Energy management (Enlog), stress detection (Solh) and agentic automation (Weam AI) all show how businesses are using real-time data and AI-enabled triggers to make decisions that would otherwise require intensive manual oversight.

Democratization through Open-Source and Accessibility

Weam AI, in particular, brings forward themes of open-source AI, tool unification and cost transparency, showing a desire for scalable, inclusive platforms that can adapt to team-specific workflows without vendor lock-in.

Across sectors, AI is being viewed not just as a technology, but as a strategic co-pilot – one that must be agile, ethical, context-aware and rooted in business problems that matter. The convergence of automation, personalization, governance and empathy marks a shift from AI as a capability to AI as a culture.

Part B: Secondary Case Studies

While the primary cases offered deep insights from direct interviews, this section highlights globally recognized organizations whose AI strategies have been well-documented in the public domain. These cases illustrate how established firms across diverse industries have adopted AI at scale – sometimes incrementally, sometimes transformationally – to solve real-world business problems.

To maintain brevity and coherence, we summarize each organization's AI journey using a consistent structure, drawing from verified reports, academic reviews and trusted business media. The aim is to extract cross-sectoral insights and best practices that students and professionals can transfer to their own contexts.

Across the companies listed in Table 12.2, AI adoption reflects both breadth and depth. From finance and healthcare to retail, agriculture and logistics, organizations are deploying AI in areas that directly impact efficiency, customer experience and decision-making. Some, like Pfizer and John Deere, use AI for innovation – accelerating drug discovery or transforming farming operations – while others, like Walmart, FedEx and Shell, have focused on optimization: cutting costs, enhancing logistics and improving asset reliability.

Companies like Procter & Gamble and Meta showcase the impact of AI on productivity and creativity when seamlessly integrated into daily tools and workflows. Kölner Stadt-Anzeiger[1] demonstrates how even smaller companies can benefit from AI through personalization and automation when strategically executed. As highlighted in the table, effective implementation relies on alignment of AI initiatives with business objectives, emphasizing targeted goals alongside measurable impact and taking a slow but strategic approach to scaling.

Cross-Case Analysis

The analysis of primary and secondary case studies shows balanced, noteworthy distinctions. Every organization embraced AI technology to address and resolve crucial business challenges; however, the scale, approach and maturity differed markedly. Primary cases such as Solh, Enlog and Ridge focused on targeted innovation, frequently within a singular domain (stress detection, energy optimization) and were resource-constrained. AI adoption in these firms was opportunistic and problem-driven due to the vision of the founding team.

The secondary cases, which include global leaders like JPMorgan, Pfizer and Walmart, showcased holistic AI adoption at the enterprise level, fuelled by strategic alignment, significant funding and large-scale cross-functional collaboration. These companies viewed AI as a systemic capability and not a tactical option. Despite these divergences, a number of common patterns surfaced:

- Success stems from clear problem definition and alignment within the business.
- Gaining incremental trust from users over time was crucial for adoption.
- Both groups faced ethical concerns, with more established companies covering governance issues more deeply.

[1] https://www.twipemobile.com/12-ways-journalists-use-ai-tools-in-the-newsroom/

Table 12.2. Comparative Summary of Secondary AI Case Studies.

Company	Industry	AI Use Case(s)	Business Function(s)	Key Outcome
JPMorgan chase	Finance (Banking)	Generative AI for wealth advisory, fraud detection, trading optimization	Customer advisory, risk management, operations	95% faster research retrieval, $1.5B saved, 20% increase in asset sales
Pfizer	Healthcare (Pharma)	Drug discovery acceleration, AI in manufacturing, generative AI for docs	R&D, manufacturing, supply chain	Drug development time reduced by months, 20k extra doses/batch, +10% yield
Volkswagen (Audi)	Automotive	AI in manufacturing QA, predictive maintenance, procurement AI bots	Manufacturing, quality control, procurement	30% faster bid analysis, 20% energy savings, 100+ AI apps in production
FedEx	Logistics	ML for routing and delivery ETAs, AI network optimization	Operations, customer service	10% pickup and delivery cost reduction, improved delivery time prediction
Walmart	Retail	Generative AI for listings, AI chatbots, demand forecasting	E-commerce, customer service, supply chain	850M listings updated 100Ã – faster, 21% e-commerce growth
Procter & gamble	Consumer goods	GPT-4 in R&D and marketing, AI for consumer insight	R&D, marketing	Innovation output tripled, junior staff performed at expert level
Kölner Stadt-Anzeiger (KStA)	Media	Personalized homepage AI, NLP tools	Editorial, user engagement	+80% CTR, 13% increase in article reads, 80% homepage AI-curated

Meta (Facebook/ Instagram)	Technology	Feed ranking, recommendation AI, generative AI chat tools	Product, advertising, UX	7%+ increase in time spent on Facebook, 42% uplift in ad conversions
John Deere	Agriculture/ Industrial	Computer vision sprayers, autonomous tractors	Product, farming operations	65% herbicide savings, autonomous 24/7 field ops
Shell	Energy	Predictive maintenance, AI optimization for safety and operations	Maintenance, safety, ops	$2B+ annual savings, 35% downtime reduction, 40% fewer failures

Overall, the success of AI is not limited to the size or the sector of the company. The main concern is on how well the technology is integrated, contextualized and scaled.

Chapter Summary

This chapter demonstrated the use of artificial intelligence across industries through both first-hand interviews and publicly recorded instances. The two-case format – consisting of primary and secondary research – depicted a range of AI uses, from individualized mental well-being tools and creative automation to industrial fine-tuning and corporate-level transformation. Across all cases, several patterns stood out:

- Successful AI initiatives start with clear business alignment and measurable goals.
- Incremental deployment and trust-building are crucial, especially in early-stage organizations.
- AI adoption is increasingly seen not as a technical upgrade but as a strategic enabler of personalization, automation and agility.
- Ethical considerations – such as transparency, privacy and human-AI collaboration – are gaining prominence, particularly in sensitive domains like health and finance.

Together, these case studies provide a practical roadmap for managers seeking to deploy AI – not just as a tool, but as a driver of sustained value and innovation.

Future Outlook

As AI technologies continue to evolve, the next wave of case studies will likely demonstrate deeper integration, greater personalization and more autonomous decision-making. Businesses across sectors are expected to move beyond pilots and isolated tools towards AI-infused systems that shape core strategy, customer experience and organizational design. Key trends shaping the future of AI in business include:

- More firms will shift from using AI to assist tasks to allowing AI systems to lead certain decision flows independently.
- Responsible AI governance will become a competitive differentiator, not just a compliance necessity.
- AI will increasingly break silos – connecting marketing, operations, finance and HR through unified data intelligence.
- With no-code and open-source platforms, AI adoption will extend to smaller firms and non-technical teams.

- Organizations will focus on designing work in which AI and people complement each other rather than compete.

> In every great business transformation, tools evolve – but what truly matters is how people choose to use them. AI is no different. It's not just about smarter machines but about building smarter intentions.

Discussion Questions

(1) How do the AI use cases presented in primary and secondary case studies differ in terms of scale, function and industry focus?
(2) Which business functions appear to benefit most consistently from AI adoption across the cases? Why do you think this is the case?
(3) What are the potential risks of relying on self-reported or secondary data when assessing AI success stories? How can these be mitigated?
(4) If you were advising a mid-sized enterprise considering AI adoption, what lessons from this chapter would you prioritize, and why?
(5) How should companies balance innovation with responsibility when implementing AI, especially in sensitive sectors like healthcare or finance?
(6) Based on the trends discussed, how might the next generation of AI case studies differ from those in this chapter?

Further Readings

Davenport, T. H., & Mittal, N. (2023). *All in on AI: How smart companies win big with artificial intelligence*. Harvard Business Review Press.

Ganesan, K. (2022). *The business case for AI: A leader's guide to AI strategies, best practices & real-world applications*. Opinosis Analytics Publishing.

Gibbs, J. (2024, April 12). *Netflix is not the only company that's good at AI and data*. LinkedIn. https://www.linkedin.com/posts/joshuagibbs_how-uber-optimizes-the-timing-of-push-notifications-activity-7209827485272735744-ozjS

Sequoia Capital. (2024, June 20). AI's $600B question. *Sequoia Capital*. https://www.sequoiacap.com/article/ais-600b-question/

Index

Printed and bound by CPI Group (UK) Ltd, Croydon, CR0 4YY

13/09/2026

14961026-0004